FRAGMENTED GODS

"It is necessary to analyze continually the signs of the times, in order that the Gospel proclamation might be more clearly heard and that the activity of the Church...might become more intense and efficacious."
—Final Report, Extraordinary Synod of Catholic Bishops, Rome, December 8, 1985

"To gain a proper impression of the needs of a country, it is necessary to study other than spiritual facts."
—J. Edwin Orr, evangelical cross-Canada traveller from England, 1935

"To attempt to evangelize in a vacuum or talk of ministry if we have only a vague idea of what service is necessary seems to me to repeat acts of futility."
—Lewis S. Garnsworthy, Archbishop, Toronto Anglican Diocese

"Our world is desperate for another Luther. For someone who has the courage to read the signs of the time, and the wisdom to discern therein a new window through which to view and understand God's activity in the world today."
—Rodney Booth, United Church of Canada

FRAGMENTED GODS

THE POVERTY AND POTENTIAL OF RELIGION IN CANADA

REGINALD W. BIBBY

FOREWORD BY GEORGE GALLUP JR.

IRWIN PUBLISHING

TORONTO CANADA

Copyright © 1987 Reginald W. Bibby

Foreword Copyright © 1987 George Gallup Jr.

Canadian Cataloguing in Publication Data

Bibby, Reginald W. (Reginald Wayne), 1943–
  Fragmented gods : the poverty and potential of religion in Canada

Bibliography: p.
Includes index.
ISBN 0-7725-1666-9

1. Canada — Religious life and customs. 2. Canada — Religious life and customs
— Statistics.
3. Canada — Religion — 20th century. I. Title.

BL2530.C3B52 1987   306'.6'0971   C87-093684-0

The author wishes to thank various publishers for generously giving permission
to use excerpts from copyrighted works. Material from *Straight From the Heart*
by Jean Chrétien (1985) and *Both My Houses: From Politics to Priesthood* by
Sean O'Sullivan (1986). Reprinted by permission of Key Porter Books Limited.
From *An Anecdotal Memoir* by Charles Templeton (1983). Used by permission
of the Canadian publishers, McClelland and Stewart, Toronto. From *An Invitation to Sociology* by Peter L. Berger. Copyright © 1963 by Peter L. Berger.
Reprinted with permission of Doubleday & Company. From *Ethics and Economics: Canada's Catholic Bishops on the Economic Crisis* by Gregory Baum
(1984). Reprinted by permission of James Lorimer & Company, Publishers.
From *The Church in the Canadian Era* by John Webster Grant (1987). Reprinted
by permission of G.R. Welch Company Limited. From *Religion in Sociological
Perspective* by Bryan Wilson (1982). Reprinted by permission of the Oxford
University Press.

Also gratefully acknowledged are excerpts from *Why We Act Like Canadians* by
Pierre Berton (McClelland and Stewart, 1982) and *Jehovah's Witnesses in Canada* by James Penton (Macmillan of Canada, 1976), reprinted by permission of
the respective authors.

DESIGN: Brant Cowie/Artplus Limited
COVER ILLUSTRATION: Ken Suzana
Typeset by Compeer Typographic Services Limited
Printed in Canada by Webcom Limited

  2 3 4 5 6 7 8   WC   94 93 92 91 90 89 88

Published by Irwin Publishing Inc.

CONTENTS

FOREWORD BY GEORGE GALLUP JR. ix

PREFACE xi

INTRODUCTION 1
Religion as History and Memory 3
Religion Through the Eyes of Social Science 6

1
THE GREAT CANADIAN ATTENDANCE DROP-OFF 11
The Protestant Exodus 12
The Roman Catholic Exodus 16
The Exodus of Others 21

2
WHERE HAVE ALL THE PEOPLE GONE? 24
The Conservative Protestant Option 25
The Electronic Church Option 31
The New Religion Option 36
The Invisible Religion Option 40
The No Religion Option 43
A Cause for Pause 45

3

THE DROP-OUT MYTH 46

Identification Stability 47
A Monopolized Mosaic 48
Following in Parental Footsteps 49
Correcting a False Equation 51
Precarious Paranoia 52
Pluralism and Stability 54
A Postscript on Defection 61

4

RELIGION À LA CARTE 62

Ultimate Questions 62
Conventional Fragments 63
Less Conventional Fragments 73
The Right to Rites 76
Religious Self-Images 78
Religious Fragments 80
The Consumption Self-Recognition Test 84

5

THE FRAGMENTED MOSAIC 86

From Sea to Sea 87
The Secular City...and Farm 91
The End of an Era 94
The Impact of Reason 96
On Godly Women 100
The Splintered Pew 102
The Fragmented Mosaic in Summary 108

6

SERVICING RELIGIOUS CONSUMERS 111

The Dominant Companies 112
The Stable Establishment 118

Competition for Consumers   121
Menu Diversification   125
Keeping the Customers   131
The Servicing Success Story   134

7
WHY FRAGMENTS WORK   137
The Social and Cultural Sources   138
Role Specialization and Commitment   139
Institutional Specialization and Authority   142
Selective Consumption   144
The Supernatural Marketplace   146
The Fragment Success Story   148

8
RELIGION AS A CONSUMER ITEM   150
Sexuality   153
The Increasingly Small Voice   164
Values   166
Social Concerns   170
Personal Concerns   172

9
RELIGION AND QUALITY OF LIFE   176
Views of Other Canadians   178
Social Attitudes   190
A Personal Cost-Benefit Analysis   205
The Bottom Line   211

10
BEYOND THE GREAT WHITE NORTH   214
We Are Not Like the Americans   214
Maybe a Little Like the English   222
Some Will Follow in Our Footsteps   227

CONCLUSION 233

Religion in the Twenty-First Century 234
Implications for the Nation 243
Implications for Individuals 246
Implications for Religious Groups 251
Beyond Fragments: The Great Possibility 259
The Necessity of Reconnection 267

APPENDIX 273

NOTES 281

BIBLIOGRAPHY 297

INDEX 309

FOREWORD

I n the best traditions of sociology and journalism, Reginald Bibby has given us a careful and objective assessment of religion in Canada.

His is a much-needed book, because no society can be fully understood without insight into its religious dynamic.

Drawing upon a number of major surveys in recent years, Bibby has woven a mass of data into a coherent and meaningful whole. His is also a book that will be valuable to American as well as Canadian readers, for Americans can see much of themselves in the picture that emerges from his analysis: religion important but not having primacy in our lives, and consumers telling the Churches the type of religion they want — and, for the most part, getting it.

Despite similarities, there are some striking differences between religion in Canada and in the United States. Canadians, for example, appear to be somewhat less enthusiastic about religion, somewhat more tolerant than Americans of religious and moral diversity, and less interested in evangelism. These differences to some extent can be explained by the fact that Roman Catholics outnumber Protestants five to four in Canada, while Protestants outnumber Catholics two to one in the United States.

Bibby dissects and examines, but he also builds. He writes about the "Great Possibility," pointing out that religion could have an important place in Canada and the world if it can reconnect God, self, and society in a meaningful way. Actually, Bibby notes, much is already in place: people long for a relationship with God; they can find in the Bible a basis for feeling good about themselves, as children of God; and finally, their need to be loved and to have meaningful relationships with others can be met by sensitized religious institutions.

Bibby writes: "If religion in Canada and elsewhere is to move beyond its current state of impoverishment, the numinous, self, and society must be linked in a manner historically insisted upon by religion."

He further notes: "The recognition of religion's poverty will open up the possibility of rediscovering its potential."

In the final analysis, *Fragmented Gods* speaks to the age-old need of religious institutions both to transcend and to be responsive to society — a difficult middle road, but perhaps the only one left open for winning the soul of modern man.

GEORGE GALLUP JR.
The Gallup Organization
Princeton, New Jersey

PREFACE

T his book is an attempt to synthesize about twenty years of research embracing six major studies of my own and important work by others. It started with a 1970 Master's level inquiry into the kinds of people joining Calgary evangelical churches. In 1975, at York University in Toronto, I fulfilled a graduate-school dream by carrying out — on a $14,000 shoe-string budget and with no little pain — a comprehensive national mail survey. That naiveté-laden project probed social issues, intergroup relations, and religion, and carried a title that drew chuckles from the people at *As It Happens* — *PROJECT CANADA: A Study of Deviance, Diversity, and Devotion.* That first survey has given birth to complementary 1980 and 1985 surveys, along with *PROJECT TEEN CANADA,* a pioneering 1984 national survey of teen-agers. The evangelical study was replicated in 1982, and the national research findings evaluated and corroborated in a detailed 1985 study of the Anglican diocese of Toronto.

For almost two decades I have been sifting through this growing body of data, publishing a large number of articles, presenting papers throughout North America and Europe, speaking to religious leaders, appearing on numerous television and radio programs, and trying out ideas on almost anyone else who has been willing to listen.

The story is now finally ready to be told. What follows is hardly the last word. But I think it is an important, informed word, badly needed in an area of Canadian life that is commonly characterized by conjecture and impression, excessive optimism and excessive cynicism. Never before in Canadian history has so large a body of information on religion been available. Moreover, the magnitude and scope of the material will probably never be replicated. This is not the summary of a solitary survey; it is a comprehensive study, based on a series of interrelated surveys, examining religion in the context of contemporary social and cultural developments. You, the reader, will be looking at unique material; you, the historian of the future, will have a detailed baseline from which to reconstruct religion in Canada at the end of the twentieth century.

This is not a one-man show. My debt to others is extensive. They include my early teachers, Merlin Brinkerhoff, Armand Mauss, and John Finney, along with the two people who have probably had the most direct influence on my work — my post-graduate friends and mentors, Charles Glock and Rodney Stark. Glock's survey-research stamp and Stark's market-model emphasis will be obvious.

Research, especially on a national level, does not come cheap. The data culled from my six research projects have had fixed costs — not including my time — of about $175,000; they carry a market value of more than $300,000. I wish to extend sincere thanks to the various funding sources that have made the work possible, notably the Social Sciences and Humanities Research Council of Canada (*PROJECT CAN85* and much of *PROJECT CAN80*), the Social Trends and Multiculturalism Directorates of the Secretary of State (*PROJECT TEEN CANADA*), and the Toronto Anglican Diocese (*ANGLITRENDS*), along with the University of Lethbridge, the University of Calgary, the Solicitor General of Canada, the Canadian Broadcasting Corporation, and the United Church of Canada. I especially thank former United Church Research Officer Dave Stone, who had the vision and faith to procure the first $2,000 for the 1975 survey; he was there in the beginning. Beyond offering research-funding assistance, the University of Lethbridge for some twelve years now has provided me with superb resources that are the envy of colleagues throughout the world. I sincerely thank the university for its generosity, including a year's study leave to complete this manuscript.

I've also benefited greatly from some exceptional research assistants, notably Michèle Coté, Debby Gordon, Denise Spisak, and Margaret McKeen. My close friend and colleague Don Posterski, my collaborator on the ongoing *PROJECT TEEN CANADA* phase of the research program, has been a great resource since the early 1980s. The managing editor at Irwin Publishing, Donald G. Bastian, has been deeply valued for his keen mind, his pursuit of excellence, and his sense of humour. He has done much to enrich this book, as he did two years ago with *The Emerging Generation: An Inside Look at Canada's Teenagers.*

I also thank some close friends for standing by me and believing in me — Grant, Dick, Gwen, Stan, Mark, Marilyn, Ted, and, especially, Laural. I also thank my sons — Reggie, Dave, and Russ — who haven't always understood what I have been up to, but who have had the wisdom and kindness to respect its importance to me. These people and sources have made it enjoyable as well as intriguing to explore the role of the gods in our time.

REGINALD W. BIBBY
Lethbridge, Alberta
April 1987

To my
Mother and Father

INTRODUCTION

I t's an old but critical question: "Did the gods create us, or did we create the gods?" It has been asked through the ages by theologians, philosophers, social scientists, and, of course, reflective ordinary people. The current Canadian religious situation requires that the question be asked again.

While the question of the reality of the gods cannot be addressed by the sociologist, the question of the nature of culture can. And if there is little difference between the nature of culture and the nature of the gods, we are left with two possibilities: either the gods are not "getting through" or they don't exist at all. In either event, they are insignificant to everyday life.

As Canada approaches the dawn of the twenty-first century, the gods are in trouble. There is little difference between the look of culture and the look of religion. Whereas Pierre Berton's primary criticism two decades ago in *The Comfortable Pew* was that the Church was playing it safe by lagging behind culture,[1] the Church of today has largely caught up to culture, but has in no way passed it. *The Comfortable Pew* has been replaced by The Cultural Pew.

For some time now, a highly specialized, consumer-oriented society has been remoulding the gods. Canadians are drawing very selectively on religion, and the dominant religious groups are responding with highly specialized items — isolated beliefs, practices, programs, and professional services, notably weddings and funerals.

The problem with all of this is that religion, instead of standing over against culture, has become a neatly packaged consumer

1

item — taking its place among other commodities that can be bought or bypassed according to one's consumption whims. Religion has become little more than a cultural product and is coming precariously close to acknowledging that culture creates the gods.

The possibility that culture will devour religion has always existed. Indeed, the reason that the question of "who created whom" has been raised in the past is that people have frequently worshipped gods that strikingly resembled their own personal and cultural characteristics. Psychologists like Gordon Allport have noted how people tend to emphasize supernatural features that reflect their own needs — if they are weak, then God is all-powerful; if they are friendless, then God is a companion; if they need guidance, then God is all-knowing.[2] Sociologists since at least Max Weber have pointed out that the conceptions of the gods closely resemble the characteristics of societies and groups — agricultural peoples develop gods of sun and rain and ocean peoples worship gods of the sea; masters and slaves, the rich and the poor, the upper class and the lower class — all have very different views about God, life, and death.[3]

When rival nations go into battle with simultaneous claims that "God is on our side"; when advocates of capitalism and socialism use the same "God" to legitimize their own position and condemn the other; when homosexuality is denounced as "sin" by Christian heterosexuals and declared "acceptable to God" by homosexuals who say they too are Christians; when people within the same denomination or even the same congregation say they have sought the will of God and have come to opposite conclusions — in such cases the neutral onlooker can be excused for wondering, "Where does the human contribution stop and the non-human begin?"

Some people conclude that no such division exists, that it's all human-made. The match-up between human and divine characteristics is so tight that there is no need to consider an intervening supernatural factor. Sigmund Freud argued that the hopes of humans resemble the alleged characteristics of "God" so closely that people simply transfer their hopes and wishes to an imaginary being.[4] Emile Durkheim concluded that the characteristics of social groups are so similar to those of "God" that "God" is nothing more than the groups' experience of themselves.[5] Karl Marx found that the nature and will of the gods closely reflected power relations. He declared, "Man makes religion; religion does not make man," and man has "found only his own reflection in the fantastic reality of heaven, where he sought a supernatural being."[6]

Historically, Judeo-Christian religion has claimed to be much more than individuals and culture. It has asserted that there is a God back of life who, as the German theologian and preacher Helmut Thielicke put it, brought history into being, oversees it, and will be there at its end.[7] This God is more than a mirror image of individuals and culture; indeed, "It" speaks to all of personal and social life, pronouncing and, when necessary, denouncing.

The extensive research unveiled in this book suggests that a religion with this kind of God is largely dead in Canada. Consumers tell religion what type of religion they would like; culture accordingly tells religion how to update and upgrade its content and forms. But, ironically, in trying to get in step with the modern age, organized religion — by dismantling the gods and serving them up piecemeal — is running the risk of becoming increasingly trivial. However, there is hope. As Berton wrote in his important critique twenty years ago, "If the Christian Church is ailing, it is certainly worth reviving."[8] Rejuvenation is not beyond the realm of possibility.

RELIGION AS HISTORY AND MEMORY

The gods weren't always so fragmented. In the beginning, religion was a central feature in the lives of Canada's Native peoples. They may not have produced systematic theologies in European terms. But our founding Indians and other indigenous Canadians have been described as "deeply committed to religious attitudes, beliefs and practices" that were grounded in "communion with nature and a connectedness with all of life."[9]

Along the way, religion in Roman Catholic and Protestant form sailed across the Atlantic from France and England and became an integral part of the earliest settlements. Religion has been an important travelling companion of virtually every other newly arriving group. Its presence has been physically acknowledged in the myriad churches, synagogues, mosques, and temples that dot the urban and rural landscapes of the nation to this day.

Accordingly, religion has had a significant place in Canadian history. As one thinks of the past, it is impossible to imagine Quebec with no Roman Catholics, Ontario with no Anglicans or Presbyterians, the Prairies with no evangelical Protestants, and British Columbia and the Atlantic region without the Church of England.

Religion has also claimed a place in most of our personal lives. Two in three of us were attending services almost every week or more when we were growing up. Religion calls forth various memories of grandparents and parents, white shirts and dresses, Sunday schools and Latin Masses, after-service meals, and, in many cases, a reduced level of activity that was strangely becoming to that different day in the week.

For some, religion is associated with good feelings — a family alive and together, close friends, a world that seemed peaceful and somehow less complex than the one we know today. For others, the thought of religion brings back memories of forced attendance, rigid morality, unbelievable beliefs, and contact with people who often seemed different from everybody else — and were aptly dubbed, by some clergy, "God's peculiar people."

Today, in the twilight of the twentieth century, things have changed. Religion no longer occupies centre stage in our society. Protestantism is not a pivotal feature of Anglo culture; Roman Catholicism is no longer at the heart of Québécois culture. Religion's importance to other cultural groups has similarly declined as those groups have become increasingly integrated into mainstream Canadian life.

It is true that our society continues to give lip service to the importance of religion. The Canadian Charter explicitly states that "Canada is founded upon principles that recognize the supremacy of God and the rule of law." We welcome visits by the Pope and other figures such as Bishop Desmond Tutu, Mother Teresa, Coretta King, and Billy Graham.

But it is also readily apparent that religion has little influence when it comes to political and economic decision-making, higher education, entertainment, and even personal morality. At the level of the federal government, for example, Robertson Davies, the novelist and Master emeritus of Massey College, maintains:

> *Our houses of Parliament open their sessions with daily prayers, asking for divine guidance, but what they discuss is necessarily broadly materialistic, sometimes quasi-scientific, and when prayers are over God is rarely invoked.* [10]

In trying to tell us what we are like in his best-selling 1985 book, *The Canadians*, Andrew Malcolm gives virtually no attention to religion.[11] The Anglican Archbishop of Toronto, Lewis Garnsworthy, has summed up the situation well in his 1984 Charge to the Synod:

> *We survive — great at Coronations, charming at weddings and impressive at funerals as long as we don't eulogize. We are welcome mascots at family do's and offer respectability to the Christmas cocktail circuit. We grace any community as long as we stay out of social issues and do not change a jot or tittle of well-worn liturgy.* [12]

Religion has also ceased to be life-informing at the level of the average Canadian. For most, it is extremely specialized in content and influence. People hold some beliefs and pray at least once in a while. They occasionally find themselves at a wedding, perhaps a funeral, and maybe a christening. But for the majority of Canadians, religious commitment is a former acquaintance rather than a current companion. In the poetry of Kris Kristofferson, the things that remind them of religion, such as a church bell or a Sunday School chorus, tend to ''take them back to something that they lost somewhere, somehow along the way.''[13]

The implications of it all are not clear. Many Canadians say they are no worse off, and are maybe even better off, without religious involvement. Still, I suspect that many silently wonder if they really are — if something beyond just religion has been ''lost somewhere along the way.'' A good number also wonder if their children in turn will experience any loss, aware that, because of their choices, that old-time religion that was "good enough for grandma, their parents, and them" is frequently a stranger to their sons and daughters.

RELIGION THROUGH THE EYES OF SOCIAL SCIENCE

While a number of means of data collection are available to the researcher who wishes to examine religion, the probing of beliefs, attitudes, and values, along with some types of behaviour, such as organizational involvement, is particularly amenable to surveys. Yet, somewhat surprisingly, up to the mid-1970s there had never been a comprehensive national survey of religion carried out in this country. Survey research had been limited to denominational studies and a limited number of poll questions that primarily probed attendance at worship services.[14]

This lack of survey-based information has been unfortunate, for religion has played a highly visible role in Canadian life. It is undoubtedly a commentary on the small number of social scientists who are interested in the topic, and the smaller number who in turn make use of surveys in carrying out their research. It may also be a commentary on a belated recognition by the country's religious groups that the social sciences can assist them in understanding themselves better — that religious commitment, in the words of sociologist Peter Berger, "involves commitment to clear perception."

Now, thanks to the generous response of people across the country, we have a much clearer understanding of the nation's religious situation. More than three thousand adults have participated in three carefully designed national surveys that have provided more information on religion than we have ever had before. They have also yielded valuable data on social concerns and intergroup relations. Carried out in 1975, 1980, and 1985, the three surveys have each involved highly representative samples of about twelve hundred cases. They allow us to generalize with a high level of accuracy about Canadians from Newfoundland to British Columbia. Further, they have been unique in including a sample core of about six hundred people who have participated in all three of the surveys, generating intriguing "panel data" that assist us in charting change over time.

These three adult surveys, part of the *PROJECT CANADA* research program at the University of Lethbridge, have been complemented by my 1984 national youth survey, *PROJECT TEEN CANADA*. This survey, conducted in collaboration with the Toronto youth expert Donald Posterski and analysed in our book, *The Emerging Generation*,[15] involved some 3,600 young people 15 to 19 years old. Regional analyses — of 1,700 Anglicans in the diocese of Toronto in 1985 and twenty evangelical Protestant congregations in Calgary between 1965 and 1980 — have provided further valuable information on religion, helping to fill in some of the details suggested by the more general "aerial photographs" of the national surveys. Details on these surveys and studies, including documentation of sample representativeness, are provided in the Appendix.

Together, the national and regional studies offer an extremely rich body of information — one highly respected reviewer has gone so far as to refer to the work as "a national treasure." But good research does not stop with good data. Rod Stark, who has gathered more than a little data himself, quipped at an informal gathering a few years ago, "We don't lack data; what we lack is good ideas." This book is anything but a mere compilation of statistics. On the contrary, my interest is in understanding how the world works — in the present instance, what is happening to religion in this country.

To that end, the surveys have been carefully designed to probe ideas, not merely to include an array of isolated "I wonder if?" items. The questionnaires used have been "knit together like quilts," with a rationale existing for the inclusion of every item. The surveys have been designed both to monitor change and to be sensitive to change, retaining key old items and adding key new ones.

Most important, an interpretative framework has gradually evolved, taking shape in about 1983 and tested and refined in research since that time. The result is that this book spares the reader the pain of wading through endless unwieldy numbers.

Rather, it lays out a systematic argument, drawing on the research with an interest not in numbers but in ideas.

Precisely because of my focus upon trying to comprehend the reality of Canadian religion, I will be drawing extensively on varied census, academic, media, and ecclesiastical sources. This includes the fine work of a number of other Canadian researchers, along with the important contributions to an understanding of religion in the modern world offered by American and European colleagues.

Some quick qualifications. First, in terms of religious affiliation, the Canadian picture is of a country that is about 50% Roman Catholic and 40% Protestant, with most of the remaining 10% claiming no religious affiliation. Only 1% are Jewish, with less than one-half of 1% either Hindu, Islamic, or Buddhist. Consequently, these smaller groups are necessarily grouped together in many of the statistical tables. Also, references to "the churches" do in fact usually refer to Christian groups, but are also meant to be all-inclusive to avoid cumbersome references, for example, to "Canadians attending churches or synagogues or mosques or temples." Also, while I realize many Anglicans see themselves as "Catholic" in the sense that they are part of a universal Church, for purposes of succinct discussion, I am including Anglicans in the "Protestant" category, where they stand in contrast to *Roman* Catholics.

Second, while the overall national sample sizes of twelve hundred cases allow us to have a high level of confidence when generalizing to the entire nation, the accuracy level for specific religious groups decreases as the groups grow smaller (e.g., as we move from Roman Catholics to Presbyterians). Nevertheless, general trends and tendencies are worth observing. Practical or substantive significance overrules statistical significance when the findings are consistent with other data sources such as policies, publications, and self-understanding. The statistics used are very basic; I refer readers who are concerned about such issues as control variables and multivariate regression to the journal publications cited.

Third, no, I haven't done everything. There undoubtedly are holes that will be disconcerting to some. I invite the critics to do some of the hole-filling; your contributions to this understaffed and under-researched area of religion in Canada will be most welcome.

A general comment. As mentioned, my primary interest is in ideas, not numbers. I encourage readers neither to get lost in numbers nor to ignore the ideas because they don't like the numbers. The reality of a culturally produced, fragmented religion is there for the eye to see, using the method of your choice. It is that depiction and its significance that I hope will be taken seriously.

This is a book about religion in cultural context. It will describe in detail the nature of religion in contemporary Canadian culture and show how social and cultural change have been remoulding the gods. It will conclude with an assessment of the implications of Canada's new-look religion for the nation, for individual Canadians, and for the country's religious groups, posing what I refer to as the great possibility — religion's largely unrealized opportunity to confront culture in the modern age.

I expect the book will be greeted with enthusiasm by many, with disappointment, chagrin, and even a little anger by more than a few. But my greatest hope is that it will shed considerable light on the nature and role of religion in Canada in our age and the coming age — and that the ensuing illumination will lead all to contemplate the personal and social consequences of ''the fragmentation of the gods.''

1

THE GREAT CANADIAN ATTENDANCE DROP-OFF

B ack on that spring 1946 Sunday morning in Edmonton, it seemed the natural thing to do. My father and mother bundled the three of us pre-schoolers into their 1938 Chev, setting out for the First Nazarene Church. They waved at the Jamiesons to the east, who were leaving to attend Mass at the nearby Roman Catholic church. Down the street, the Proctors and the Fieldings, adorned in their "Sunday best," could be seen strolling towards their respective United and Anglican church services.

The scene was hardly peculiar to Edmonton or Alberta. In Montreal, the Roman Catholic who did not appear at Mass would be a 15% exception to an 85% rule. In Halifax, Toronto, Winnipeg, or Vancouver, some 60% of Protestants and 80% of Catholics were entering church doors on that same morning. In smaller communities and rural areas, the attending proportion would be even higher. Overall, two in three Canadians were sitting there in the churches on that Sunday in 1946.

Today, that 1946 scene looks increasingly old-fashioned. My parents have been among those astonished to find that, just forty years later, a typical Sunday finds only one in three adults making their way to the nation's places of worship. Two-thirds to one-third in merely forty years!

The drop-off has been spectacular, not only because of its magnitude, but also because of its sheer speed. Little wonder it has left religious leaders and laity in a state of bewilderment. It has also done little for morale. A 1986 national survey of some 2,500 practising Roman Catholics carried out by the Canadian Conference of Catholic Bishops found that 57% think the health of the Church in Canada is fair (48%), poor (7%), or very poor (2%); a minority, 43%, view its condition as very good (5%) or good (38%). The most common lament is that there has been a decrease in church attendance.[1]

Observers have been inclined to think of the late 1950s and early 1960s as representing a time of "religious revival" in Canada. This was a time when Protestant, Roman Catholic, and Jewish membership figures were supposedly on the rise. Buildings were being erected at an unprecedented pace. Gordon Turner of the United Church expresses a common view of the period when he writes,

The decades of the 1950s and '60s were ones of expansion and growth for the Christian church in Canada. Mainline denominations dipped deep into their stewardship pockets to fund church extension projects in various parts of the nation. It was to be the new boom era of church development.[2]

Between 1945 and 1966, the United Church alone built fifteen hundred churches and church halls, as well as six hundred manses (parsonages).[3] It looked like a golden age for religion. But looks can be deceiving.

THE PROTESTANT EXODUS

The truth of the matter is that the numerical trends were being badly misread. Gallup poll data reveal that in 1946 some 60% of Protestants claimed they had been in church in the previous seven days. However, that figure dropped to 45% by the mid-1950s, and to less than 30% by the mid-1960s. It seems to have stabilized at around 25% over the past twenty years.

If Protestant church attendance has been declining at least since the end of World War II, why all the confusion? The problem seems to lie, in part at least, with the failure to take population increase into account. Leaders were focusing on sheer numbers and forgetting about proportions. A Lutheran planning consultant, Larry Wolfe, explains the numbers-proportion issue this way:

Because population is growing, we have to grow a little just to stand still. Let's assume the population in the Vancouver region increases by five percent from 1986 to 1991. To increase our membership by five percent over 5 years we need to add 12.5 new members over that period to each congregation. That is what we require in order to stand still. Now let's suppose we want to grow by two percent a year faster than the population. To do this, we would have to add an additional five new members a year to each congregation.[4]

The statistical truth of the matter is that most of Canada's religious groups were essentially standing still when they thought they were enjoying tremendous growth. In sheer numbers, a 43% weekly attendance level for Protestants in the mid-1950s represented about 3.4 million weekly attenders (43% of 8 million adults). But because of the rise in population, a decrease in regular attendance to about 38% by 1960 actually represented an increase in absolute numbers — to around 3.8 million weekly attenders (38% of 10 million adults).

This "numbers up, proportions down" argument receives strong support when we examine membership figures for the major Protestant bodies during the period. Through about 1965, most groups experienced numerical increases in membership (see TABLE 1.1). This was especially true for the Anglicans and the United Church. Baptists, Pentecostals, Lutherans, and Presbyterians also experienced modest gains. Not everyone grew, however. The Baptist Convention of Ontario and Quebec, for example, actually lost members—declining from 53,000 to 48,000 between 1950 and 1970. Generally speaking, it is easy to see why the groups felt they were enjoying numerical prosperity.

TABLE 1.1. **Membership of Select Denominations
in Thousands: 1926-85**

Year	Total	UC	Ang	Bapt	Pent	Luth	Pres
1926	1611	610	700	138	*	*	163
1931	1778	671	794	132	*	*	181
1936	1869	698	861	133	*	*	177
1941	1886	717	861	134	*	*	174
1946	1991	768	872	132	45	*	174
1951	2408	834	1096	135	45	121	177
1956	2737	933	1282	137	50	147	188
1961	2966	1037	1358	138	60	172	201
1966	2946	1062	1293	137	65	189	200
1971	2791	1017	1109	132	150	200	183
1976	2571	940	1008	128	117	209	169
1981	2458	900	922	128	125	218	165
1985	2417	881	856	130	179	208	163

*Figures unavailable.

Baptist = Canadian Baptist Federation; Lutheran = Evangelical Church of Canada,
Lutheran Church-Canada and in America-Canada section.

SOURCES: United, Anglican, Baptist, Presbyterian: Yearbooks of these groups; Lutheran:
McLeod, 1982; Pentecostal: estimates through 1971, 1976, and following from
directories of clergy (1976 based on 1979).

However, over the century, in relation to the nation's population, all the major Protestant denominations have experienced a pronounced decline in membership (see TABLE 1.2). United Church membership, for example, comprised 6% of Canadians in 1946, about 5% by 1966, and only some 3% by 1986.

Even during the time of alleged peak expansion in the mid-1950s and early 1960s, Canada's dominant religious groups saw their membership proportions shrink. No group — including the Pentecostals — increased their proportional share of the national population during religion's alleged golden era.

While the number of members in most Protestant groups was increasing, then, the proportion of members was decreasing. Paradoxically, more people than ever before were staying away at precisely the same time as more people than ever before were attending. In the mid-1950s, 4.6 million Protestants were *not* in church on a typical Sunday. By the mid-1960s, that figure had risen to 6.2 million. The Protestant churches were losing propor-

TABLE 1.2. **Membership of Select Denominations as Percentages of Total Population: 1926-85**

Year	Total	UC	Ang	Bapt	Pent	Luth	Pres
1926	16.4	6.2	7.1	1.4	*	*	1.7
1931	17.2	6.5	7.7	1.3	*	*	1.7
1936	17.1	6.4	7.9	1.2	*	*	1.6
1941	16.4	6.2	7.5	1.2	*	*	1.5
1946	15.6	6.0	6.8	1.0	.4	*	1.4
1951	17.3	6.0	7.8	1.0	.3	.9	1.3
1956	17.1	5.8	8.0	.9	.3	.9	1.2
1961	16.3	5.7	7.5	.8	.3	.9	1.1
1966	14.7	5.3	6.5	.7	.3	.9	1.0
1971	12.9	4.7	5.1	.6	.7	.9	.9
1976	11.2	4.1	4.4	.6	.5	.9	.7
1981	10.1	3.7	3.8	.5	.5	.9	.7
1985	9.5	3.5	3.4	.5	.7	.8	.6

*Not available.
SOURCE: Computed from TABLE 1.1 and census figures.

tional ground when they seemed to be enjoying their greatest numerical hour.

One result, in many instances, has been financial strain. John Webster Grant makes the interesting observation that since few of the buildings erected during the explosion of the 1950s and 1960s were paid for by the 1970s, "a large proportion of the time and effort [suburbanites] could spare for church activities was devoted to the raising of money."[5] Difficulties continue to be felt in the late 1980s. Financial problems have frequently been one of the legacies of Canadian religion's "boom to bust" experience.

Take the United Church, for instance. Gordon Turner notes that "many of these huge cathedral-like structures now hold a handful of the faithful [who] are left to carry the heavy mortgages of a once-booming vision."[6] A recent article in *The United Church Observer* carried the title, "Hard Times Have Arrived as Forecast." The article pointed out that the church's "Mission and Service Fund" — pivotal to the operation of the national structure and program — had experienced a 1986 shortfall of $1.5 million. William Davis, General Secretary of the Division of Finance, has projected that over the next three years the church will have to balance the books by drawing between $6 and $7 million from its Stabilization Fund, which now stands at $11 million. In Davis's words, "It sounds rather gloomy."[7] The reasons for the dollar problems, according to the article, are increased costs, the tendency to give locally rather than nationally, and the boycotting of national giving by some disenchanted members.

What the article failed to mention is the obvious: as membership drops, so does revenue. To lose people is to lose financial as well as human resources.

And the numbers game is claiming a large number of Protestant casualties. Other groups, including the Anglicans, acknowledges *The Canadian Churchman*, can expect "a serious financial shortage in the next few years."[8] Yet Ted Byfield, columnist and founder of *The Alberta Report*, in drawing attention to the numbers-dollars relationship, claims that "at both the Anglican general synod and the United Church general council [in 1986], no mention was made of any crisis in membership."[9] Mentioned or not, the negative financial news coming from decreasing membership is not good.

THE ROMAN CATHOLIC EXODUS

Canadian Roman Catholics have not been exempt from the drop-off in attendance. The chronology, however, has been quite different.

At the end of World War II, more than 80% of Catholics maintained they had been to Mass in the previous seven days — some 20 percentage points above the Protestant level (see TABLE 1.3). By the mid-1960s, the Roman Catholic figure stood virtually unchanged, then 40 points above that of Protestants.

However, in the late 1960s, just as the Protestant dip in attendance seemed to be levelling off, the Catholic Church, until then seemingly immune, began to experience a devastating decline. By the mid-1970s, weekly attendance at Mass had dropped to about 60%. At present, the level has slipped further, to almost 40%. The Canadian Conference of Catholic Bishops says that the "celebration of the Eucharist on Sunday is the centre and culmination

TABLE 1.3. **Service Attendance for Protestants and Catholics, 1946 to the Present** *(In %s)*

"Did you yourself happen to go to church or synagogue in the last seven days?"

	1946	1956	1965	1975	1986
Roman Catholics	83	87	83	61	43
Protestants	60	43	32	25	27
ALL OF CANADA	67	61	55	41	35

SOURCE: Canadian Institute of Public Opinion.

of the whole life of the Catholic community, especially the parish community."[10] A minority of Roman Catholics now share regularly in that celebration.

THE VATICAN II FACTOR   Many observers have been inclined to attribute much of this change in attendance to the after-effects of Vatican II. That historic Council was convened in Rome by Pope John XXIII in 1962 and lasted through December of 1965, in the papacy of Paul VI. The primary goal of the Council was the modernization of the Church; Pope John used the now well-known term *aggiornamento,* meaning "updating." Among the changes were the celebration of Mass in the vernacular; greater participation by the people in hymns and responses; revised catechisms; increased "dialogue" with other disciplines and other religions; greater consultation of leaders and even laity in the governing of the Church at all levels ("collegiality").

But leaders deny that Vatican II's effects have been primarily negative. In calling bishops to Rome in late 1985 to reflect on Vatican II twenty years after its conclusion, John Paul II, considered a conservative himself, nevertheless asserted that "the Second Vatican Council remains the fundamental event in the life of the contemporary church." At the conclusion of this special Synod, the bishops noted in their final report, "The large majority of the faithful received the Second Vatican Council with zeal; a few, here and there, showed resistance to it." Of liturgical change specifically, the bishops wrote: "Even if there have been some difficulties, it has generally been received joyfully and fruitfully by the faithful.''[11]

In reporting the response to Vatican II in Canada, Bernard Hubert, Bishop of Saint-Jean-Longueuil and President of the Canadian Conference of Catholic Bishops, told the Synod:

> We find movements of the Spirit which have deeply changed the Roman Catholic Church in the past twenty years: evangelical reading of the signs of the times, direct contact of the baptized with the Word of God, a church serving the world, concern in each diocese for all the other local churches, vital links between Christian faith and social justice, search for unity among Christians, dialogue with world religions, involvement of the laity...and many other things. [12]

Bishop Hubert acknowledged that these realities are embryonic, but added that they nevertheless contain seeds of life for the renewal of the Church and the salvation of the world.

Practising Canadian Catholics tend to concur. The 1986 national survey by the Bishops—focusing on lay involvement—found that some 86% feel the changes in the Church since Vatican II have been mostly for the better. Only 4% feel the changes have been for the worse, with the remaining 10% asserting they have made little difference.

On the plus side, Catholics cite liturgy in the language of the people and greater participation of the laity; on the minus side, some mention the downplaying of doctrine, moral demands, and popular devotions. Still further, the survey found that about 50% of practising Catholics think there have been enough changes, 40% want more, and a remaining 10% feel there have been too many innovations. [13]

Obviously the views of these practising Catholics — 95% of whom are attending Mass once a week or more — are not representative of all Catholics, especially the 60% who are not weekly attenders. The 1975 PROJECT CANADA survey asked Canadians who are no longer as involved in the Church as previously why they had dropped off. Among Roman Catholics, the most frequently cited reason was disenchantment with what the Church was doing (60%). [14] But it seems that many are not so much concerned with the changes that have taken place as they are about the changes that still need to occur. As one Drummondville Catholic said in explaining why he is no longer as involved as before, "The Church did not adjust to the contemporary world."

To be sure, as the 1985 Synod in Rome acknowledged, Vatican II has had its detractors. Anne Roche Muggeridge, who describes herself as "an orthodox defender of the Council," has recently published *The Desolate City*, in which she describes the Catholic Church as being "in ruins." Vatican II is seen by Roche Muggeridge as having eroded the orthodox Church's authority, reflecting Protestant anti-dogmatic and anti-hierarchical principles. She sees the emphasis upon dialogue and collegiality, for example, as an attempt to remove authority from a divinely designated hierarchy.[15]

Critics of the Council are not limited to Roman Catholic ranks. Anglican Robertson Davies, for example, decries many of the liturgical changes, saying that

> much of the splendour and beauty which Protestants covertly envied has disappeared. The heaviest loss is undoubtedly the poetic splendour of the Latin Mass, which was truly numinous. . . . It seems that Rome has turned her back on the poetry in which lay much of her power.[16]

And such disenchantment with Vatican II has not lacked for some clergy casualties. Janice Newson, in a study of priests who quit, found that some left not so much because they were unhappy with the Council as because of lay reaction and lack of Church support. She writes that "resigned priests often found themselves alienated from the lay and clerical community which criticized their efforts, or from superiors who withdrew support, or from the council Fathers who endorsed renewal."[17]

Nevertheless, the alleged negative impact of Vatican II on overall Roman Catholic attendance and participation in Canada has probably been grossly exaggerated. People have been looking to Rome when they should have been looking to Montreal and Quebec City.

THE QUEBEC FACTOR In support of such an argument is the very significant finding that the extent of the Roman Catholic

TABLE 1.4. **Service Attendance of Roman Catholics, 1965, 1975, and 1985** *% Attending Twice a Month or More*

	1965 N (902)*	1975 (481)	1985 (481)
QUEBEC CATHOLICS	88	46	38
NON-QUEBEC CATHOLICS	69	55	49
NATIONALLY	83	50	43

SOURCE: 1965, Mol (1976); PROJECT CAN75; PROJECT CAN85.
*Bracketed figures refer to the number of cases on which the percentages are based.

attendance drop-off is far from uniform across the country. While characteristic of every region, it has been particularly dramatic in Quebec (see TABLE 1.4). In a mere twenty years, Roman Catholic attendance in that province has declined from 88% to 38% — a full 50 percentage points. Elsewhere, the drop has been substantial but less spectacular — from 69% to 49%.

These differences strongly suggest that much more is involved than merely the aftereffects of Vatican II. Of central significance is the post-1960 acceleration of Quebec's modernization. With industrialization has come specialization, with religion and other institutions playing more specific and more limited roles.

What has taken place in Quebec since 1960 mirrors changes in Canada as a whole during this century. Until then the Catholic Church had dominated the life of the province. Social organization and social institutions were fused with the Church. But when the Liberal Party came to power in Quebec in 1960, the alliance of Church and State began to come to an end. The "Quiet Revolution" included the secularization of trade unionism, the revision of labour, health, and welfare laws, and the nationalization of electricity. Institutions previously under the control of the Church — such as education, social welfare, and health — were largely taken over by the government.

Remarkably, the transfer of power was relatively quiet. J.P. Rouleau of Laval University notes:

There were no ideological struggles in the specialized journals and magazines, in the press, on radio or television. There were no mass rallies either for or against the legislation implementing the evolution. [18]

Rouleau suggests a number of reasons for the relatively calm transition: the transfer was essentially from Catholic clerics to Catholic laity; religion was permitted a place in the new institutions, such as the school and the hospital; equity was observed in the purchase and sale of assets; there was continuous consultation and an avoidance of confrontation and conflict by both Church and State; and, finally, the Church had become increasingly aware that the nature of the modern era and the aspirations of the people called for physical and human resources beyond its own.

Modern industrialization and post-industrialization have tended to lead to a loss of significance for religion in Canada and other western nations. Quebec's secularization has been only as belated as its modernization. The factors are virtually the same as elsewhere; only the timing is different.

The role of social and cultural change in altering the face of Catholicism in Canada has been far more important than the developments emanating from Vatican II. Such an interpretation is very similar to the conclusion arrived at by sociologist Dean Hoge in his extensive examination of Catholicism in the United States. Hoge writes that, in the 1960s, social pressures contributing to the assimilation of Catholics into American life ''were very high, and the main effect of the Council was to open the gates and legitimize a general direction of change.''[19] In Canada, the modernization of Quebec was likewise a far more important factor in shaping Catholicism than the developments arising from the historic Rome Council. At best, Vatican II may have played something of a complementary role.

THE EXODUS OF OTHERS

While Roman Catholics (47% of the population), Protestants (41%), and the non-affiliated (7%) dominate the Canadian religious scene, this is not to say that the religions of the cultural minorities have been spared this pattern of decline in participation. Ukrainian Catholic membership dropped from 58% of Ukrainian Canadians in 1931 to 33% by 1971; those choosing to be Ukrainian Orthodox declined from 25% to 20% during the same period. Manitoba professors Stella Hryniuk and Roman Yereniuk identify a decline in the Churches' functions "as [hubs] of religious life and as focal centers for the maintenance of a separate Ukrainian identity." The result is that they "have suffered a decline in numbers of members and prominence."[20]

Jewish congregations are regarded as voluntary associations founded to hold services and provide other benefits for their members. Yet synagogue attendance has been regarded as low for some time, with only about half of Canadian Jews currently members of synagogues. Specific weekly attendance figures are not known, but are thought by some to be probably similar to those of the United States; since the mid-1950s, American weekly attendance for Jews has ranged from 27% to 15%.[21] According to a national survey of Jews carried out in 1971, 13% were frequent synagogue attenders.[22]

The participation of Buddhists, Moslems, and Hindus—although not well documented to date—nonetheless appears to be declining as followers and their offspring become increasingly integrated into Canadian economic and social life.

The picture is clear. Organized religion in Canada has experienced a startling decline in service attendance. First the Protestants saw their numbers drop, but as we have seen, they had been in proportional decline long before they noticed there were fewer people in the pews. Next came the Catholics, somehow immune to the attendance plague until the 1960s, when modernization hit Quebec and assimilation was increasingly experienced by Roman Catholics elsewhere in the country. The result is that the Catholic attendance figure is closing in on its Protestant counterpart. Canada's other religious groups give no indication of having greater vitality when it comes to participation, particularly with the passage of time and cultural assimilation.

At the same time that attendance is down, there are strange signs that religion is far from dead. People seem to have a heightened interest in the supernatural, including astrology and psychic phenomena. Groups like the Pentecostals seem to be alive and well, and charismatics have been springing up in a number of unexpected places, like the Anglican and Roman Catholic Churches. Newspapers cover the social pronouncements of the major groups and the private lives of television preachers. The current Pope seems to have increased the profile and influence of the Catholic Church, while people like former Anglican Primate Ted Scott have become known worldwide for their efforts to bring about peace and international well-being. And then, too, we still have all those church weddings, baptisms, and christenings, not to mention funerals.

In the midst of the mass exodus, the paradox is that religion lives on, even showing occasional signs of health. The key to understanding the Canadian religious scene lies in resolving the apparent contradiction between exodus on the one hand and the persistence of religion on the other. We'll begin by looking for missing members, touring a few interesting religious camps along the way.

2
WHERE HAVE ALL THE PEOPLE GONE?

I n a recent interview, Roy Bonisteel commented that there is a need in Canada "that's not being met by the churches or broadcasting." Bonisteel, the highly regarded host of CBC's twenty-year-old program, *Man Alive*, added, "This is why I think people are walking away from churches, joining cults and being swayed by charismatic evangelists."[1]

His impression is a common one. The dramatic post-war drop-off in attendance has led virtually everyone — religious leaders, the media, academics, and the public in general — to conclude that traditional religion has been losing ground. The obvious related question is one I personally have been asked again and again by journalist and religious leader alike: "Where have all the people gone? If they are not interested in conventional religion, then to what are they turning?"

Five major alternatives have been highly touted: the Conservative Protestants, the electronic church, new religious movements, privatized religion, and the possibility that people are opting for no religion. Until fairly recently, we had lots of speculation but very little systematic information on the extent to which these options are being taken. Considerable data are now in, and this is what we have found.

THE CONSERVATIVE PROTESTANT OPTION

Queensway Cathedral in Toronto opened its doors in 1985. This Pentecostal Assemblies of Canada building seats four thousand people, has an annual budget of $3.2 million, and at its opening claimed a full-time staff of twelve ministers. The Cathedral broadcasts a taped version of its Sunday-morning service on television stations across the country. Its senior minister, the Reverend Ralph Rutledge, claimed in a 1985 interview on CBC Radio's national phone-in show, *Cross Country Checkup*, that the church was growing primarily because it was preaching a clear-cut version of the gospel. As the guest for the day, I was asked to respond. On the basis of research now brought together in this book, I diplomatically disagreed.

The Burnaby Christian Fellowship in Greater Vancouver started out as an informal, interdenominational gathering of charismatically inclined people in the spring of 1981. By the mid-1980s the group had grown to about eight hundred members, with a full-time ministerial staff of three. George Mallone, its affable senior minister, attributes much of the expansion to the desire of people to experience a faith with substance and significance. In the course of discussing the congregational make-up with me at some length in the summer of 1983, he acknowledged that the outreach to the unaffiliated might, in fact, be suspect.

"Phenomenal is the best way to describe the rapid growth of the newest Baptist Convention of Ontario and Quebec church in the city of London, Ontario," reports Milton Swaren in the March 1986 issue of *The Canadian Baptist*. In just over four years, he writes, Westview has developed from a congregation of forty charter members to an average Sunday attendance of 125 to 135 people. It also has a large number of weekday group activities, along with a radio broadcast of the Sunday service, which is further distributed via cassettes to shut-ins. Westview also has a prayer line, with thirty-five women committed to pray for specific concerns that are phoned in. Swaren does not address the question of where exactly the new recruits are coming from.

In suburban Ottawa, the Bethel Pentecostal Church erected a new $4-million church in 1986. Within two months of its dedication, attendance at the Sunday-morning service had grown from 515 to 700, with Sunday-school attendance expected to increase from 350 to 1,000 in a few months. The church's pastor, Donald Feltmate, said that his church's experience reflected "evangelical church growth in general and the strong need people feel these days for direction and moral support."[2] He was not clear, however, about just who these newcomers were.

And in February 1986 the Council of the Canadian Baptist Federation affirmed a plan to reach two hundred thousand members by the year 2000, as well as adding two hundred new churches and as many missionaries. The Baptist Federation leader Richard Coffin claims that the goals "have received the acclaim of our people coast to coast."[3] The Federation has approximately 130,000 members at present; this compares with about 135,000 members in 1950 and some 130,000 in 1910.

High-profile, evangelical church success stories and would-be success stories such as these have contributed to a general impression that fundamentalist and evangelical Protestant groups are flourishing. These denominations include Baptists, Pentecostals, Nazarenes, the Christian and Missionary Alliance, Mennonites, the Salvation Army, Free Methodists, the Evangelical Free, and others, as well as an array of independent community churches. Sociologists commonly refer to them as "the Conservative Protestants" — a designation I will be using throughout this book.

While the groups vary theologically, they nevertheless come under the umbrella of "the Believers' Church," in which a central criterion for membership is "regeneration" or "rebirth" — the belief that the individual has to have a personal, life-changing encounter with Christ in order to become a Christian and join the Church. They also stress the authority of Scripture.

As so often happens in Canada, the image of evangelical vitality is largely based on events in the United States. Since the 1970s, considerable American media and academic attention has been given to the alleged resurgence of evangelical Protestantism in that country. The industrialization of the American South and the election of a Southern Baptist President, Jimmy Carter, in 1976, awakened the media to the tremendous numerical strength of Baptists and evangelical Methodists.

The 1970s also saw evangelicals become far more strident in the social and political realms, most notably in the form of the Moral Majority, headed by Baptist preacher Jerry Falwell. Evangelicals came to dominate Sunday television offerings in many parts of North America. They also claimed some very high-profile conversions: Watergate figure Charles Colson, former radical Eldridge Cleaver, and singer Bob Dylan, to name just a few.

Gallup poll findings in 1976 that about one in three Americans claimed to be "born again"[4] further enhanced the picture of accelerated evangelical success. And in contrast to the decline of mainline Protestant groups, the membership gains of the American Conservatives were impressive. In 1972, Dean Kelley, a leading figure in the U.S. National Council of Churches, attempted to lead the mainline bodies into self-evaluation by contrasting them with Conservative groups. In his *Why Conservative Churches Are Growing*, Kelley attributed the superior growth of the evangelical churches to their effort to provide clear answers to the ultimate questions, and to their insistence that commitment costs something in terms of lifestyle and personal resources.[5] After the publication of his book, many church leaders and academics conceded that evangelicals were significantly penetrating secular America.

Strange though it may sound, it has never been demonstrated that Conservatives have actually been successful in reaching unaffiliated or inactive Americans. However, I have examined the question in some detail in Canada. The results are surprising.

Some theologically conservative Protestant groups, such as the Pentecostals, the Christian and Missionary Alliance, and the Salvation Army, have grown faster than the population during this century. Others, however, including the Baptists and Mennonites, have not (see TABLE 2.1). The Conservative Protestant groups currently form about 7% of the nation. But in 1921 the Baptists (now

TABLE 2.1.   **Conservative Protestants as a Percentage of the Canadian Population: 1921-81**

	1921	1941	1961	1981
TOTAL (Rounded)	8.0	7.0	7.0	7.0
Baptist (all)	4.8	4.2	3.3	3.1
Church of Christ, Disciples	.2	.2	.1	.1
Christian and Missionary Alliance	.0	.0	.1	.1
Christian Reformed	*	*	.3	.3
Free Methodist	.1	.1	.1	.1
Mennonite	.7	1.0	.8	.8
Pentecostal	.8	.5	.8	1.4
Salvation Army	.3	.3	.5	.5

SOURCE: Canadian Censuses, 1921-81.
* Not available.
NOTE: As of 1981, the percentages for all other Conservative Protestant groups are under 1%: Associated Gospel .03, Brethren .09, Canadian Reformed .05, Church of God .04, Church of the Nazarene .05, Evangelical Free .02, Missionary .03, Plymouth Brethren .03, Wesleyan .03.

3%) all by themselves made up 5% of the population. Conservative groups have thus experienced a negligible gain in proportion to population during the twentieth century.

If such groups are to experience significant proportional increases, they clearly have to recruit large numbers of people from outside the evangelical community. Yet Conservatives are no more successful than the mainline Protestant denominations in reaching people not active in other religious groups.[6] The Conservatives have been found to have, among their weekly attenders, some 17% who were not regular churchgoers when they were growing up. This compares with about 20% for mainline groups. The Conservatives don't appear to be reaching people outside church life any better than mainliners.

These national findings are consistent with research that Merlin Brinkerhoff and I have been conducting in Calgary.[7] In 1971, we analysed the backgrounds of about three thousand people who had joined twenty randomly selected Conservative churches between 1966 and 1970. Ten years later, we went back to the same congregations and examined their membership additions for 1976 through 1980. During those periods, the churches were engaged in a wide range of evangelistic efforts, aimed at reaching outsiders. Methods included door-to-door visitation, city-wide crusades, and regular evangelistic services at particular churches.

However, we found that, for all their efforts, 70% of the new additions had come from other evangelical churches, including a sizable number of people moving into Calgary from rural areas. Another 20% were the children of evangelicals. Only about 10% of the new members had come from outside the evangelical community, almost without exception as a result of social ties, notably friendship and marriage (see TABLE 2.2).

In interpreting these results to evangelicals, I have somewhat facetiously, and yet accurately in the light of the findings, suggested that if they are serious about recruiting "real live sinners,"

TABLE 2.2. **Sources of New Members for Select Calgary Conservative Protestant Churches, 1966-70 and 1976-80** *(In %s)*

		Transfers	Children	Outsiders	Total
Alliance	1976-80	69	19	12	100
	1966-70	69	19	12	100
Baptist	1976-80	74	17	9	100
	1966-70	70	22	8	100
Brethren	1976-80	51	27	22	100
	1966-70	72	24	4	100
Missionary	1976-80	53	22	25	100
	1966-70	100	0	0	100
Nazarene	1976-80	62	20	18	100
	1966-70	82	14	4	100
Pentecostal	1976-80	75	12	13	100
	1966-70	78	13	9	100
Salvation	1976-80	78	12	10	100
Army	1966-70	72	9	19	100
TOTAL	1976-80	70	17	13	100
	1966-70	72	19	9	100

SOURCE: Bibby & Brinkerhoff, *Circulation of the Saints Research Project.*

the best approach is either to befriend them or to marry them. For that is how the majority of outsiders are actually recruited.

Overall, the twenty evangelistic churches managed to recruit an average of about 1.9 outsiders per church per year. It is very clear that for these Calgary churches—and probably evangelical churches elsewhere — church growth is largely internal, related to a birth rate higher than the national average and greater success in holding on to children and geographically mobile members.

This does not necessarily mean that Conservative Protestant churches lack members who are committed. A recent study of eight Conservative congregations in Winnipeg by sociologists Irwin Barker and Raymond Currie found that life-long converts who claimed to be "born again" exhibited equally high levels of commitment as the "outsiders" who had been recruited.[8] Viability does not necessarily dissipate when the outreach does not extend very far.

Incidentally, this conclusion about the importance of retaining the geographically mobile is hardly new. Back in 1903, the Committee on the State of Religion for the Baptist Convention of Ontario and Quebec wrote in its annual report:

> *Many whose names have been erased by change of residence have been lost sight of by the church where their membership had been. In connection with the losses by erasure, it is well to notice large numbers of non-resident members. . . . Do not the foregoing statements demand on the part of our churches a more solicitous guardianship of those that have removed to other parts and have not united with the nearest Baptist church?*[9]

In following the twenty churches through the early 1980s (we will look again in 1991), Brinkerhoff and I have found that the congregations with numerical problems have not been solving them by intensifying their efforts to recruit outsiders. Rather, they have tended to move into newer neighbourhoods with younger families, where they can rely on the much easier membership pathways — namely, other newly arrived evangelicals and their children.[10]

It appears that these churches evangelize outsiders almost as a last resort, pursuing them vigorously only when reaffiliation and birth pathways fail. Even so, intensifying such evangelistic efforts is frequently a second choice to relocating the church altogether.

In the light of the census figures and research to date, it is difficult to support the assertion that many Canadians no longer regularly attending their own groups' services are turning to the Protestant evangelicals. It is not welcome news to these Churches, but the Conservatives are not functioning as alternatives for many Canadians. Outreach is tough in this country. Ironically, however, the seemingly dismal annual average of 1.9 new outsiders may represent a feat of sorts. The reasons for the lack of evangelistic success will soon become clear.

THE ELECTRONIC CHURCH OPTION

The late twentieth century has seen mass-appeal religion move from the outdoors to the indoors, from the tent, arena, and stadium to the television screen. One prominent Canadian communications expert describes the "televangelist" this way:

> His sanctuary is your TV set. His pulpit is a television screen. Your pew is the easy chair in your living room. . . . In lieu of sermons he delivers brief chats, and wouldn't dream of preaching on hell — it's bad for ratings. Some don't preach at all, but sit behind a Johnny Carson desk. . . .[11]

The vast majority of religious programs seen in Canada originate in the United States where, according to religion writer Tom Harpur, business is booming. Harpur reports that the February 1987 annual convention of the National Religious Broadcasters (NRB) in Washington, D.C., drew 4,200 people, with guest speakers including President Ronald Reagan and Vice-President George Bush. Some twenty new religious radio stations and two new TV stations are being opened in the U.S. every month. In the past five years, says Harpur, the number of radio stations with mainly religious programming has jumped from 1,069 to 1,370; the number of TV stations, from 65 to 221. In early 1987, an on-line TV and radio news service, "NRBNet," became available to all members of the NRB.[12]

This emergence of religion on television has led some observers to suggest that the decline in church attendance reflects technological change. Communication is not what it used to be. In the past people literally had to *go* to services. Now it is possible and more convenient to "attend" by watching them in the comfort of their own living rooms. Many argue that religion on television is a substitute for formal church attendance. It's not that people are less interested in worship but that technology has simply transformed the manner in which many worship. People are not turning off; they are simply tuning in.

A cursory glance at Sunday-morning television offerings suggests that there has been a sharp increase in the number of religious programs gracing the tube. Over the years, past and present figures like Oral Roberts, Rex Humbard, Jerry Falwell, Kathryn Kuhlman, Robert Schuller, Jimmy Swaggart, Jim Bakker, and Pat Robertson have become widely known, along with Canadians such as David Mainse and Terry Winter. Assisted by the claims of these programs about the size of their audiences, it is easy to assume that the number of Canadian viewers has grown substantially.

We now have considerable hard information on this question, and it gives little support to the "attendance substitute" thesis. Religious programs are literally more visible through television. But there has actually been a significant decline in the inclination of Canadians to watch the programs or listen to them on radio. In 1958, a Gallup poll claimed that 29% of Canadians were regular patrons of religious broadcasts (see TABLE 2.3). In 1985, that figure stood at only 4% — a drop of 25 percentage points in three decades!

Furthermore, the majority of people who watch religious programs on TV are also regular churchgoers. Almost 80% attend either weekly (68%) or monthly (11%) (see TABLE 2.4).

This finding, however, should not be taken to mean that most regular service attenders are also regular viewers. On the contrary, only 10% of weekly attenders and a mere 1% of people who

TABLE 2.3. **Religious Television Program Viewing Since 1958** *(In %s)**

	N	Regularly	Sometimes	Seldom	Never
NATIONALLY					
1985	1187	4	16	26	54
1980	1294	6	23	18	53
1975	1188	10	26	23	41
1958*	1873	29		46	25

SOURCE: PROJECT CANADA surveys and *Canadian Institute of Public Opinion* (1958).
* 1958 options: "Yes, regularly," "Yes, sometimes," and "No, or practically never."

TABLE 2.4. **Religious Program Viewing by Attendance** *(In %s)*

RELIGIOUS TV Viewing	N	SERVICE ATTENDANCE			
		Weekly	Monthly	Yearly	Never
Regularly	44	68	11	16	5
Sometimes	183	52	14	29	5
Seldom	309	31	15	48	6
Never	641	12	9	55	24
TOTAL	1177	25	12	47	16

SOURCE: PROJECT CAN85.

never attend are tuned in regularly to "the electronic church." Consistent with these findings is the Bishops' 1986 national survey of practising Roman Catholics, which found that only 9% said religious TV or radio programs are "very important" in helping them "to grow as a Christian." In contrast, 73% cited the Mass, 70% personal prayer, 29% participation in lay organizations, and 19% books on faith.[13]

The nature of the audience for religious programs is further clarified when the sample is analysed by age. Almost 80% of the regular audience are 55 or over; conversely, almost 90% of those who never watch such programs are under 55, more than half are under 35 (see TABLE 2.5).

TABLE 2.5.   **Religious Program Viewing by Age**   *(In %s)*

RELIGIOUS TV Viewing	AGE 18-34	35-54	55+	Total
Regularly	4	17	79	100
Sometimes	18	33	49	100
Seldom	38	37	25	100
Never	54	32	14	100

SOURCE: PROJECT CAN85.

Many of that fairly small viewing segment who seldom attend services are therefore probably not outsiders. They are predominantly older people who were once active but now don't attend regularly because of health and lack of mobility. My examination of the infrequent attenders who watch religious programs regularly reveals that 79% are over the age of 55, 17% are 35 to 54, and a mere 4% are under 35. And 77% describe themselves as "committed Christians."

The rule of thumb with Canadian religious television programs, then, is that, except for the committed elderly, they tend to function as a *supplement* to church attendance, rather than as a *substitute* for it. The pattern is hardly unique to Canada. Summing up international findings, Swedish professor Thorleif Pettersson recently wrote:

> *Most of the research, American as well as European, on the audiences of religious broadcasting, has, as a main finding, reported the audience to be rather restricted in size . . . and church-involved. Thus, neither the electronic church's claims of high viewer ratings, nor the main-line churches' charges of "pulling-people-away-from the local church" have been supported.*[14]

In the light of these viewing patterns, it is encouraging to see that the proposed Canadian Interfaith Network (CIN) pay channel has made a number of important modifications in the course of preparing for its launching. Up to the middle of 1986, CIN was an interdenominational project aimed at providing alternative programming for Canadians. However, it was unable to enrol many key groups, most notably the Roman Catholics and Anglicans, who to varying degrees had reservations about its potential audience.

As a result, CIN evolved into Vision TV, which according to Paul De Groot of the *Edmonton Journal* "is more like a commercial network, offering time for sale to religious organizations." Religious groups, including Roman Catholics and Anglicans, have reacted more favourably to the new model; David Nostbakken, the executive director, describes the early commitments as "an extremely strong showing."[15]

One final note: it is clear Canadians not only pay limited attention to the American-style religious programs on television but also hold them in contempt. A November 1986 national poll found that 73% of adults feel uncomfortable about "the increasing number of evangelists appearing on television."[16] The skepticism was fuelled by the January 1987 on-air declaration of Oral Roberts to the effect that God would take his life if $8 million was not forthcoming within three months. His pronouncement received extensive national publicity, with media clearly catering to a cynical majority.

Coverage of the Roberts incident was mild, however, compared with the publicity given the 1987 resignation of Jim Bakker as head of the PTL ("Praise the Lord") Club. This classic kind of religious soap opera, in which minister seduces church secretary, became a tongue-in-cheek media event. Little concern was shown for the relevance of the incident for Canadians, most of whom had previously never heard of Jim Bakker. Unfortunately, even less sensitivity was shown to the 4% of Canadians — mostly elderly people—who in many instances had been shaken and saddened by the fall of one of their religious media stars.

Still, in fairness to the critics of American "televangelism," some of the cynicism is not without warrant. The casual, channel-flicking observer can be excused for thinking the fund-raising is a major emphasis and financial crisis an inherent problem. On a spring 1987 trip spanning Toronto, Ottawa, Montreal, and Quebec City, I found myself browsing through the late-evening offerings, which included a sprinkling of religious programs. Despite the bad publicity given the Roberts affair, the centrality of the appeal for funds was unmistakable, blatant, and annoyingly tedious. Charles Templeton, a former evangelist whose media expertise includes television performance and production, assesses religion on television this way:

> *Television Christianity is an undemanding faith; a media-apostasy that tells listeners that, to become a Christian, all they have to do is 'believe.' . . . The offerings, [extracted] mostly from the poor, the elderly and lonely women, amount to millions of dollars annually. Few of these dollars are used to give succour to the needy, to put food in empty bellies or to help the helpless and dispossessed. . . . There are, among the host of television evangelists, exceptions to those I have described, but they are a minority. . . . On balance I think the contemporary television evangelist is deleterious to society.*[17]

I find it difficult to disagree. When looking stateside, however, as the United Church pointed out on the heels of the Bakker affair, many and probably most Canadian TV evangelists — including David Mainse and Terry Winter—are considerably different from their American counterparts. The style of religion is much more low-key; there are few efforts at empire-building.[18] Winter, for example, recently told me that less than 10% of his show's revenues come from the donations of viewers — funding is provided through private contributions. I would like to think Canadians are plentiful among the ''exceptions'' to which Templeton refers.

THE NEW RELIGION OPTION

One night in 1972, Armand Mauss and I arrived early for a Seattle storefront mission service we were attending as part of our study of skid road religion. We decided to go for a walk in the area, and about two blocks away came across an old theatre where a religious meeting was in progress. We decided to go in. For about half an hour we listened to an impassioned evangelist clothed in what seemed to be a tattered white robe. He claimed to be seeing visions of good things to come for various people who were present. "I see a name!" he exclaimed, and called it out loud, leading exuberant individuals to bound down the aisles to the front to be prayed over. The audience was predominantly composed of working-class whites and blacks, seemingly looking for better things.

In the midst of a long appeal for funds, we had to leave for our mission service. This was my brief and only encounter with the man whose name would one day be known to just about everyone — Jim Jones.

The media have played a major role in creating the impression that new religious movements have been making significant headway in Canada. With the 1970s and early 1980s came a flood of stories about such groups as the Children of God, Hare Krishna, Scientology, and the Unification Church ("Moonies"). The topic was paramount, but the numbers were incidental. A Calgary paper ran a four-part series on the success of the Children of God in that city, mentioning almost by way of footnote that "the threat" consisted of about eight young people living in two houses.

But then, cults made great copy. They therefore received widespread publicity. *Ticket to Heaven*, a movie telling the true story of the conversion and subsequent kidnapping and deprogramming of a Montrealer in California, was chosen Canada's best film of 1982. The average Canadian could be excused for having thought that carefully disguised cult members were lurking everywhere, ready to kidnap and brainwash just about any unsuspecting young person.

With the Jim Jones tragedy in Guyana in 1978, paranoia reached an all-time high. *Maclean's*, in covering the story, included an item on mind control allegedly being used at the Wyevale Mill Christian commune near Midland, Ontario. The magazine concluded:

> *The Wyevale Mill story was just one more sad entry into a file in the attorney general's department thick with descriptions of those seekers of the way, the truth, and the light who have disappeared into various cults and sects never to be seen again, or have emerged psychologically damaged.*[19]

The Ontario government, which five weeks before Guyana had appointed the civil libertarian Daniel Hill to decide if a public inquiry should be held, proceeded with the investigation. "After the saga of the Peoples' Temple," *Maclean's* had prophesied, "the answer seems in little doubt."[20]

For all the publicity and anxiety, the available data have told a different story. It is estimated that in the 1980s this country of 25 million people has about 700 full-time Scientologists, 450 Hare Krishna members, 350 to 650 Moonies, and 250 Children of God.[21] The 1981 census lists 4,100 people who identify with New Thought, Unity, and Metaphysical organizations. Allowing for the possibility that the record-keeping here is far from perfect, it is nonetheless clear that these movements are numerically on the extreme fringe of the Canadian religious scene.

With media hype comes predictable public interest in new religions. However, few of the interested appear to proceed to commitment. As of 1980, 3% of Canadians reported that they had had a strong interest in some of the new religions at one time or another, but only 1% still did at that time. Frederick Bird and William Reimer of Concordia University surveyed evening university students and found participation in new groups to be highly transitory.[22] Interest in new religions appears to have been at best a passing fancy.

Less than one-half of 1% of Canadians are actually participating in any new religion activities. The most popular of these has been transcendental meditation (TM). However, many of the participants view it more as a meditation practice than as a religion.

Here, as with the electronic church, the opposition and hostility towards some new religious movements should not be underestimated. The 1975 *PROJECT CANADA* survey found that, apart from interest in new movements, 42% were *opposed* to satanist groups, with similar negative sentiments expressed by 17% for Hare Krishna, 11% for the Children of God, 8% for Zen, 7% for TM, and 6% for Yoga. A 1983 study of Canadian and American University students by Calgary sociologists Brinkerhoff and Marlene Mackie found that less than 3% would want to see a family member marry a Unificationist ("Moonie"), Hare

Krishna, or Scientologist. Further, some 50% would exclude Moonies from their respective countries, 30% Hare Krishnas, and 15% Scientologists.[23]

Religious brainwashing and deprogramming have been far more prevalent in Canadian newsrooms and TV and radio studios than in everyday life. The media have been dabbling in religious deviance, rather than depicting what is real for an appreciable number of Canadians.

Some people, most notably American observers Rodney Stark and William Bainbridge,[24] have argued that in Canada, as elsewhere, cult centres are most abundant in areas such as British Columbia where conventional religion is weakest. They predict that, in time, new religious movements will make inroads, recruiting people who have abandoned the traditional groups. But national survey results to date offer no support for this thesis.[25] Canadians who seem to have abandoned their own religious groups have shown little inclination to adopt the new religions, no matter how plentiful or active the groups may be. Stark's reaction in a personal conversation with me was: "I guess it's not showing up so far." Persistent with his argument, he encourages ongoing readings.[26]

It's easy to underestimate the impact of conventional religious socialization on the average Canadian mind and heart. Most of us have been raised in a predominantly Judeo-Christian culture and find it difficult to deviate very far from familiar religious ideas and practices. Alternative expressions that exceed our "range of religious familiarity" are sometimes received with psychological responses we had not consciously expected. To put it another way, most of us cannot handle new religions that differ very dramatically from the old ones.

Take "New Age" worship forms, for example. For many people, the New Age movement is associated with Marilyn Ferguson (*The Aquarian Conspiracy*)[27] and Shirley MacLaine (*Out on a Limb* and *Dancing in the Light*).[28] The term "New Age" has come to embrace a wide range of ideas seen as belonging to a new era—in keeping with the astrological prediction of the dawn of an Aquarian Age with the coming of the twenty-first century. It combines a pro-human outlook, eastern mysticism, and, for some, contact with the spirit world.

However, while individual New Age congregations exist, the movement is not tied to any particular organization, has no overarching hierarchical structure, and is extremely diverse in both practice and belief. Evidence of its lack of content uniformity and monolithic structure are the varied people linked with the New Age movement — celebrities like MacLaine, Yoko Ono, and John Denver, Werner Erhard of *est* and *The Forum* and the author Fritjof Capra.[29]

During the past year, I attended the morning service of a New Age congregation in Edmonton, the Centre for Self-Awareness. The centre is a member church of Religious Science International and the International New Thought Alliance. The Bible reading was referred to in the calendar as a "Metaphysical Interpretation of the Bible," prayers as "Treatments," the responsive reading as an "affirmation," the hymns as "songs." The "songs" included "This Land Is Your Land," "Let There Be Peace on Earth," and "It's in Every One of Us." The offertory song was "Put on a Happy Face." It was not clear to the novice to whom or where the prayers were being addressed. Nor was their termination obvious, since they carried no "Amen" endings.

Without being disparaging, it seems accurate to assert that the forms are familiar to people raised in the Judeo-Christian tradition, but the content is not. While some New Age emphases, such as belief in human potential and various kinds of meditation, might be fairly readily adopted, exclusive commitment to a New Age group would probably be a fairly drastic transition for most people who have been brought up on traditional religion.

New religions are being used as alternatives to old religions by relatively few people. In view of the conventional religious socialization of most Canadians, the situation is unlikely to change markedly in the foreseeable future.

THE INVISIBLE RELIGION OPTION

Two decades ago, European sociologist Thomas Luckmann wrote a provocative and popular book entitled *The Invisible*

Religion.[30] Early in the summer of 1981, he and I sat together at an outdoor restaurant in Constance, Germany, overlooking the Rhine. For about three hours, while we enjoyed the warmth of a bright sun, he clarified the ideas he had tried to convey in his book. He had not found the decline of church-oriented religion in modern societies surprising. But that didn't mean that he felt religion in a more general sense was disappearing. Instead, it has been taking on new, personal, "privatized forms." In the course of acquiring identity and thereby becoming self-transcendent, says Luckmann, individuals develop "systems of meaning." These systems run like thread through the various sectors of a person's life, giving it coherence.

Until relatively recently, he continued, church-oriented religion was the dominant source of these integrating systems of meaning. Industrialization and ensuing secularization, however, have made traditional religion just one of a variety of themes around which such systems are developed. Theme possibilities for Luckmann include the family, sexuality, mobility, self-expression, and self-realization. The present interest in certain supranatural phenomena — such as astrology, ESP, bio-rhythms, and human auras — might suggest other potential system themes. Tom Sinclair-Faulkner of Dalhousie University, for example, has gone so far as to argue that "hockey is more than a game in Canada: it functions as a religion for many."[31] According to the criteria used here, it is an interesting but precarious claim.

In practice, Luckmann's invisible religions or alternative systems of meaning have largely eluded researchers. Various "exploration attempts" in the United States by such eminent researchers as J. Milton Yinger, Charles Glock, Andrew Greeley, and Robert Wuthnow have generally been judged unconvincing.[32]

Glock, for example, joined forces with Thomas Piazza in an attempt to explore what they call "reality structures." People who responded to their mailback questionnaire were presented with a number of problems on the personal and social levels and asked to try to account for them. The two researchers identified six major answer-types or structures — environmental, individual, cultural, supernatural, conspiratorial, and hereditarian. One of the problems with their findings is that many people use a number of structures to account for what is happening personally and socially, rather than giving evidence of having one dominant structure that provides meaning to all of life.

The inconclusiveness of these American results corroborates the findings of research in England conducted by Melanie Cottrell, a sociologist.[33] She carried out three-hour in-depth interviews with a sample of some forty people in a southern English community near Oxford in an attempt to uncover "invisible thread." After carefully analysing these interviews, she concluded that such threads could seldom be identified. Most people were simply not in the market for integrative meaning systems. In her words:

> *The people I have interviewed do not require "meaning" in any way and do not seek functional equivalents to religion. One ancient religion appears to be near to death, but no new religions are being born.* [34]

Using data from the *PROJECT CANADA* surveys, I have carefully probed the presence of invisible religion in Canada.[35] Following Luckmann's suggestion, my strategy was first to try to identify the presence of some possible meaning-system themes. The data allowed me to explore the themes of the family and feminism, along with science, mysticism, and paranormal interest. I then examined the extent to which these themes are associated with the provision of answers to questions of meaning regarding life and death. I also explored the extent to which they "tie" the various spheres of our lives together — family, work, leisure, and so on.

The results were consistent with the American and British research: some Canadians, notably those committed to a traditional version of Christianity, give evidence of having access to a system of meaning that addresses both immediate and ultimate concerns. However, most Canadians either do not exhibit highly integrated personal lives, or tie the various facets of their lives together without drawing upon an identifiable meaning system. The thread of which Luckmann spoke is commonly neither church-like nor invisible; rather, it is missing altogether. Added to the earlier studies, the findings for Canada suggest that it may not be true that all people require meaning systems. The search for them by social scientists may be largely futile.

In our country and elsewhere, people who give up conventional religion cannot be assumed to be adopting alternate systems of meaning, such as political conviction, humanitarianism, hedonism, and so on. Indeed, the evidence is strong in the opposite direction—if people are not visibly religious, the likelihood is that they are not informed by any system of meaning at all.

Stark and Bainbridge have come to much the same conclusion in the light of their American findings. They note that meaning systems are difficult to construct and sustain. They require social support in the form of organizations to which people are tied through social relationships. As a result, they write, "It may be only in the sphere of [conventional] religion that it is feasible to create and sustain a really general meaning system."[36]

It seems that if people do not have some kind of social support for their religion, they are seldom inclined to "go it alone" in a private one. A well-worn phrase in social psychology is that ideas are socially created, socially sustained, and socially changed.[37] Religion shows no sign of having been granted an exemption from that pattern.

THE NO RELIGION OPTION

Many Canadians are disenchanted with conventional forms of Roman Catholicism and Protestantism but are not inclined to turn to the Conservatives, the electronic church, the new religions, or privatized religion. But there is one more obvious possibility: they may simply be abandoning religion altogether. This would be in keeping with the prophecies of the likes of the father of sociology, Auguste Comte, who saw religion as giving way successively to metaphysics and science,[38] and the founder of psychoanalysis, Sigmund Freud, who expected religion to give way to reason.[39]

There seems to be some support for this argument. As mentioned earlier, some 7% of Canadian adults now indicate "None" when asked for their religious group preference. This represents an increase of more than six percentage points since 1961 and three points since 1971.

But these figures are misleading. Before 1971, "None" was not regarded by the census-takers as a valid response. They literally would not take "nothing" for an answer, probably because the pervasiveness of affiliation seemed to make the category unnecessary. It seems that "the Nones" partly made the new category necessary and partly were created by it.

Still, the increase of three percentage points between 1971 and 1981 at the very least reveals a culture in which a decreasing number of Canadians feel compelled to indicate a preference for any religious group. It may also indicate that a growing number of people have no religion at all.

The PROJECT CANADA survey samples, as I mentioned earlier, have included a core of people who have participated in all three of the surveys. The surveys consequently offer unique "panel data," making it possible to explore what happens to "religious Nones" over time.[40] Most of the non-affiliated were found to be under the age of forty. Within ten years, almost half of those we have been able to follow left the None category and adopted a Protestant or Catholic affiliation — usually that of their parents. Of the 1975 "Nones," close to four in ten became Protestants or Roman Catholics by 1980. A further one in ten adopted those labels by 1985.

Why did these Nones appear to affiliate? An examination of their belief, practice, and involvement levels suggest that few of the Nones affiliate because of intensified religious commitment. If anything, the Nones who become "something" exhibit slightly lower levels of religiousness than the population as a whole (see TABLE 2.6). Affiliation appears to be associated not with spiritual urgency but with the need for rites of passage pertaining to marriage, baptism of children, and, in some cases, death.

When "religious Nones" marry, many desire church rites and tend to look to the affiliation of their parents. The same is true when, as some crassly put it, people want their children "done," and, frequently, when death occurs.

TABLE 2.6. **Beliefs and Practices of Switching Nones and Others** *(In %s)*

	N	Switching Nones (28)	Protestants Roman Catholics (1106)	All Canada (1308)
Belief: God		41	75	66
Belief: Divinity Jesus		30	77	68
Private prayer		50	76	70
See self as committed Christian		19	47	40
Church membership		14	46	42
Weekly attendance		0	32	38

SOURCE: Derived from Bibby and Weaver, 1985.

For many and perhaps most of the Nones, then, non-affiliation is a temporary category adopted in early adulthood, foreign both to one's past and to one's future. Few Canadians set up permanent residence among "the religious Nones."

A CAUSE FOR PAUSE

The exodus from the churches has led observers to look in a variety of places for the alleged defectors. But the extensive searches of the past few decades have largely been exercises in futility.

As one of the people who have helped to lead a number of those unproductive expeditions, I'd like to try to save face by making a suggestion. Having looked for the recalcitrants in every conceivable place and found few, perhaps we should retrace our steps, trek back home, and renew the search there — just in case.

3

THE DROP-OUT MYTH

The dramatic downturn in attendance has created panic in the Churches. Infrequent attenders and outright non-attenders have been viewed as drop-outs who have been lost to the Church, and possibly to the faith. They have been variously dubbed "inactives," "lapsed members," "defectors," "switchers," "disaffiliates," "apostates," and, of course, "backsliders."

Consequently, a major preoccupation of religious groups has been re-recruitment. Some groups speak of the need for "re-evangelization."[1] The central question is "What will it take to bring them back?" This equation of non-attendance with disaffiliation has been widely shared by academics, who have searched high and low for these alleged dissidents in order to account for their apparent departure.

This drop-out mind set has blinded us to the possibility that we may be "looking in all the wrong places." After all, as was seen in the previous chapter, we have failed to locate the apparent defectors outside their previous groupings — even, for any appreciable length of time, in the "None" category.

The religious institutions of Canada are overdue for a new strategy. Before embarking on further exhaustive searches, why not stop long enough to let Canadians speak for themselves, through census and survey data?

IDENTIFICATION STABILITY

If religious defection is characteristic of Canadians, it should show up in the national census. A cursory glance at the most recent census figures, however, shows that almost 90% of Canadians continue to claim Roman Catholic (47%) or Protestant (41%) ties (see TABLE 3.1). Another 5% are associated with other religions. The remaining 7% have no affiliation.

TABLE 3.1.   **Population Proportions of Select Religions Groups: 1871-1981**   *(In %s)*

	1871	1881	1901	1921	1941	1961	1981
RC	43	42	42	39	42	46	47
UC	na	na	na	na	19	20	16
Congregationalist	.6	.6	.5	.3			
Methodist	16	17	17	13			
ANGLICAN	14	14	14	16	15	13	10
CONSERVATIVE PROTESTANT	8	8	8	8	7	7	7
Baptist	7	7	6	5	4	3	3
Mennonite	*	*	.6	.7	1.0	.8	.8
Pentecostal	*	*	.0	.1	.5	.8	1.4
Salvation Army	*	*	.2	.3	.3	.5	.5
LUTHERAN	1	1	2	3	3	4	3
PRESBYTERIAN	16	16	16	16	7	4	3
OTHER	1	1	2	5	6	2	7
Eastern Orthodox	*	*	.3	2	3	1	1
Jewish	.0	.1	.3	1	1	1	1
Jehovah's Witness	*	*	*	.1	.1	.4	.6
Mormon	.0	*	.1	.2	.2	.3	.4
Hindu	*	*	*	*	*	*	.3
Islam	*	*	*	*	*	*	.3
Sikh	*	*	*	*	*	*	.3
Buddhist	*	*	.2	.1	.1	.1	.2
Confucian	*	*	.1	.3	.2	.0	.0
NONE	.0	.0	.0	.2	.5	4	7

* Not available. na = Not applicable.
SOURCES: Canadian censuses, 1961 & 1981; 1871-1941: 1941 Census, Vol. 1:288-92.
NOTE: Mennonites included with Baptists in 1871 & 1891; Hutterites included with Mennonites.

Despite their increasing tendency to stay away from worship services, Canadians are not abandoning the historically dominant groups. The point is simple, but extremely important.

In the midst of attendance bedlam, changes of affiliation during this century have been relatively minor. It is true that there have been some internal changes, attributable primarily to immigration and birth.[2] The proportion of Roman Catholics has increased while the United Church and Anglican proportions have decreased. As noted earlier, some of the theologically conservative Protestant groups — such as the Pentecostals, Christian and Missionary Alliance, and the Salvation Army — have grown slightly faster than the population. Other Conservative groups, however, including the Baptists and Mennonites, have not.

Jews have remained fairly constant at about 1% since about 1940. Recent immigration has resulted in a slight increase in the number of Hindus and Sikhs, yet proportionately, both still constitute less than 1% of the population. Buddhists have remained at under 1% throughout the century.

Jehovah's Witnesses and Mormons have the reputation of growing rapidly, but the two groups combined still form only 1% of the population. The Witnesses reached .8% in 1971 but have declined slightly since that time (.6% in 1981). Mormons have enjoyed impressive growth in the United States and a number of other countries, but have failed to make noteworthy proportional advances here.

Canadians, then, offer the census-taker little evidence that they are deserting the nation's prominent religious groups. Few report that they have no religious preference; even fewer say they have ties with the newer groups.

A MONOPOLIZED MOSAIC

Since the eighteenth century, a small number of Protestant groups, along with Roman Catholics, have monopolized the religious scene. The census figures point to a continuing Canadian religious establishment. This establishment consists of four dominant groupings — Roman Catholics (47%), the United Church

(16%), Anglicans (10%), and Conservative Protestants (7%): about 80% of the population altogether.

Some other groups, notably Lutherans (3%), Presbyterians (3%), and Jews (1%), are also solidly entrenched. (Most Presbyterians joined the United Church in 1925.) They have stable followings and fairly high profiles. However, numerically they are on the outer edge of the religious establishment.

From the early years, and certainly during this century, the four "establishment" groupings have monopolized the Canadian religious market. They have been and continue to be Canada's four major "religious companies." As University of Waterloo sociologist Kenneth Westhues has put it, "If Canadian churches exist in a free market, it is a market like that of North American auto companies, a handful of which account for the bulk of sales."[3]

FOLLOWING IN PARENTAL FOOTSTEPS

The high level of stability of Canada's religious market is apparent in findings on intergenerational affiliation (see TABLE 3.2). Almost 90% of Canadians with Roman Catholic or Protestant parents have retained those ties themselves. Only 1% affiliate with a different religious tradition. The remaining 8% are located in the highly transitory "None" category.

TABLE 3.2. **Intergenerational Affiliation: All Canadians**
(In %s)

PARENTS' AFFILIATION	N	PRESENT AFFFILIATION					Total
		RC	Prot	Jew	Other	None	
Roman Catholic	457	88	3	0	1	8	100
Protestant	461	3	88	0	1	8	100
Jew*	12	0	0	100	0	0	100
Other*	7	0	7	0	93	0	100
None	54	13	32	0	2	53	100

SOURCE: PROJECT CAN85.
* The number of cases in the sample (12 and 7, respectively) are obviously insufficient to permit stable percentaging. They are included for interest value.

It is consistent with our earlier findings in tracing "religious Nones" over time that almost half the people with no religious parentage affiliate with Protestantism or Catholicism. The "Other Religions," although showing relative stability, nevertheless do lose a number of their affiliates to Christianity.

These intergenerational stability patterns are unlikely to change. The *PROJECT TEEN CANADA* analyses of the nation's 15- to 19-year-olds have found that approximately 90% of Roman Catholics and Protestants are claiming the same religious-group preference as their parents.[4] A further 27% of teens with "parental Nones" are opting for Protestant or Catholic affiliation. The same is true for 16% of young people with "parental Others."

Tightening the focus, the stability of religious ties between generations is also present at the Protestant denominational level (see TABLE 3.3). Protestants do some switching, but they still show a strong tendency to remain within their groupings.

The general pattern is readily observable: the smaller the group, the greater the inclination to move out. This seems to reflect marriage opportunities within the groups, given the different sizes of their "marriage pools." United Church affiliates have some 16% of the opposite sex to choose from, Anglicans 10%, the rest 7% to 3%; Roman Catholics, in contrast, have almost a 50% population pool.

Still, Protestant movement out of the Protestant category is relatively infrequent, happening in no more than about one in ten instances.

TABLE 3.3. **Intergenerational Switching: Protestants**
 (In %s)

PARENTS' AFFILIATION	N	PRESENT AFFFILIATION						
		Ang	UC	Cons	Luth	Pres	RC	Oth
Ang	138	71	12	4	1	1	5	6
UC	140	11	75	1	1	4	1	7
Cons	58	7	12	65	0	3	1	12
Luth	39	1	5	2	75	1	4	12
Pres	41	17	15	1	1	54	3	9

SOURCE: PROJECT CAN85.

It is now clear why our searches for disaffiliates have come up mostly empty. Regardless of their levels of attendance at services, relatively few Canadians actually desert their religious groups. The alleged defectors have seldom left home. They may not be attending services to the extent their parents and grandparents did, but most of them have not jumped ship.

Canada's established groups might be surprised to learn that an amazingly small number of people have been lost. Switching to other groups and to the "no religion" category is fairly rare. For better or worse, religious affiliation is extremely stable and should remain so in the foreseeable future.

CORRECTING A FALSE EQUATION

As must be clear by now, the equation of irregular service attendance with religious defection is inaccurate. In the colourful phrase of the Anglican Archbishop of Toronto, Lewis Garnsworthy, "It's not that they're leaving; it's just that they're not coming!"[5]

The Archbishop knows first-hand what he is talking about. Diocesan officials in the past have seen inactives as largely lost to the Church. In 1985 I was asked to study affiliates in the diocese. I found that close to 80% of self-proclaimed inactive Anglicans — only 8% of whom attend services weekly — maintain that "being Anglicans" is important to them. Very few indicate any inclination to turn elsewhere. And these are the inactives! Needless to say, the loyalty level approaches unanimity for the actives: some 96% place a high value on being Anglicans.

Canadians are not attending religious services in numbers comparable with the past. But the overwhelming majority still continue to identify with the historically dominant groups. It has been a major error to equate attendance drop-off with religious disaffiliation. The ties remain strong.

Ironically, rather than readily losing people, the major religious groups in reality have extreme difficulty losing them. Over generations, religion has been fused with one's family, biography, and culture. The bond is not readily dissolved.

If that is not enough, it should be remembered that in the case of Roman Catholics and some other groups such as Mormons, one is not allowed to wander far from home even in a psychological sense. The reason: such groups do not give individuals the right to quit. In the Catholic case, the Church regards baptized Catholics as irrevocably and forever members of the Church.[6] The Mormons have very involved procedures for the revocation of membership. In these and other cases, even when one wants to leave, it's tough.

PRECARIOUS PARANOIA

The myth of the drop-out created by the decline in service attendance carries a psychological price-tag.

Some leaders masochistically blame themselves for the fall in attendance. If people stop attending, they surely must be disenchanted with the organizations generally and religious leaders specifically. It's not an easy thing to maintain a positive clerical self-image in the face of an ever-dwindling congregation. Nor is one's self-image elevated by the seemingly constant complaints about irrelevant ministry, hypocrisy, preoccupation with money, and incompetent leadership.

Clergy and other officials have frequently felt stigmatized. An Anglican priest — and he is certainly not alone — joked to me how he finds himself playing down his ministerial role whenever possible, frequently abandoning his clerical collar. He stresses that he "is just like anyone else."

His feelings of stigma seem to be grossly exaggerated. The 1975 PROJECT CANADA survey found that about 80% of Canadians were feeling at ease in the presence of a minister, priest, or rabbi; some 15% said they felt "a bit" uneasy; less than 5% indicated they were "very uneasy."

In the more than forty years since World War II, the polls have shown that about half of Canadians have consistently viewed organized religion as a relevant part of their lives. Organized religion has tended to be among the nation's leaders in the respect and confidence it has been accorded — outdistancing, for example, the Supreme Court, public schools, the House of Commons, newspapers, corporations, political parties, and labour unions (see TABLE 3.4).

The *PROJECT CANADA* adult and teenage surveys have documented similar positive views of religious leaders. In general, teenagers are more positive than adults about leadership in almost every sector. The confidence levels of both teens and adults regarding church leaders are similar to those for the schools, the court system, and science (see TABLE 3.5). The confidence in religious leaders is less than that shown the police, but well above the confidence accorded the media, government, and labour.

Some will say, "But what about Quebec? Hasn't the post-1950s disenchantment with the Church been a major factor in declining attendance? Haven't many Quebeckers, in the style of René Levesque, seen their Church as the perpetrator of the old, oppressive structures and therefore worthy of little time or respect?"

In some cases, the answer is surely "yes." The 1975 *PROJECT CANADA* survey found that in Quebec, specifically, the two most commonly cited reasons Roman Catholics gave for decreased participation were disenchantment with the Church and a reaction to having had religion forced on them as children. The latter factor, while mentioned by 26% of Canadians who were no longer

TABLE 3.4. **Confidence and Respect Accorded Select Institutions and Organizations**
% Indicating "A Great Deal" or "Quite a Bit"

	1974	1979
Church, organized religion	58	60
Supreme Court	53	57
Public schools	*	54
House of Commons	42	38
Newspapers	*	37
Large corporations	26	34
Political parties	*	30
Labour unions	25	23

SOURCE: *Canadian Institute of Public Opinion*, September 18 & 21, 1974; August 4, 1979.
* Not included in 1974.

TABLE 3.5. **Teenage and Adult Confidence in Institutional Leaders**
"How much CONFIDENCE do you have in the people in charge of . . ."

% Indicating "A Great Deal" or "Quite a Bit"

	Teens (3599)	Adults (1201)
The police	77	74
The schools	68	56
The court system	67	48
Science	65	66
The churches	62	50
Television	57	43
Newspapers	48	39
Your provincial government	40	30
The federal government	39	29
Labour unions	35	21

SOURCE: PROJECT CAN85 and PROJECT TEEN CANADA.

as involved as previously, was cited by no less than 66% of less involved Catholics in Quebec.[7]

In general, the decline in attendance has not been signalling disenchantment with conventional religion and religious leaders. Few people, young or old, are "mad" at the churches or critical of their leaders. Contrary to widespread belief, the overwhelming majority of Canadians are neither leaving nor upset.

PLURALISM AND STABILITY

Some observers are mystified by continuing religious identification in the face of sporadic attendance. One evangelical visitor from Britain, in deploring the spiritual state of the land, commented fifty years ago, "Strange to say, the people are often loyal to [the churches] — why I cannot say."[8]

It is no accident, however, that religious affiliation in Canada has remained so stable. In virtually every society, religion is strongly tied to an individual's biography and culture. That link comes to have profound psychological and emotional dimensions. Religion is learned in childhood family settings and is present in rites of passage associated with life's crucial events. The impact of these passage rites should not be underestimated. Participation in them can almost indelibly link individuals with religious groups and traditions. To be baptized a Roman Catholic or confirmed as a Lutheran, to be married in a United Church or have a parent buried as an Anglican — all of these ceremonies contribute to psychological and emotional attachment.

A classic example of the role of rites in identification is the Jewish bar mitzvah for males and the bat mitzvah for females. According to rabbinic law, the transition into adulthood takes place at age 13 for boys and 12 for girls. In a Friday night or Saturday morning service, the young person (the bar or bat mitzvah) reads from the Torah for the first time. A number of social events surround the ceremony, typically including a dinner for close family, refreshments for those attending the service, and a dinner and dance for invited guests. The last often includes speeches by the bar or bat mitzvah and his or her relatives. Presents are given and a permanent record made in the form of a photo album or a video tape.[9]

But what is of central importance, says Stuart Schoenfeld of York University, is that the bar and bat mitzvahs are far more than merely ceremonies acknowledging movement into adulthood:

The group gathers together to renew its moral bonds, to symbolically assert its cohesiveness. . . . They are modern rituals of identification more than they are traditional rituals of initiation.[10]

The importance of one's affiliation, therefore, can hardly be measured only by such a crude indicator as service attendance. Long after weekly attendance is a thing of the past, the children of the English immigrant regard themselves as Anglicans, the Québécois see themselves as Roman Catholics, the grandchildren of the Methodist or Congregationalist identify with the United Church. Similar tendencies characterize countless other Canadians who have ceased to attend their churches with regularity. Low synagogue attendance in major cities, says Marshall Sklare, would lead one to think the synagogue is peripheral to Jewish life. "Nothing," he says, "could be further from the truth."[11] Religious identification goes far beyond occupying a pew or having one's name on a congregational list. It is psychological and emotional in nature. Consequently, it commonly continues to live on, even when the plugs on the organizational support systems have been pulled.

Pierre Berton, who acknowledged some twenty years ago in *The Comfortable Pew* that he had left the Anglican Church, nonetheless speaks of the emotional weight of a heritage in which religion has had a place. Berton recently wrote:

> *My earliest memories are tied up with that same family Bible in which [great-great-great-grandfather] Peter Berton described his arrival on those cold and barren Atlantic shores. My [Church of England] father used to read those passages aloud to us, showing us the cramped, brown handwriting, then 150 years old. Thus, in far-off Dawson City, we felt the tug of our heritage. I still have that Bible and I cannot turn those brittle pages without feeling a little tingle, as if a ghost had just brushed past.* [12]

But beyond personal biography and group culture, another critical factor has contributed significantly to the stability of religious group identification in Canada: the national norm of pluralism. Such an ideal has been increasingly incorporated into the Canadian psyche, with implications for a wide variety of aspects of national life. I'm talking about those Canadian "buzz words," bilingualism and multiculturalism, concepts largely created as the federal government's official response to the human diversity of the country.

This emphasis on pluralism appears to have moved beyond the linguistic and cultural spheres to human rights more generally. A sampling of survey comments illustrates the trend. A 53-year-old gas-station operator in rural Nova Scotia comments, "Everyone has the right to express their views, no matter how objectionable they are to you." "Each adult should be entitled to his or her own opinion," says a 29-year-old Quebec City woman, who adds, "Freedom of speech can help people develop intellectually." Many Canadians express some concern about coercion, especially where young people are involved. A Mission, B.C., housewife and mother of two children maintains, "Everyone should have the right to their own opinion, but it should not be forced on young, impressionable minds." Concern is also expressed about the abuse of free speech. A 59-year-old Toronto caretaker, for example, says, "Freedom of speech should be allowed, but not to such an extent that people be harmed or maligned."

The pluralistic ideal in Canada has not left the moral sphere untouched. It seems accurate to speak of a Canadian "moral mosaic."[13] In the United States, the likes of Jerry Falwell can crusade successfully for moral truth under the banner of the Moral Majority. In Canada, however, moral crusades are felt to be rather distasteful, even among Conservative Protestants. A recent poll of 126 Canadian leaders and lay people by the evangelical magazine *Faith Today* found that only 10% would approve of a Moral Majority operation in Canada; a minority of just 24% said they approved of the American Moral Majority's approach and programs. A number of people in the same poll indicated that an Ontario-based movement headed by the Reverend Kenneth Campbell, known as Renaissance International, "is too right wing and abrasive."[14] The thirteen-year-old movement, described by some of the media as Canada's Moral Majority, has had little success in mounting a significant following. There are virtually no efforts to carry out general moral crusades in other parts of the country. Canadians have not been imbued with an ideology valuing "the pursuit of truth," but with one valuing "the pursuit of appreciation for diverse views."

This ideal of pluralism has been spilling over into the sphere of religion. In a country placing paramount value on the positive co-existence of diversity, it is not at all clear how "appropriate" it is for churches aggressively to recruit people who bear other groups' labels. Evangelism borders on imperialism. However heart-warming these words of Jacques Cartier may have been around 1630, they produce a cringe from most of us in the 1980s:

[Finding the aborigines] living without God and without religion like brute beasts, I thereupon concluded in my private judgment that I should be committing a great sin if I did not make it my business to devise some means of bringing them to the knowledge of God. [15]

Rather than applauding Cartier's evangelistic fervour, most of us, I suspect, would find ourselves cheering the remarks of Saskatchewan Cree Chief Thunderchild in the late nineteenth century:

The white men have offered us two forms of religion: the Roman Catholic and the Protestant. But we in our Indian bands have our own religion. Why is that not accepted too? It is the worship of one God, and it was the strength of our people for centuries. [16]

The United Church, at its General Council in 1986, voted to extend an official apology to Canadian Native peoples for being blind to their spirituality and for imposing White culture on them. The apology was delivered almost immediately by moderator Robert Smith and some five hundred Council delegates, and was readily accepted. [17]

A 1987 editorial in the Anglican national newspaper, *The Canadian Churchman*, deplored the fact that the first Anglican missionary to the Nishga Indians in northern British Columbia

was horrified by Nishga culture, which he interpreted as rampant paganism. He ordered the totem poles cut down. He forbade ceremonials and dances. Singlehandedly he was responsible for the virtual destruction of centuries of Nishga culture.

It was also noted that this was far from an isolated response. [18]

A 39-year-old United Church woman in rural Manitoba may well reflect prevalent Canadian sentiments when she says, "I feel if a person wishes to be religious it is their business. But in the same breath, they should not try to force their religion on others."

The Roman Catholic Church is among the religious groups that have readily recognized the need for intergroup respect, not only in a multinational Canada but in a world community that calls for universal human rights. It therefore speaks of "dialogue" with other Christians and emphasizes the respect for freedom of conscience in attempting to evangelize non-Christians:

> *In spreading religious faith and introducing religious practices, everyone ought at all times to refrain from any manner of action which could seem to carry a hint of coercion or of a kind of persuasion that would be dishonourable or unworthy.*[19]

Intergroup protocol calls for mutual respect—whether the organizations involved are religious or secular. In June of 1986, Dave Nichol of Loblaws proclaimed in a widely circulated newspaper advertisement for cat food, "Cats are like Baptists — they raise hell — but you can't catch them at it." Wrong thing to say. Nichol found himself apologizing not only to Baptists, but also to his 83-year-old Baptist mother, who called his ad "distasteful."[20]

The visit of Pope John Paul II in 1984 was seen, accordingly, as "good for all Canadians," not only by the predictable eight in ten Roman Catholics, but also by a polite six in ten Protestants and five in ten Others.[21] Brian Stiller, executive director of the Evangelical Fellowship of Canada, said that the Pope was not the authentic leader of all Christendom and therefore was not being welcomed as such by all Christians.[22] His remarks bordered on being "un-Canadian."

But as pluralistically inappropriate was an amazing letter from Dalton Camp in the spring of 1985, addressed to "concerned Canadians" and written—ironically—in support of the Canadian Civil Liberties Association. In the letter, Camp stated:

> *Evangelical movements are becoming increasingly well organized, vocal, and influential. Just look at the groups south of the border. They want their religious doctrines enacted into law and imposed on everyone else.*[23]

Should a reflective bystander point out that that kind of thing may have been taking place stateside, but not in this country, Camp was determined to proceed undaunted:

> *Sure Canada is different, but* we can't afford to be complacent. *There is no denying that many of the same signs are surfacing here. Trends do have a habit of moving north.*[24]

Needless to say, Brian Stiller did not lack for a response to such an "un-Canadian" attack. In an October letter to Camp on behalf of the Evangelical Fellowship of Canada, Stiller said:

> *By your name [CCLA], the implication is that you defend the civil liberties of our citizens. Given that we are a pluralistic society within a democratic environment, isn't it fair to conclude that evangelicals, with whom you obviously have disagreement, also have a civil right to their own point of view and to the expression of that view within the public forums of this nation?* [24]

I have no doubt most people would concur with Stiller.

Even in the immediate aftermath of the 1978 Jim Jones cult tragedy in Guyana, only one in two Canadians thought that smaller, cult-like religious groups should be more closely supervised by government.[26] As Calgary sociologist Harry Hiller points out, as long as religious groups' norms are not in sharp conflict with societal norms such as national loyalty or the monogamous family, tolerance is usually forthcoming.[27]

Pluralism also has the effect of making sheer critiques of society precarious. The reason? Criticism runs the risk of stepping on the toes of individuals and groups and thus being seen as an attack on others. Anglican Archbishop Lewis Garnsworthy has been severely stigmatized for questioning the public funding of Roman Catholic schools in Ontario. In the Archbishop's own words, "To speak is to risk being called a bigot."[28] In the educational matter, incidentally, Protestants, says one academic observer, "seem to have acquiesced," leaving Roman Catholics "in a favoured position regarding education in most provinces."[29]

Affiliational stability is hardly new. Some observers think that the religious market was much freer in the past, when gains were more easily made. Canadian Baptist Federation minister and official Maurice Boillat recently stated, "There is no doubt in my mind that a monumental strategical error was made some 50 years ago when we sent countless missionaries to Africa but none to Spadina [an area in Toronto]." Things may have been easier. But there is good reason to believe that well before "50 years ago," the situation was already tough.[30] In 1857, a Catholic priest who turned to evangelical Protestantism started a work in Quebec City. After ten years, he had a church of *twenty* members.[31] The tight market persists. The general pluralistic ideal has only solidified religious affiliational loyalty in Canada. In such a cultural milieu, in which recruitment is in questionable taste and where claims to the truth are virtually unacceptable outside the group in which they are made, people would not be expected to move in random fashion from one group to another.

A POSTSCRIPT ON DEFECTION

The fact is, Canadians seldom move away from the religious preferences of their parents. Over this century, there has been an extremely high level of affiliational stability. Attendance levels may be down, but relatively few Canadians are disenchanted with the churches or their leaders. The established groups have continued to dominate the twentieth-century religion market, and have "lost" relatively few Canadians.

But this is not to say for one moment that things have remained the same.

4
RELIGION À LA CARTE

During the 1960s, it was common to assert that modern men and women could no longer give credence to supernatural doctrines. Picking up a phrase from the nineteenth-century philosopher Nietzsche, some theologians announced that God as "He" had traditionally been conceived was "dead."[1] Supernatural ideas were said to have lost their relevance to our times. We now know that such claims were inaccurate. North American and European research reveals that while religion is perhaps taken less seriously now than before, modernity has done little to slay supernatural beliefs and related practices. Canada is no exception.

ULTIMATE QUESTIONS

Canadians continue to have a very strong interest in what many refer to as the "ultimate questions"—issues pertaining to the meaning and future of our existence. The national surveys have found that more than eight in ten Canadians say they "often" or "sometimes" think about why there is suffering in the world (see TABLE 4.1). Some seven in ten report that they reflect on what happens after death, life's purpose, and whether or not there is a God or Supreme Being. Six in ten find themselves pondering the world's origin, while about the same number say they "sometimes" or "often" think about how they can find real happiness.

An additional 10% to 20% report they no longer raise these questions, presumably either because they think they have found

TABLE 4.1.   **Interest in Ultimate Questions**   *(In %s)*

"To what extent would you say you think about the following questions?"

	N	Often or Sometimes	No Longer	Never Have
Why is there suffering in the world?	1263	82	10	8
What happens after death?	1257	73	15	12
What is the purpose of life?	1248	71	14	15
Is there a God or Supreme Being?	1256	69	15	16
How did the world come into being?	1259	63	20	17
How can I find real happiness?	1253	61	22	17

SOURCE: PROJECT CAN80.

answers, or because they have simply stopped looking. Fewer than two in ten Canadians say they have never thought about these issues.

A majority of Canadians raise such questions, but that does not mean they rely very heavily on their religious groups in attempting to answer them. Some 70% ask the question of life's purpose, a question Christianity obviously attempts to address, but more than 40% of the population say there probably is no answer (see TABLE 4.2). Another 30% are uncertain they have found the answer. Only about 30% think they have resolved the question, including just 10% who are very certain. This is merely the tip of the fragment iceberg.

CONVENTIONAL FRAGMENTS

BELIEFS   Canadians continue to work within a conventional belief framework when it comes to God, Jesus, and life after death. At the same time, they exhibit a wide range of ideas about the three themes.

TABLE 4.2. **Posture on the Meaning of Life** *(In %s)*

"How sure are you that you have found the answer to the meaning of life?" *(N = 1286)*

I don't think there is an answer to such a question	42
Rather uncertain	27
Quite certain	21
Very certain	10

SOURCE: PROJECT CAN80.

The *PROJECT CANADA* surveys have found almost nine in ten Canadians express belief in God or a Supreme Being. This finding is consistent with Gallup polls that have reported levels of 87% (1985), 88% (1975), 92% (1969), and 95% (1949);[2] a *Weekend Magazine* poll in 1977 found the level to be 88%.[3] Although observers frequently argue that the term "God" is so relative that it can scarcely be used, the average Canadian seems to conceptualize "God" as either a personal being or a higher power of some kind (see TABLE 4.3). Some, like this 41-year-old Winnipeg woman, however, see "God" in quite different terms:

"God" is the positive side of life — the rhythm and balance that keeps the world functioning — the existence of beauty, physical and spiritual, in all aspects of life and death — the continuity of cycles of life and seasons. "God" is goodness.

About 7% of Canadians are agnostics. One such person, a 21-year-old Roman Catholic student, expresses the problem this way: "The answer is somewhere out in space." Only about 4% are self-acknowledged atheists. Robertson Davies is accurate in his recent assertion that "hard-rock atheists are few."[4] He further suggests that those who claim to be agnostic include many who "are religious illiterates: they have not examined what they say they do not believe." In support of his argument, the surveys have found that only 33% of agnostics know, for example, who it was who denied Jesus.

Close to seven in ten Canadians maintain that Jesus was divine, although 20% acknowledge having some doubts. Most of the

TABLE 4.3.   **Belief in God**   *(In %s)*

"Which of the following statements comes closest to expressing what you believe about God?"
, *(N = 1276)*

* I know God exists and I have no doubts about it	46
* While I have doubts, I feel that I do believe in God	20
* I find myself believing in God some of the time, but not at other times	6
* I don't believe in a personal God, but I do believe in a higher power of some kind	16
* I don't know whether there is a God, and I don't believe there is any way to find out	7
* I don't believe in God	4
* Other	1

SOURCE: PROJECT CAN80.

remaining 30% view him as an exceptional man, although a small minority are not convinced he ever lived at all (see TABLE 4.4).

It would seem that Allan Stratton — subsequently called "a fundamentalist" by a reader — expressed the dominant Canadian sentiment about the person of Jesus when he stated, in *The United Church Observer,* that

> *faith in the divinity of Christ is the defining core of Christianity, as both Scripture and the word itself underline. . . . If Christ is just a prophet . . . why bother with a religion at all? Why not follow Gandhi? Or Mother Teresa? Or Pierre Trudeau?*[5]

When the Gallup organization has probed belief in life after death, the response options used have simply been "Yes" and "No." In 1976, Gallup found that 54% of Canadians asserted belief in an afterlife, about the same as in 1969 (55%) but a slight drop from 1960 (68%).[6] The *PROJECT CANADA* surveys have found that when the response possibilities are broadened, belief in life after death receives greater endorsement, reaching about 65%.

The reason for making this methodological point is that it appears that opinions about life after death are so diverse in

TABLE 4.4. **Beliefs About Jesus** *(In %s)*

"Which of the following statements comes closest to expressing what you believe about Jesus?"
(N = 1282)

* Jesus is the divine Son of God and I have no doubts about it	46
* While I have some doubts, I basically feel Jesus is divine	21
* I feel that Jesus was a great man and very holy, but I don't feel Him to be the Son of God	9
* I think Jesus was only a man, although an extraordinary one	16
* Frankly, I'm not entirely sure there really was such a person as Jesus	6
* Other	2

SOURCE: PROJECT CAN80.

this country that a simple choice of "Yes" or "No" fails to express what people have in mind (see TABLE 4.5). Some four in ten Canadians believe there is *something*, but have no idea what it will be like. About two in ten think in terms of rewards and punishment, with just under one in ten expecting reincarnation. Only 13% rule out completely the possibility of life after death. Comments like the following illustrate the general fuzziness surrounding the issue:

There will be a resurrection and several degrees of heavens.
—a 31-year-old Salvation Army woman,
St. John's

I think we simply move to another dimension.
—a 26-year-old in Edmonton,
no affiliation

As for heaven, hell, and purgatory, I probably will spend time in all three.
—a 63-year-old Roman Catholic man
in Charlottetown

I would like to believe that there is such a thing as reincarnation, but who knows?
—a 70-year-old Jewish housewife, Montreal

TABLE 4.5. **Beliefs About Life After Death** *(In %s)*

"Which of the following comes closest to your view of life after death?" *(N = 1298)*

* I believe that there must be something beyond death, but I have no idea what it may be like	40
* There is life after death, with rewards for some people and punishment for others	18
* I am unsure whether or not there is life after death	16
* I don't believe in life after death	13
* The notion of reincarnation expresses my view of what happens to people when they die	7
* There is life after death, but no punishment	4
* Other	2

SOURCE: PROJECT CAN80.

Certainly one day if we live right here we will meet Christ to live with him always.
> —a 64-year-old retired Anglican woman, rural New Brunswick

I will stop existing until I am resurrected to life on this planet with the prospect of living forever on it, while it is brought back to the paradise state God intended.
> —a 26-year-old male evangelical, Regina

I really don't know what will happen after death, but I am not worried about it. I enjoy today.
> —a 33-year-old United Church office worker, Toronto

The description of the pre-settlement Indian view of death offered by anthropologist Diamond Jenness seems hauntingly appropriate:

Not for one moment did he believe that death put an end to all existence; but so dense a fog obscured the after-life, so conflicting were the opinions about it, that he planned his course for an earthly existence only and blindly resigned himself to whatever fate awaited him hereafter.[7]

PRACTICES The stereotype most of us have of Canadians hardly includes the idea that we are "a praying people." It might therefore come as something of a surprise to find that three in four of those people who sit across from us in subways or push past us in crowded malls pray privately at least once in a while (see TABLE 4.6). Some 30% say they pray daily, commonly gaining considerable gratification from their efforts to "talk to God." As one 68-year-old Edmonton woman puts it, "God is only a prayer away; He hears my needs and the needs of others." For many other people, prayer is less frequent, yet functions as a resource one draws on in living out life.

Table grace, however, does not fare as well. According to Gallup, in 1962 grace was being said at least once a week by 52% of Canadians. By 1981 that figure had tumbled to 28%.[8]

TABLE 4.6. **Select Religious Practices** *(In %s)*

"How often do you pray privately?"

Regularly once a day or more	28
Regularly many times a week	9
Regularly once a week	2
Sometimes but not regularly	30
Only on special occasions	8
I never pray, or only in religious services	23

"How often, if at all, are table prayers or grace said before or after meals in your home?"

At all meals	10
At least once a day	7
At least once a week	5
Only on special occasions	27
Never or hardly ever	51

"How often do you read the Bible privately?"

Regularly once a day or more	4
Regularly many times a week	3
Regularly once a week	2
Sometimes but not regularly	27
Only on special occasions	9
Never or rarely	55

SOURCE: PROJECT CAN80.

Currently, only 22% regularly give thanks for food, with just 10% saying grace at all meals. What this finding corroborates is the decline in the explicit place of religion within Canadian homes. Many adults readily acknowledge that they are not as devout as their parents. The religious socialization of children has declined significantly in the past four decades: in the late 1940s two in three parents with school-age children were exposing them to religious instruction outside the regular school day; the same is true of only one in three parents in the late 1980s.

Even less common than table grace is the private reading of the Bible and other Holy Scriptures. At present, only 9% of Canadians read the Scriptures weekly or more; just 4% are daily readers (see TABLE 4.6). It appears there has been a significant decline in the tendency of people to read the Bible and other Scriptures. Some twenty-five years ago, in 1960, 42% did so at least weekly and the "never" readers — now one in two — numbered only one in four.[9] The big drop-off is symptomatic of Canada's accelerated secularization. People no longer read the Scriptures with regularity (if at all), because they are no longer a highly valued element of religion.

EXPERIENCE   American and British researchers have reported that they have been surprised at the widespread claims of supernatural experiences. People have increasingly been feeling they can admit to such phenomena without being labelled as "weird" or "fanatical." It now appears that a majority of people in the United States and Britain have actually had religious, mystical, and other "transcendent" experiences.[10]

Some fairly conventional supernatural experiences have been explored through the national surveys. What we have found is that close to five in ten Canadians acknowledge the possibility of having experienced God's presence (see TABLE 4.7). A similar proportion report having experienced a sustaining presence of some kind, be it God or something else. Further, about three in ten think they have probably encountered an evil presence.

Contrary to what some might expect, these claims are certainly not limited to older people or adults in general. More than 40% of

TABLE 4.7. **Select Religious Experiences** *(In %s)*

"Have you ever had any of the following experiences?"

	N	Yes, I'm Sure I Have	Yes, I Think I Have	No
A feeling that you were somehow in the presence of God	1006	20	23	57
A feeling that you were being sustained by a power beyond yourself	980	22	24	54
A feeling that you were somehow in the presence of evil	1016	10	18	72

SOURCE: PROJECT CAN80.

the nation's 15- to 19-year-olds also think that they have experienced God.[11] When sociologist Raymond Currie extended the range of experiences of God in a 1979 study of seven hundred Calgary youth—to include not only God's presence but a sense of fear, punishment, union, salvation, and enlightenment or direction —the alleged experiences were even higher. Some three-quarters of Currie's 15- to 24-year-olds indicated that they had had at least one religious experience, with more than one-quarter of all respondents saying that at least one experience was still important to them.[12]

KNOWLEDGE People have frequently maintained that one of the reasons why modern men and women are turning away from religion is that they are unable to resolve conflicts between religion and science. Such an argument assumes that people have studied religion, have been exposed to scientific thought, and have come to a rational, intellectual conclusion that the two are incompatible. A second possibility is that Canadians are socialized into a cultural milieu in which the merits of science are maximized, the merits of religion minimized. They therefore seldom reject religion because its content is incompatible with science; most simply never confront the claims of religion.

One way of probing the question is to try some simple questions on Canadians and see how familiar they are with the basics of Christianity and Judaism. If they can get past the basics, then we can consider further the "rational rejection" hypothesis we just mentioned. If they cannot, we can safely lay that argument to rest.

The national surveys have included a number of tests of knowledge, aimed at probing the awareness people have of Biblical and historical material.

More than 40% of the population think they could essentially recite the Ten Commandments, although less than 10% have confidence they could remember the exact words (see TABLE 4.8). When we get more specific, we find that about 50% know that Elijah, Ezekiel, and Jeremiah were Old Testament prophets, and that Paul was not. The Old Testament books of Deuteronomy and Leviticus, however, are recognized as non-prophets by only about 25% of the population.

TABLE 4.8. **Select Judeo-Christian Knowledge Items** *(In %s)*

"If you were asked, do you think you could recite the Ten Commandments?"

Yes, the exact words	9
Yes, but not the exact words	34
I'm not sure I could remember all ten	44
No, I couldn't	13

"Can you pick the Old Testament prophets from the following?"

	Correct
Elijah	52
Jeremiah	51
Ezekiel	47
Paul	43
Deuteronomy	28
Leviticus	21

"Do you happen to know which of Christ's disciples denied him three times?"

Peter	54
No, I don't know	24
Judas	18
Thomas	2
Paul	1
John	1

SOURCES: PROJECT CAN75 and PROJECT CAN85.

As for familiarity with the New Testament, we asked Canadians if they could identify the disciple who "denied Jesus three times." Under six in ten were able to cite "Peter." About two in ten acknowledged that they didn't know, while the remaining two in ten — not lost for an opinion — gave wrong answers.

It is obvious from these probes of basics that most Canadians who reject Judeo-Christianity hardly do so on the basis of a studious examination of content. The majority have little familiarity with the tradition.

CUMULATIVE COMMITMENT   These findings clearly document the general health of conventional beliefs, practices, and experiences in Canada.

However, in exploring religious commitment as such, it is important to go beyond single, isolated characteristics. For example, people committed to Christianity and other world religions have been expected not only to hold some core beliefs, but also to engage in certain practices. Further, they have claimed to have experienced the supernatural and have possessed a rudimentary knowledge of their traditions.[13] Commitment embraces all four of these facets or dimensions. In examining commitment in Canada, it is therefore necessary to explore the extent to which belief *and* practice *and* experience *and* knowledge characterize Canadians.

Using such criteria to probe Christian commitment specifically, we find that only about 60% of Canadians hold all three of the above central beliefs concerning God, the divinity of Jesus, and life after death (see TABLE 4.9). When the additional criterion of practice in the form of occasional private prayer is added, the proportion dips to just under 50%. The introduction of experiencing God brings the figure down a further 10 percentage points. When knowledge is added (the Peter question), the cumulative proportion of Canadians who exhibit positive belief, practice, experience, and knowledge settles at 20%.

The people of Canada do not lack for an array of conventional beliefs and practices. Only about two in ten, however, give preliminary evidence of embracing what might be regarded as a traditional expression of Judeo-Christian commitment. The religion of the vast majority is a religion of isolated fragments.

TABLE 4.9. **Cumulative Commitment**   *(In %s)*

		Positive	Cumulative
BELIEF	God	83	83
	Divinity of Jesus	78	76
	Life after death	65	59
PRACTICE	Private prayer	53	48
EXPERIENCE	God's presence	42	38
KNOWLEDGE	Who denied Jesus	54	20

SOURCE: PROJECT CAN85.

LESS CONVENTIONAL FRAGMENTS

If Sigmund Freud could have been at Exhibition Place in Toronto in the first week in February 1987, I suspect he would have been astonished — perhaps disappointed, maybe troubled. For there was advanced technology at its glorious best, aiding and abetting, rather than destroying and replacing, supernatural ideas.

The occasion: the annual "Psychics, Mystics and Seers Fair." The fair, like many others elsewhere in the country, was jammed with more than 150 exhibitors, showcasing numerology, New-Age thought, iridology, reincarnation, and tarot-card, crystal-ball, palmist, and psychic readers. Broadcaster and lecturer Henry Gordon comments,

> But high tech has really taken over. The computer and the printed readout dominate. And that's where the real bargains are. A mere $3 will satisfy your curiosity. At most of the computerized booths, you need only fill in a card with your name and birthdate and you get an immediate reading. . . . Three bucks in 15 seconds — seems like a fairly profitable operation. [14]

In Canada, an abundance of Judeo-Christian beliefs and practices are supplemented by a wide array of less conventional ideas and behaviour. Just under 25% think it is possible to communicate with the dead; 35% say they believe in astrology; more than 60% in ESP; the same proportion believe some people have psychic powers (see TABLE 4.10).

TABLE 4.10.   **Less Conventional Beliefs**   *(In %s)*

"Do you believe:"

	N	Yes, I Definitely Do	Yes, I Think So	No, I Don't Think So	No, I Definitely Do Not
* That it is possible to communicate with the dead	1163	7	15	41	37
* In astrology	1147	9	26	38	27
* In ESP (extra-sensory perception)	1139	24	37	24	15
* That some people have psychic powers, enabling them to predict events	1160	21	42	23	14

SOURCE: PROJECT CAN85.

Interest does not stop at beliefs, but extends to practices and experiences. Horoscope readers easily outnumber the nation's Bible readers. Some 75% say they read their horoscopes at least occasionally, easily above the 45% level for Bible-reading; the daily proportions are 13% and 4% respectively (see TABLE 4.11). For many, horoscope reading seems merely a form of entertainment. A number of respondents comment that they turn to the "sign column" in the newspaper "just for the fun of it." One respondent from a small Alberta community said, "My newspaper arrives a day late. I like to read my horoscope to find out what was supposed to have happened to me yesterday." An Ontario respondent reminds us, however, that for some, like herself, "astrology is a science."

As for experiences, about one in two Canadians think they have personally experienced mental telepathy. Even more — some 60% — maintain they have experienced premonition (the anticipation of a future event). A 45-year-old Regina woman tells us:

Many times I have a fleeting glimpse of something. Then, when it happens, I recall that instant vision that seemed to

TABLE 4.11. **Less Conventional Practices and Experiences**
(In %s)

"How often do you read your horoscope?"	
Daily	13
Occasionally	62
Never	25
I'm not sure what a horoscope is	0
"Have you ever had any experience that you think is an example of mental telepathy (awareness of others' thoughts)?"	
Yes, I'm sure I have	19
Yes, I think I have	32
No	49
"Have you ever had any experience that you think is an example of premonition (anticipation of a coming event)?"	
Yes, I'm sure I have	20
Yes, I think I have	38
No	42

SOURCE: PROJECT CAN80.

have passed. Usually it turns out to be a tragedy. It passes through my mind and it happens weeks or months later. Feelings really seem to warn me. Really weird, yet these forewarnings happen.

As the 60% figure indicates, her claim is far from rare. In exploring such experiences informally with people over the past decade or so, I have found they are innumerable. My mother, a devout Christian, recalls the night when she had a nightmare that my father, returning home from a trip, had slid off the icy highway into the ditch. Awakening suddenly, she looked at the clock beside her bed — it was 2:15 A.M. She learned within the hour that my father had indeed gone off the highway, at precisely 2:15 A.M.

As a result of such experiences and exposure to the claims of others, Canadians seem to embrace fairly readily both conventional and less conventional ideas about the supernatural. People who attend religious services weekly are only slightly less inclined than others to believe in astrology, ESP, and psychic powers (see TABLE 4.12). Those who "never" attend services are just as likely to hold such beliefs as other people.

TABLE 4.12.   **Less Conventional Traits and Service Attendance**   *% Positive*

Attendance Level	N	Commun Dead	Astrol	Horo Read	Psychic Powers	ESP	Precog	Telep
Weekly	369	24	27	33	56	48	47	42
Monthly	113	21	45	41	72	64	61	57
Yearly	571	23	36	42	65	63	61	55
Never	242	22	37	33	63	68	49	52

SOURCE: PROJECT CAN80.

Bryan Wilson observes that people "might go through the motions of accepting orthodoxy, but they may not always accept that orthodoxy is enough."[15] Supplementation of conventional ideas among Canadians is common.

THE RIGHT TO RITES

The national surveys have also found that Canadians continue to look to the churches for an array of services such as baptisms, confirmations, marriages, and funerals. These are commonly referred to as "rites of passage," because they surround the critical life stages of birth, adulthood, marriage, and death.

Approximately seven in ten Canadians indicate that the church (or synagogue) has carried out baptisms and marriages for them in the past, while some five in ten have had confirmations and funerals performed (see TABLE 4.13). Reflecting the age structure of the Canadian population, about 15% expect to have future baptisms and confirmations carried out, and 20% expect church weddings. Almost 50% expect to have church funerals. The market for rites of passage continues to be extensive.

People who worship irregularly are almost as likely as weekly attenders to expect to be "serviced" by the nation's religious groups, also primarily in times of birth, marriage, and death (see TABLE 4.13).

Data from the aforementioned 1986 analysis of the Toronto Anglican diocese has helped to clarify the thoughts of some Canadians on passage rites.[16] For starters, inactive Anglicans are just

TABLE 4.13.   **Previous and Expected Professional Services by Attendance**   *(In %s)*

"Which of the following have been performed for you by the church (1) in the past or, as you see it, (2) will probably be carried out for you by the church (or synagogue) in the future?"

		N	Bapt	Confirm	Wed	Fun'l
Past	Nationally	1201	71	52	66	46
	Weekly	299	81	67	72	51
	<Weekly	892	67	47	64	45
Future	Nationally	1201	14	13	20	45
	Weekly	299	12	11	17	51
	<Weekly	892	15	13	21	43

SOURCE: PROJECT CAN85.
NOTE: At least one in the past, 84%; in the future, 52%; in either, 92%.

as likely as active Anglicans to expect to have these rites carried out for them. It is also clear that inactives are not just thinking of rote performances. One 30-year-old inactive mother in Toronto comments:

> *I have witnessed public Baptisms which seemed almost assembly line (eight children at once). I think this many at once takes away from the specialness of this event for each individual child. To have so many children and parents lining up seemed somehow "not the Anglican way." If I am to be honest here, at the end of this service (at which I was a Godmother), there was no longer awe — only boredom.*

Given this demand for professional services on the part of infrequent attenders, the obvious question facing Anglicans and other religious groups is how to respond. Anglican inactives, for example, have very strong feelings about their "right to rites." In the Toronto diocese, some 90% or more maintain they should be allowed to have church burials, marriages, and baptisms. The logic involved is diverse. A 40-year-old Brampton inactive argues, "Just because people don't attend Church doesn't mean they don't believe in God and shouldn't be able to be baptized, married, and buried in a church, which represents God."

It is important to note that religious inactives have allies in their expectations. More than 80% of active Anglicans, according to the Toronto study, say inactives should be allowed church marriages and baptisms, and 94% support their right to church burials. One 63-year-old active, for example, says:

I'm against making young people go to church regularly to have their babies baptized. I feel we are turning our young married couples away from the church by demanding they come. I feel no child should be refused.

A 32-year-old illustrates the support of younger actives as well. In agreeing that rites should be extended to inactives, she adds, "Perhaps they will return in the future. Why alienate them?" And finally, concerning burials specifically, one active offers this rationale: "God wouldn't deny it, so why should we?"

Some religious leaders have argued for a tough stance. It is not uncommon, both in conservative and in more liberal churches, for couples to be required to complete pre-marriage counselling classes. In a few cases, couples are refused ceremonies if they are not prepared to profess commitment.

What would the costs be if religious organizations collectively denied rites of passage to their inactive affiliates? In the case of weddings, many people would probably turn elsewhere and thereby be lost to the religious groups. It is possible that quasi-religious rites-of-passage "businesses" would come into being to meet the new marriage-market need. One can readily imagine the emergence of "religious-like retail outlets," providing weddings — perhaps even additional services — in attractive settings with congenial and competent personnel.

The somewhat brash comment of one 38-year-old Anglican woman puts the consumer outlook in blunt terms: "I'm inactive! If I weren't married, baptized, confirmed, and allowed to attend when I wish, I wouldn't be an Anglican, and that would be your loss."

RELIGIOUS SELF-IMAGES

Beyond relying on responses to questions about belief, practice, experience, and knowledge in probing religious commitment, another obvious method is to let people speak for themselves. The *PROJECT CANADA* surveys have done so, asking people to describe the nature of their religion. A number of options have been offered to them, with an opportunity to write in more applicable responses if they so desire.

The results: some 40% of Canadians say they regard themselves as committed Christians, with about 2% indicating they are committed to other faiths (see TABLE 4.14). Almost another 40% are uncommitted, either seeing themselves as interested in religion but not strongly committed, or as religious in somewhat unconventional ways. The remaining 20% do not regard themselves as religious.

To be sure, the content of Christian faith for the four in ten who profess to be committed Christians varies dramatically. Only about one-third, for example, exhibit the aforementioned traditional style of commitment—believing in God, the divinity of Jesus, and life after death, praying privately, experiencing God, and having some knowledge of the Christian tradition.

The other two-thirds of the committed Christians exhibit fragments—to varying degrees not holding conventional beliefs about

TABLE 4.14.   **Self-Reported Nature of One's Religion**   *(In %s)*

"Which of the following statements comes closest to describing the nature of your religion?"

I regard myself as a committed Christian	42
I have a mild interest in Christianity and an inquisitive interest in other religions, but I hardly regard myself as a strongly religious person	24
I am not a religious person	19
I find myself interested in a variety of religions, but not committed to any particular one	4
I am deeply committed to a religion other than Christianity	1

Write-in
    Regard self as Christian, practice irregularly (5)
    Other (5)
	10

SOURCE: PROJECT CAN85.

TABLE 4.15.   **Self-Reported Commitment Styles and Select Beliefs and Services**   *(In %s)*

	N	Tradit Commit	Astrol	ESP	Weds Future	Fun'ls Future
Committed						
To Christianity	494	35	33	55	20	47
To other religions		—	17	23	14	42
Un-committed	383	9	39	70	24	47
Non-religious	224	2	32	54	15	38
Other	53	27	48	77	17	57

SOURCE: PROJECT CAN85.

God, Jesus, and immortality, not praying, not claiming to have experienced God, or having a limited knowledge of Christianity.

The religion of most of the remaining 60% of Canadians seems to be characterized by specialized consumption rather than religious commitment (see TABLE 4.15). They readily adopt "religious fragments"—isolated beliefs, isolated practices, and isolated professional services. But they make no pretence that religion informs their lives.

RELIGIOUS FRAGMENTS

Canadians give little indication of abandoning their ties with the established religious groups. Nonetheless, things have changed. As the century draws to a close, people in greater and greater numbers are drawing upon religion as consumers, adopting a belief here and a practice there. Additionally, they are calling on clergy to perform various rites of passage relating primarily to birth, marriage, and death.

At the same time, Canadians appear to be moving away from Christianity or other religions as meaning systems addressing all of life. They are opting for Judeo-Christian fragments. To borrow a phrase one of France's sociologists used in telling me about religion in his country, Canadians are into "religion à la carte."

The national drop-off in attendance at services is merely a symptom of the increasing tendency of Canadians to consume religion selectively.

It appears that a major shift in religious styles has been taking place in Canada during the twentieth century, involving the increasing movement from religious commitment to religious consumption.

Invariably people raise the question, "But are things really any different now than they were in the past? Haven't most people always been adopting religious fragments?"

Four quick responses: First, yes, fragments are not new. But there are indications that the extent of their adoption is. What is different from the past is our current cultural reality — a highly specialized, consumption-oriented Canada. That culture is dramatically eroding religion as a system addressing all of life. (More about this in Chapter 7.)

Second, we need only look at Quebec to see how religion at one time coloured culture and the structure of society. As historian Ian Rennie concludes in examining the question, "Was Canada Ever Christian?", those people who settled and governed early French and English Canada "developed its laws and governing policies on the basis of what they conceived to be a Christian world view."[17] That religious tone is largely gone.

Third, the fact of the matter is that there has been a downward turn in service attendance over time. As we will see shortly, there also is a much greater tendency for older Canadians to profess commitment, and for younger people to adopt fragments. Such findings suggest that, at least since the turn of this century, there has indeed been an increase in the tendency of Canadians to order off the religion à la carte menu.

Fourth, in some ways the question is academic. In the minds of many proponents of religion, the important issue is not how recent widespread fragment adoption is, but rather, how pervasive the pattern is at present. Whether new or ongoing, fragment selection is not what religion has been all about.

According to John Webster Grant, a consumer attitude towards Christianity was prevalent by at least the 1950s. Grant writes:

[People] were selective in what they took. They crowded church buildings on Sunday morning, but except for conservative evangelicals, stayed home to watch [television] in the evening. . . . Newly active members sought a product called religion in buildings that increasingly resembled attractive retail outlets. They went to church not so much to express convictions as to seek answers to questions, solutions to problems, and guidance in decisions. [18]

The social forecaster John Naisbitt has written that society, in a relatively short time, "has fractionalized into many diverse groups of people with a wide array of differing tastes and values." The idea of "a multiple-option society," he says, has spilled over into a number of areas, including the family, music, food, entertainment, and religion. [19]

In Canada, increasing institutional specialization has been associated with the tendency for people to look to the Church to provide very specific commodities. These include isolated beliefs and practices. Thus it is that Canadians believe in God but are not sure about the divinity of Jesus or the nature of life after death. They find themselves praying once in a while, even if they seldom read a Bible or say grace. Indeed, as we have seen, a higher proportion of Canadians say they pray (77%) than say they believe in a personal God (66%). They attend services occasionally, but hardly weekly. And, of course, they look to the Church to provide the critical rites of passage.

Canadians tend to pick and choose religious fragments at will. An Anglican housewife and mother in a small New Brunswick community comments, "I believe in God but do not believe in the divinity of Jesus." From an Edmonton science administrator comes the acknowledgement, "I believe in Jesus Christ but have doubts about immortality." And a pragmatic, retired Roman Catholic living in rural British Columbia attends services only infrequently, but quips, "I have to believe in God — I'm too old to take a chance!"

Canadians also readily supplement their conventional Christian menu with an assortment of other supernatural beliefs and practices, including astrology, psychic phenomena, auras, bio-rhythms, demon possession, and communication with the dead.

Significantly, however, beyond a certain investment of time and money, the returns are diminishing. Attendance at services is a case in point. The fact that decreasing numbers of Canadians attend services every week suggests that many feel weekly attendance is unnecessary for experiencing what religious groups have to offer. Less than once a week is sufficient. Aldous Huxley seemed to know what was coming. In *Brave New World*, Bernard attends his "Solidarity Service" only twice a month.[20]

The same principle seems to hold for money—putting a little in the offering plate is fine, but putting in a lot is too much. When Canadians are asked why they are no longer as involved in churches as they once were, the dominant response is not that they are "down" on the Church or opposed to contributing; it is simply that they prefer to spend more of their time on other things.

Some, of course, solidly endorse religious groups. A 67-year-old Mulgrave, Nova Scotia, man, for example, says, "For me there's no substitute for the Roman Catholic Church." But many are quick to deny the necessity of involvement in religious groups. A Toronto man working in public relations comments, "I object to the assumption that any person not subscribing to an organized religion is not religious. Anyone can develop their own religious attitudes." A young rural Alberta mother with United Church ties says,

> I've been through a great deal in life and my faith is very strong. But I believe that one is closer to God in their own home and garden than a church. I see going to church these days as "keeping up with the Joneses."

A 30-year-old man in St. John's notes, "I have no specific denomination, but I consider myself to be a Christian." A similar view is offered by a Montreal man, 48, who says, "I believe in a supreme power or force, but I am not involved in organized religion."

But even if such people are not attending, few are disenchanted and turning elsewhere. In the words of Raymond Currie, a sociologist at the University of Manitoba, belonging exceeds commitment.[21] Canadians are not "dropping out." As a student in one of my classes pointed out, it probably would be more accurate to describe them as "dropping in."

THE CONSUMPTION SELF-RECOGNITION TEST

During my research, I have tried to take seriously a comment made a few years ago by the American sociologist Howard Becker. Becker suggested that there is something seriously wrong with our research if people have difficulty recognizing themselves in our descriptions of them. Carrying out national and regional studies from Lethbridge has had important benefits. But I must confess that as I work with my computer and questionnaires and look out at the barren coulees of southern Alberta in the middle of the night (my favourite work time), I feel a shade apprehensive about how well my analyses depict Canadian reality. As a critical check on methodology, I find it essential, therefore, to give people various "mirrors" to try out.

The 1985 *PROJECT CANADA* survey included an item that explicitly probed how clearly Canadians recognize themselves in the "fragment" description I have been outlining. The item was directed to the 75% of the population who "do not attend services regularly." It read as follows:

> *Some observers maintain that few people are actually abandoning their religious traditions. Rather, they draw selective beliefs and practices, even if they do not attend services frequently. They are not about to be recruited by other religious groups. Their identification with their religious tradition is fairly solidly fixed, and it is to these groups that they will turn when confronted with marriage, death and, frequently, birth. How well would you say this observation describes YOU?*

Almost 80% said that the observation "very accurately" (45%) or "somewhat accurately" (33%) described them; only 12% said that it did not depict them "accurately at all," with one-third of these being people who currently claim no religious affiliation.

The fragment thesis reflects the reality of religion in Canada. Modern industrialization and post-industrialization have seen neither the death of conventional religion nor the inroads of new religious expressions. But the nature and role of religion has been radically transformed. The gods of old have been neither abandoned nor replaced. Rather, they have been broken into pieces and offered to religious consumers in piecemeal form.

5

THE FRAGMENTED MOSAIC

Bearers of bad news are not particularly popular. Messengers get slain and carrier pigeons get roasted. I am well aware that for some people, notably the religiously committed, the fragmented-gods story is not good news. It would be unfortunate, however, if the analysis were to ignore the reality of Canadian religion and slay the sociologist who delivers the news. Sociologists will come and go, but unless the Canadian situation is taken seriously, the gods will remain dismantled.

During some fifteen years of disseminating research findings, I think I have been on the receiving end of the whole gamut of possible responses from the country's dominant religious groups. My work has been taken seriously, passively ignored, and vigorously contradicted.[1] For the record, my main criticism of my criticizers is that their reactions have been excessively dependent upon whether the news is good or bad, rather than on whether the research itself is sound or unsound.

But by this time, the data are virtually conclusive. The case for the fragmentation of religion rests on solid ground. It is there for any objective eye to see, regardless of whether the method of exploration be surveys, observation, record analysis, or any other means of data collection.

Nonetheless, it would be unfortunate if the story were ignored by one last neutralization technique. I have found that when all else fails, some critics shrug their shoulders and say, "It might be happening elsewhere, but it's not happening here." In this chapter, I want to demonstrate the pervasiveness of fragments throughout *all* of Canadian society. The movement from commitment to consumption is not limited to some parts of the country or some individuals or some religious groups. Fragment adoption is virtually everywhere.

The Bible Belt of the Prairies is no exception; in fact, what remains of the Bible Belt isn't even located on the Prairies. The farms and villages are no longer havens for the committed. The people who value religion the most — older Canadians — are literally passing from the scene. Higher education is joined by lower education in omitting religion as a significant aspect of life. These days women, historically a key source of religious commitment in at least the Christian case, are scarcely any more committed than men. Inside the doors of the churches, fragments have become the norm. And it scarcely matters whether you are looking at Roman Catholics or Anglicans, United Church members or Conservative Protestants, Lutherans or Presbyterians, or just about anyone else. Fortunately, you don't have to take my word for it; the survey results speak for themselves.

FROM SEA TO SEA

Conventional and unconventional beliefs and practices are thriving in each of the country's five major regions. A majority of people everywhere claim to believe in God, the divinity of Jesus, and life after death (see TABLE 5.1). The greatest support for these three beliefs is found in the Atlantic region, followed by Quebec, Ontario and the Prairies, and finally, British Columbia.

In the case of Judeo-Christian practice, experience, and knowledge, the "Atlantic High, Pacific Low" pattern continues with only minor exceptions (e.g., Bible-reading is lowest in Quebec). Differences between Ontario and the Prairies are very slight.

TABLE 5.1. **Beliefs, Practices, and Commitment by Region** *(In %s)*

	N	Can (1201)	Atl (109)	Que (312)	Ont (431)	Prair (212)	BC (137)
BELIEF							
God		83	93	90	79	83	73
Jesus' divinity		79	91	82	77	78	66
Life after death		65	78	64	62	66	64
PRACTICE							
Private prayer		53	71	54	52	54	41
Bible reading		25	40	16	26	29	26
EXPERIENCE: God		42	50	54	36	38	36
KNOWLEDGE: Peter		46	55	54	45	38	39
LESS CONVENTIONAL							
Horoscope reading		39	44	36	39	43	33
ESP		60	62	44	64	68	74
Communication with dead		22	17	33	17	20	24
NATURE OF RELIGION							
Committed to Christianity		44	66	38	45	47	31
Committed to other faiths		1	0	1	2	0	1
Uncommitted		29	20	27	27	33	41
Not religious		20	10	20	25	15	19
Other		6	4	14	1	5	8

SOURCE: PROJECT CAN85.

Even the less conventional traits are present everywhere, including British Columbia. Old fragments may pass away, but they seem to be replaced readily by new ones. But when we move beyond fragments in the direction of commitment, we find that the percentages begin to drop. While almost seven in ten Canadians east of Quebec say they are committed Christians, the proportion slips to just under five in ten in Ontario and the Prairies, to about four in ten in Quebec, and to only three in ten in British Columbia (see TABLE 5.1).

Group participation in religious activities tends to follow the same geographical patterns (see TABLE 5.2). Quebec residents, however, are just as likely as B.C. residents *not* to be members of a local church or parish (about 25%).

TABLE 5.2. **Involvement and Rites of Passage by Region**
 (In %s)

		Can (1201)	Atl (109)	Que (312)	Ont (431)	Prair (212)	BC (137)
	N						
INVOLVEMENT							
Affiliation		89	97	88	90	90	83
Membership		35	52	25	38	38	26
Attendance		25	42	27	23	23	19
Church school: children		25	46	25	21	23	20
Enjoyment from church: high		16	24	11	16	17	18
RITES OF PASSAGE							
Past	Baptism	71	80	64	75	76	56
	Confirmation	52	65	59	51	46	35
	Wedding	66	73	62	68	68	61
	Funeral	46	49	45	48	51	30
Future	Baptism	14	10	23	9	15	12
	Confirmation	13	12	22	9	10	9
	Wedding	20	14	20	19	26	19
	Funeral	45	43	49	41	48	46
One-	Past	84	92	77	87	89	79
Plus	Future	52	52	57	46	56	54
	Either	92	96	90	91	95	93

SOURCE: PROJECT CAN85.

The demand for rites of passage is very strong in every region of the country, again including British Columbia (see TABLE 5.2). Variations to date in the performance of such rites largely reflect differences in age structure between the regions.

When the past and expected future performances of these services are combined, the situation is that some nine in ten Canadians are looking to religious groups to perform funerals, weddings, and baptisms. Only in British Columbia is the proportion less, but not by much (eight in ten for funerals and weddings, and seven in ten for baptisms). Confirmation, which is related to commitment and also is not practised by groups such as the Conservative Protestants, is slightly less in demand (65%), particularly from Ontario westward. Yet, compared with attendance, even this figure is high.

The range of Canadian religious commitment corresponds roughly to geography. It is high in the Atlantic region, moderate in Quebec, Ontario, and the Prairies, and low in British Columbia.

The findings, according to these objective and subjective criteria, are clear: at this point in Canadian history, the nation's "Bible Belt" is found, not on the Prairies, but in the Atlantic region. Religiously speaking, the Prairies bear a very close resemblance to Ontario and, to a lesser extent, Quebec — in between the Atlantic and Pacific extremes.

University of Calgary sociologist Harry Hiller would concur. Analysing census data, Hiller found no support for the notion that fundamentalist denominations have been historically over-represented in Alberta. In "the demography of Canadian society," he maintains, "the notion of a [western] Bible Belt is more fiction than fact."[2] The stereotype, he suggests, has been the result of fundamentalist religion's moving into the spheres of politics (e.g., the Social Credit Party) and education (e.g., Prairie Bible Institute). The media have responded by assuming that most Albertans have had similar religious convictions. They have not.

With the Atlantic region, we may have something of "a latter-day Quebec" — a region somewhat isolated and a step behind much of the country in its level of industrial development. The dominant pattern in the western world is for industrialization to be associated with secularization. As with post-1960 Quebec, these religious differences for the east-coast region of Canada would be expected to diminish with increasing industrialization.

British Columbia's greater secularity, like California's in the United States, seems to be tied to the province's tendency to attract many people who want a "different" way of life. Many of these Canadians, men and women who want to maximize life's enjoyment in a beautiful coastal setting, are less concerned about keeping the status quo. Surveys consistently show, for example, that B.C. residents hold more liberal moral views than residents of any other region in the country. The lifestyles of the permanent residents, combined with the aspirant lifestyles of the new arrivals, result in a less conventional, more hedonistic way of life.

Incidentally, the 1985 national survey found that if Canadians could live in any province, a majority in all ten cases would choose their own. However, the most popular second choice — you guessed it — was "beautiful British Columbia." The same is true for the nation's 15- to 19-year-olds. In fact, more Manitoba teenagers, if they had a choice, would rather live in British Columbia than in Manitoba![3]

Not all these regional religious tendencies are particularly new. J. Edwin Orr, a British evangelical, toured Canada in 1935 by train, expressly to take the nation's religious pulse. He reported:

> *The Newfoundlander is reported to be very religious and church attendance is fairly high. . . . Quebec City has always been the Vatican of the New World. . . . [In] Ontario we find entrenched liberalism and the evangelicals bickering among themselves. . . . In [Prairie] towns one may find one live church, two half-alive, three dead and the remainder breathing very heavily. . . . smug complacency is the rule. . . . In British Columbia, there are huge areas without a true gospel witness. . . . Victoria is a very sleepy place, especially spiritually.*[4]

THE SECULAR CITY . . . AND FARM

Sunday morning. In Canada's countryside it seems synonymous with tranquillity. A stillness rests over the land. People will begin to stir, but activity will be kept to a minimum. Men and women, boys and girls will eat breakfast and then begin to "dress up." In a few hours they will make their way to the country or village church. And afterwards there will be Sunday dinner, together. It all seems so natural.

In Canada's urban centres, people are beginning to come alive after having had later Saturday nights than expected. The television sets will be variously tuned in to sporting events and movies from yesteryear. More than a few fathers will be heading outside to start work on overgrown yards; many a mother will have sighed with relief to have awakened and realized there is still one more day to catch up on things before she goes back to the office; a large number of young people will be taking off to meet their friends. By noon the slumbering cities will have their eyes open; by mid-afternoon most of them will be in full flight. Was life ever any different?

These stereotypes — rural Canada as religiously committed, urban Canada as more secular — live on, no doubt partly out of nostalgia. People who have moved to the cities have a tendency to remember times past as characterized by churchgoing, committed grandparents, church socials, and so on.

The problem with such generalizations based on recollection is that they are grounded in a past which, first, may never have been unique to rural Canada, and, second, may be far removed from the current reality. But let's let the data tell the real story, broken into three community-size groupings — 100,000 or more, 99,000 to 10,000, and communities with fewer than 10,000 people, including farms.

At present, the differences in commitment many people expect to find between big city and farm simply do not exist. Canadians living in communities large and small show remarkably similar tendencies to believe, practise, experience, and know (see TABLE 5.3). Traditional beliefs about God and claims that "He" is being experienced are in no way the prerogative of people who find themselves surrounded by countryside rather than pavement. Devotional life, to the extent that it exists, is just as common in the modern high-rise as in the country farmhouse. And, yes, as crickets signal the calmness of the evening, rural Canadians are just as likely as their urban contemporaries to be reading their horoscopes in their daily and weekly newspapers.

On the dark side of this part of the Canadian religion story is the prevalence of fragments. As we travel from the metropolitan areas through the smaller cities and towns to the villages and farms, we can see them everywhere. Fewer than five in ten people in each community-size category claim to be committed to Christianity, or to any other religion, for that matter.

TABLE 5.3. **Belief, Practice, and Commitment by Community Size** *(In %s)*

	N	Canada (1201)	Large Cities (647)	Small Cities (187)	Small & Rural (367)
BELIEF					
God		83	82	85	86
Jesus' divinity		79	75	82	83
Life after death		65	64	66	67
PRACTICE					
Private prayer		53	53	58	53
Bible reading		25	23	29	27
EXPERIENCE: God		42	40	46	44
KNOWLEDGE: Peter		46	45	50	46
LESS CONVENTIONAL					
Horoscope		39	37	41	40
ESP		60	63	59	57
Communication with dead		22	22	29	20
NATURE OF RELIGION					
Committed to Christianity		44	44	44	44
Committed to other faiths		1	2	1	1
Uncommitted		29	29	28	31
Not religious		20	20	19	19
Other		6	6	8	5

SOURCE: PROJECT CAN85.

Further, although nine in ten people in all size categories claim a religious-group tie, just more than three in ten in each category are members of local churches, and fewer than three in ten attend services weekly. Rural dwellers are also no more inclined than people in the big cities to have their children in church schools on a typical Sunday morning. Overall, only two in ten Canadians living in rural areas and small towns say they receive "a great deal" of enjoyment from church life, scarcely higher than people in cities. Yet, regardless of the sizes of the communities in which they live, more than nine in ten Canadians are also just about as likely as one another to turn to religious groups when they want the various rites of passage performed.

TABLE 5.4. **Involvement and Rites of Passage by Community Size** *(In %s)*

		Canada (1201)	Large Cities (647)	Small Cities (187)	Small & Rural (367)
	N				
INVOLVEMENT					
Affiliation		89	89	91	89
Membership		35	34	34	36
Attendance		25	23	26	28
Church school: children		25	24	26	25
Enjoyment from church: high		16	16	14	17
RITES OF PASSAGE					
Past	Baptism	71	70	70	72
	Confirmation	52	50	57	52
	Wedding	66	64	67	69
	Funeral	46	46	44	46
Future	Baptism	14	13	16	14
	Confirmation	13	12	15	14
	Wedding	20	21	18	19
	Funeral	45	45	40	47
One-	Past	84	85	84	84
Plus	Future	52	53	48	54
	Total	92	93	90	92

SOURCE: PROJECT CAN85.

Whatever the urban-rural differences in religion might have been in the past, they are no longer characteristic of the Canadian demographic landscape.

The tendency for individuals to draw upon fragments in consumer-like fashion is not an urban phenomenon. The social and cultural factors that have made fragments functional in large communities have filtered down through the smaller cities and have not spared even the farm.

THE END OF AN ERA

It is difficult to assess how much the present religious situation represents a departure from the past. Ideally, we would compare our present findings to those from a variety of points in

Canadian history. Where possible, I have been trying to do just that, although seriously hampered by the lack of early survey research.

There is another way to explore change over time — using the age of Canadians not only as an indicator of life-stage but also as an indicator of era.[5] The logic is fairly simple: history and culture influence us from the time we are born. Exposure to different time-periods would therefore be expected to have the potential to affect us in different ways. Events such as the Great Depression, World War II, and today's threat of nuclear war are not without impact; the same can be said of cultural features such as the birth of rock and roll, the changing role of women, the movement towards a global economy, and microtechnology and the dawn of the computer age.

History and culture, then, have the potential to influence the nature and role of religion profoundly, and the PROJECT CANADA findings underscore the point.

Canadians born in 1930 or earlier are slightly more likely than others to assert positive belief in God and the divinity of Jesus (see TABLE 5.5). They are also far more inclined to pray privately, to claim to have experienced God, and to be familiar with Peter's denial of Jesus. And these older Canadians are considerably more likely than others to profess Christian commitment, rather than non-commitment.

Positive responses to these measures of commitment decrease progressively as we move from people born before 1930 through those born between 1931 and 1950 to those born since 1950. Christian commitment has declined from 61% to 44% to 33% among people born in the three time periods. The pattern reverses on credence given to ESP and the possibility of communicating with the dead. There is little difference on horoscope reading.

Variations in group-participation patterns are similar. Membership, attendance, and gratification levels drop noticeably as we move from older to younger Canadians (see TABLE 5.6). Yet affiliation differs only marginally. Further, younger adults continue to express a strong desire for religious rites of passage. When past

TABLE 5.5. **Beliefs, Practices, and Commitment by Era**
(In %s)

	N	Canada (1201)	1930 & Earlier (301)	1950-1931 (396)	1967-1951 (504)
BELIEF					
God		83	87	85	80
Jesus' divinity		79	84	77	77
Life after death		65	64	65	66
PRACTICE					
Private prayer		53	73	56	40
Bible reading		25	39	28	15
EXPERIENCE: God		42	51	41	39
KNOWLEDGE: Peter		46	55	49	38
LESS CONVENTIONAL					
Horoscope reading		39	44	36	37
ESP		60	47	61	67
Communication with dead		22	13	22	29
NATURE OF RELIGION					
Committed to Christianity		44	61	44	33
Committed to other faiths		1	1	2	0
Uncommitted		29	21	29	35
Not religious		20	14	18	25
Other		6	3	7	7

SOURCE: PROJECT CAN85.

and expected services are added together, there is little difference by age.

These findings offer further support for the assertion that there has been a pronounced change in the dominant role of religion in Canada. Religious commitment has been increasingly replaced by the consumption of religious fragments.

THE IMPACT OF REASON

One's view of the world is obviously influenced by other factors besides sheer exposure to select aspects of history and culture. Among the most important of these mind-shaping

TABLE 5.6. **Involvement and Rites of Passage by Era** *(In %s)*

		N	Canada (1201)	1931 Earlier (301)	1950-1931 (396)	1967-1951 (504)
INVOLVEMENT						
Affiliation			89	96	90	86
Membership			35	52	36	23
Attendance			25	43	25	14
Enjoyment from church: high			16	31	16	8
RITES OF PASSAGE						
Past	Baptism		71	73	76	65
	Confirmation		52	55	58	45
	Wedding		66	71	74	56
	Funeral		46	55	49	38
Future	Baptism		14	5	11	19
	Confirmation		13	14	15	12
	Wedding		20	8	19	28
	Funeral		45	37	44	50
One-	Past		84	84	88	82
Plus	Future		52	38	49	63
	Either		92	90	94	91

SOURCE: PROJECT CAN85.

factors is exposure to science and critical thought through formal education. Religion, with its traditional supernatural dimension, cannot be expected to go untouched in modern societies that look to science for innovation and direction and that place a high value on the mastery of information pertaining to this world.

Robert Fulford depicts the Canada of 1887 as a nation in which religion was "the driving force behind thought and action, the best excuse for the exercise of power, and the only consolation for sickness, death, and worldly failure." According to Fulford, "Religion gave life its gravity. In a way that people of 1987 can just barely imagine," he says, "it was the foundation on which everything stood." But the coming of modern science, Fulford continues, shook that foundation. He writes of Canada's great contributor to medicine, Sir William Osler, whose life spanned the years from

1849 to 1919: "Born in an age whose ultimate authority was God, he died in an age whose ultimate authority was science."[6]

In exploring the impact of formal education, it must be kept in mind that education and age are highly related. People who are younger tend to have more formal education than those who are older. Since we have already found age to be associated with religion, it is important to distinguish between the influence of the two — as we shall do.

The surveys show that an increase in the level of education tends to be associated with modest decreases in every age group in beliefs and practices regarding God, the divinity of Jesus, and prayer (see TABLE 5.7). For example, among 18- to 34-year-olds who have not gone beyond high school, 84% believe in God and 81% believe in the divinity of Jesus; the comparable figures for those with more education are 77% for God and 73% for Jesus' divinity. Clearly these differences, while consistent, are small.

Moreover, education is not related to any less inclination to believe in life after death or claim religious experiences. Among Canadians between the ages of 35 and 54, for example, 53% with post-secondary education say they have experienced God's presence, compared with 44% of those who have not gone beyond high school. Education is also associated with a slight increase in knowledge (Peter), but a mild decrease in less conventional belief (astrology).

Further, and perhaps surprisingly to many, Canadians with more education are no less inclined than others to claim to be religiously committed. If anything, the opposite is marginally true.

As for organizational involvement, education makes very little difference. Affiliation levels are similar, with membership and attendance slightly higher for those with more education. Expected rites of passage are even more prevalent among better-educated Canadians.

But an examination of the findings summed up in TABLE 5.7 shows that, overall, differences between Canadians on these criteria of belief, practice, commitment, and involvement are far greater by year of birth than education.

To the extent that there is a change in the commitment and participation styles of Canadians, the era in which one was born

TABLE 5.7.   **Select Beliefs, Practices, and Commitment by Age and Education**   *(In %s)*

	Canada	< HS	> HS
BELIEF:			
God			
18-34	80	84	77
35-54	85	90	80
over 55	87	89	85
EXPERIENCE:			
God			
18-34	39	41	38
35-54	49	44	53
over 55	51	49	56
COMMITMENT:			
Christianity			
18-34	33	27	33
35-54	44	27	38
over 55	61	58	58
AFFILIATION:			
18-34	85	87	82
35-54	90	93	88
over 55	96	96	96
ATTENDANCE:			
18-34	14	11	17
35-54	25	25	25
over 55	43	42	46
FUTURE RITES:			
One-Plus			
18-34	63	56	69
35-54	49	45	53
over 55	38	37	40

SOURCE: **PROJECT CAN85.**

and subsequent socialization experiences have played a far more important role than formal education. Cultural and historical experience, rather than rational choice, seems to be the more important determinant of the style of religion Canadians adopt. Freud once said that people learn religion pretty much like the alphabet and geometry.[7] These findings on the role of formal education are consistent with our findings concerning Judeo-Christian knowledge. Canadians don't so much reject religion; they simply are no longer learning it like the alphabet.

ON GODLY WOMEN

It is commonly thought that women are more devout than men. Because of traditional sex-role expectations, women in the past provided much of the spiritual leadership in the home. In the first of the PROJECT CANADA surveys, conducted in 1975, 40% of Canadians said that their mothers had been "very religious"; only 27% said the same about their fathers. Biographies of American politicians from Abraham Lincoln to Ronald Reagan, along with those of Canadians such as Egerton Ryerson and John Diefenbaker, are replete with statements of debts to "godly mothers." Indeed, the fates of entire nations have been seen as dependent upon the performance of devout mothers.

As Canada approaches the end of the twentieth century, a different national picture emerges, one in which women consistently but only marginally exhibit greater religious tendencies than men. More females than males endorse conventional and less conventional ideas, engage in private devotional practices, profess religious experience, demonstrate basic knowledge, and claim to be committed (see TABLE 5.8).

The same is true of involvement in formal religious groups. More women than men say they are members, attend regularly, and enjoy their participation (see TABLE 5.9). It is easy to see why people stereotype religious organizations as being "full of little old ladies." All you have to do is add our finding on age, keeping in mind that women significantly outnumber men in the upper age-groups.

In allowing for *both* age and education, I have found that gender differences persist, though only slightly. Young women with university degrees, for example, score marginally higher on these measures than young men who are university graduates.

Yet these gender differences must be kept in proper perspective. Despite slightly exceeding men on all of these commitment measures, Canadian women as a whole are hardly devout. Only

TABLE 5.8. **Belief, Practice, and Commitment by Gender** *(In %s)*

	N	Canada (1201)	Males (601)	Females (600)
BELIEF				
God		83	79	88
Jesus' divinity		79	75	83
Life after death		65	60	70
PRACTICE				
Private prayer		53	45	62
Bible reading		25	21	29
EXPERIENCE: God		42	39	46
KNOWLEDGE: Peter		46	45	48
LESS CONVENTIONAL				
Horoscope reading		39	28	49
ESP		60	53	68
Communication with dead		22	19	26
NATURE OF RELIGION				
Committed to Christianity		44	40	48
Committed to other faiths		1	1	1
Uncommitted		29	32	27
Not religious		20	23	16
Other		6	4	8

SOURCE: PROJECT CAN85.

about half claim to be religiously committed — only 8 percentage points more than men.

For their part, men are neither abandoning supernatural beliefs and practices nor breaking with their Churches. The majority continue to hold isolated beliefs, and, for example, engage in prayer. Men also show no less interest than women in having religious rites carried out for them.

The religious differences between males and females persist at this stage in our history but they are relatively minor. The more important finding is that Canadians, whether female or male, are drawing upon isolated Judeo-Christian ideas, practices, and services, rather than opting for religious commitment. The tendency to adopt religious fragments is no respecter of gender.

TABLE 5.9.   **Involvement and Rites of Passage by Gender**
(*In %s*)

	N	**Canada** (1201)	**Males** (601)	**Females** (600)
INVOLVEMENT				
Affiliation		89	89	89
Membership		35	31	38
Attendance		25	23	27
Enjoyment from church: high-mod		16	14	18
RITES OF PASSAGE: One-Plus				
Past		84	86	83
Future		52	53	52
Either		92	93	91

SOURCE: PROJECT CAN85.

THE SPLINTERED PEW

Fragments also abound in all Canada's major religious groups. What differences there are pertain not to their presence but to their pervasiveness.

BELIEFS AND PRACTICES   A good rule of thumb on beliefs and practices is that Anglican, United Church, and Lutheran affiliates tend to be the least traditional. The Conservative Protestants are the most traditional, with Roman Catholics a close second. In between, representing something of a moderate position, are the Presbyterians.

The inclination of the Conservative Protestants and Catholics to take explicit stands on theological questions is well known. In accounting for differences between the United and Presbyterian churches, Robertson Davies recently offered this succinct and provocative observation:

Those Presbyterians — about a third of the whole — who refused to join with the United Church did so on theological grounds. The United Church offered no firm theology, and has never done so, permitting its detractors to accuse it of a flabby benevolence, of being a theological boneless

TABLE 5.10. **Select Beliefs and Practices by Religious Group** *(In %s)*

	Nat (1201)	RCOQ (236)	RCQ (244)	UC (187)	Ang (144)	Cons (74)	Luth (59)	Pres (79)	Other (118)	None (122)*
N										
BELIEF										
God	83	95	96	85	82	96	85	80	69	40
Jesus' divinity	79	95	90	82	76	95	77+	82+	63	26
Life after death	65	75	69	68	65	88	62+	60+	49	38
PRACTICE										
Private prayer	53	68	57	47	50	79	60	68	53	13
Bible reading	25	23	16	26?	23	76	39	44	33	5
EXPERIENCE: God	42	42	57	34	34	82	38	37	39	18
KNOWLEDGE: Peter	46	56	56	28	36	72	39	38	34	40
LESS CONVENTIONAL										
Horoscope reading	39	46	39	43	41	27	45	49	29	24
ESP	60	64	47	74	69	51	73	81	51	61
Communication with dead	22	20	37	22	19	10	11+	25+	15	23

SOURCE: PROJECT CAN85.

* These Ns are the same in all subsequent tables for these religious groups; the Lutheran and Presbyterian totals are for 1985 & 1980— " + " indicates only 1985 Ns (39 & 37 respectively). For details, see the Appendix.

wonder. The Presbyterians knew exactly where they stood;
it was narrow ground, but it was firm. [8]

Catholics and Conservative Protestants are slightly more likely than others to profess unequivocal belief in God, the divinity of Jesus, and life after death (see TABLE 5.10). This seems to reflect the importance the groups give to the holding of these traditional doctrines. People in the two groupings are also somewhat likelier than other Canadians to engage in private prayer, claim to have experienced God, and have some basic familiarity with the New Testament.

In the face of these relative differences, it is important to remember that the majority of people in *all* the groups score high on isolated beliefs and practices. For example, a majority of people in each of the groupings continue to endorse traditional beliefs concerning God, the divinity of Jesus, and life after death. Even a sizable minority of individuals with no group ties say they hold these beliefs. More than half say they "very often" or "sometimes" pray; a quarter claim the same frequency for Bible reading (see TABLE 5.10).

And claims to have experienced God are widespread. They are hardly limited to groups widely associated with emotional and experiential religion, such as Pentecostals and "spirit-filled" charismatics. The experience of God is claimed not only by more than 80% of Conservative Protestants, but also by one in two Roman Catholics, and more than one in three people with Anglican, United Church, Lutheran, Presbyterian, and other religious ties. Two in ten people with no religious affiliation also maintain they have experienced God.

Less conventional supernatural ideas are also common among religious-group affiliates — being somewhat more prevalent among Roman Catholics in Quebec and less characteristic of Conservative Protestants.

COMMITMENT   Conservative Protestants (75%), followed by Roman Catholics (55%), are more likely than others to say they regard themselves as "committed Christians" (see TABLE 5.11). The corresponding level for the other major Christian groups is about 40%. Approximately the same proportion — 40% — of

TABLE 5.11.   **Self-Professed Nature of Religion by Religious Group**   *(In %s)*

	Nat (1201)	RCOQ (236)	RCQ (244)	UC (187)	Ang (144)	Cons (74)	Luth (59)	Pres (79)	Other (118)	None (122)
N										
Committed to Christianity	44	66	43	38	40	75	51	42	37	1
Committed to other	1	0	0	0	0	0	0	0	9	1
Uncommitted	29	21	26	41	37	21	29	38	27	31
Not religious	20	8	15	19	20	2	15	18	19	64
Other	6	5	16	2	3	2	5	2	8	3

SOURCE: PROJECT CAN85.

Anglican, United Church, and Presbyterian affiliates lay no claim to commitment. The same is true of about 30% of Lutherans and 20% of Roman Catholics and Conservatives.

People who describe themselves as not religious comprise about 20% of the Anglican, United Church, Lutheran, and Presbyterian ranks, some 10% of Roman Catholics, and only 2% of the Conservative Protestants. This description is accepted by roughly two-thirds of "the religious Nones"; most of the remainder see themselves as uncommitted.

INVOLVEMENT Here again, Conservative Protestants easily outdistance other groups—this time by a wide margin (see TABLE 5.12). They are far more likely than others to be members of a local group (73%), attend weekly (60%), expose their children to Sunday school (72%), and claim a high level of enjoyment from church life (49%).

More than one in two Catholics and Lutherans claim to be members of a local parish or church, as do one in three Presbyterian affiliates. Groups also vary on other measures of involvement. From the high of 60% attendance for Conservative Protestants, weekly churchgoing stands at about 35% for Roman Catholics, 20% for Presbyterians, and around 15% for United Church, Anglican, and Lutheran affiliates. The Sunday school levels for adults with school-age children range from approximately 30% for Presbyterians through 25% for Roman Catholics and Lutherans, 20% for Anglicans, to 15% for the United Church. It needs to be remembered that some groups — notably Roman Catholics—have alternative means of socializing children beyond Sunday (or Sabbath) schools; the implications of low church-school attendance levels vary accordingly.

Enjoyment from church life is high for some 25% of Presbyterians and about 15% of others — well below the 49% figure for Conservative Protestants.

To the extent that sheer organizational participation is valued, there is little doubt which groups are leading the nation. Conservative Protestants have a solid hold on first place. Roman Catholics come in second, with Presbyterians third. The other major

TABLE 5.12. **Organizational Involvement by Religious Group**   *(In %s)*

	Nat (1201)	RCOQ (236)	RCQ (244)	UC (187)	Ang (144)	Cons (74)	Luth (59)	Pres (79)	Other (118)	None (122)
N										
Membership	35	62	46	35	33	73	58	37	33	3
Attendance	25	40	31	13	16	60	14	20	20	1
Church school: children	25	23	26	16	20	72	23	29	33	5
Enjoyment: high	16	19	12	12	13	49	15+	24+	21	0

SOURCE: PROJECT CAN85.

denominations—Anglican, United Church, and Lutheran—are in a virtual tie for fourth place.

RITES OF PASSAGE   This is not to say that affiliates have stopped looking to their groups for rites of passage. On the contrary, some 90% or more of Roman Catholics, Anglicans, Lutherans, and Presbyterians have had or expect to have baptism, marriage, and funeral ceremonies performed. There is a somewhat lower demand for confirmation—a rite that tends to be associated with commitment (see TABLE 5.13).

In the case of most Conservative Protestant groups, baptism is an adult rite, while confirmation is not widely practised; in both instances the levels are understandably below those of the other main groups.

Significantly, even within the "None" category, there has been and continues to be a noteworthy demand for rites — some 60% for baptisms, weddings, and funerals, and about 35% for confirmation.

The majority of Canadians may no longer be highly involved. But most continue to look to their groups to carry out religious ceremonies surrounding the central events in their lives — birth, maturation, marriage, and death.

THE FRAGMENTED MOSAIC IN SUMMARY

Our exploration of differences across the country has revealed some variations. Atlantic Canada is the nation's true Bible Belt. Older Canadians are more likely to adhere to traditional commitment than are other people; era seems more important than either education or gender in shaping one's religious style. Conservative Protestants and, to a lesser extent, Roman Catholics, exceed the affiliates of other groups in both their levels of traditional commitment and the extent of their group involvement.

However, these regional, personal, and group variations are relatively minor when seen against the stark reality characterizing most regions, most social categories, and most religious groups — the pervasiveness of fragment adoption. In every part of the country, in every social grouping, within virtually every religious

TABLE 5.13. **Past and Anticipated Rites of Passage by Religious Group** *(In %s)*

	N	Nat (1201)	RCOQ (236)	RCQ (244)	UC (187)	Ang (144)	Cons (74)	Luth (59)	Pres (79)	Oth (118)	None (122)
Past	Baptism	71	86	68	66	78	74	90	82	58	46
	Confirmation	52	76	65	30	66	17	70	41	34	29
	Wedding	66	70	67	73	65	67	69	81	63	44
	Funeral	46	48	48	54	48	42	46	59	40	27
Future	Baptism	14	11	23	9	13	8	17	19	11	13
	Confirmation	13	22	36	6	13	4	16	13	10	7
	Wedding	20	19	21	15	26	20	25	32	17	18
	Funeral	45	46	51	37	50	49	45	51	42	36
One-Plus	Past	84	89	81	88	89	86	97	94	83	65
	Future	52	54	59	57	43	44	43	45	50	57
	Either	92	95	91	92	94	92	100	99	92	81

SOURCE: PROJECT CAN85.

group, belief, practice, and professional-service fragments are now the norm rather than the exception.

These are not intuitive conclusions from interpretation of the data. Canadians in their diverse forms readily recognize themselves in the fragment thesis (see TABLE 5.14). Late-twentieth-century Canada is filled with a consumer approach to religion.

Meanwhile, religious organizations have been responding to such a religious consumption style with remarkable efficiency. Ironically, they themselves, largely unintentionally, have made it possible for Canadians to move with relative ease from religious commitment to religious consumption. Consciously and unconsciously, they have become highly efficient "fragment outlets."

TABLE 5.14.   **Fragment Self-Recognition by Select Variables**   *(In %s)*

*"How well would you say this observation describes YOU?"**

	N	Very Accurate	Somewhat Accurate	Not Very Accurate	Not Accurate At All
British Columbia	104	38	37	8	17
Prairies	160	42	34	11	13
Ontario	325	44	35	11	10
Quebec	271	53	26	10	11
Atlantic	71	40	38	8	14
Large Cities	520	45	32	12	11
Small Cities	141	49	31	7	13
Small Towns/ Rural areas	271	45	34	9	12
18-34	409	41	34	14	11
35-54	309	46	33	8	13
55 and over	214	53	29	6	12
RC's: Outside Quebec	153	45	34	9	12
RC's: Quebec	209	59	26	7	8
United Church	154	56	35	5	4
Anglican	116	48	39	5	8
Conservative Protestants	40	33	43	16	8
Lutheran	31	42	33	15	10
Presbyterian	28	53	33	9	5

SOURCE: PROJECT CAN85.
* For the full text of the item, see p. 84.

6

SERVICING RELIGIOUS CONSUMERS

I t's hard to say it. But nonetheless it needs to be said. Canada's religious groups are largely responsible for the country's drop-off in attendance.

The main reason is that the groups have responded to social and cultural change by offering religion as a range of consumer goods. Rather than saying to culture, "This is what religion is," they have been much more inclined to say to culture, "What do you want religion to be?" Even in the case of Roman Catholics and Conservative Protestants, who frequently appear to resist culture, it is not at all clear at times whether they are being prophetic or simply bringing old culture to new culture.

The result is that the gods have been fragmented with the blessing of the majority, the silence of many, and the protests of few. Rather than presenting religion as a system of meaning that insists on informing all of one's life, the groups have broken it down and offered it as a wide variety of belief, practice, program, and service items. Religion is available to Canadians in all shapes and sizes, and fragment-minded consumers have before them a multitude of choices.

This plurality of choices is even applauded as evidence of religious maturity. In the words of English scholar and churchman Andrew Walker,

Nobody forces a version on us any more. There are varieties on sale vying for our attention, but we, the consumers, have

*the absolute power of either buying one version in prefer-
ence to another or withholding payment altogether.*[1]

Ironically, religious groups lament the tendency of Canadians
to treat service attendance as a fragment, yet they themselves have
done much to create their own predicament. This chapter explains
how it has happened.

THE DOMINANT COMPANIES

Back in 1970, during a late-night discussion with a church-
extension official, I found myself—for the sake of emphasizing the merits of good planning and good business — suggesting
that his denomination would probably be far more effective if it
ran its churches like Safeway stores. The official was shocked at
the crass statement.

He shouldn't have been. Many people both inside and outside of
religious organizations tend to see them as somehow different
from other bodies. They are variously viewed as created by God,
embodying God, and representing God. Christians, for example,
see the church as "Christ's creation," "the Body of Christ,"
"the servant of Christ," "the People of God," and "the Family
of God." Roman Catholic Bishops, in their 1985 Synod Report
from Rome, reaffirmed Vatican II's emphasis on "the Mystery of
the Church." Since the Church is connected with Christ, the
Bishops stressed, it is "necessary to understand the profound
reality of the Church, and consequently to avoid false sociological
or political interpretations of its nature."[2]

However, though it may sound cold to say it, in market-model
terms religion is a product and the churches are suppliers. Kenneth Westhues' aforementioned analogy to the auto industry is
helpful. In buying cars, Canadians historically have turned to the
three major American manufacturers, plus a number of smaller
foreign companies. In the realm of religion, Canadians have turned
to four major companies — the Roman Catholic, United, Anglican, and Conservative Protestant Churches. There are also a fairly
large number of smaller, primarily foreign religious companies as
well.

The Roman Catholic Church is in fact a multinational corporation. It is based in Italy but extends to every corner of the globe, adapting itself as necessary to national environments, including Canada.[3] The Catholic Church stresses the application of faith to the entirety of life and backs up this emphasis by regularly releasing statements from Rome and its Canadian Bishops on a vast array of topics. Historically, the Catholic Church has held a monopoly in Quebec. Ethnically diverse, it also has very strong Italian and Irish representation in Canada. The Church's cultural, regional, and linguistic diversity, however, has resulted in a national organization that is not much better integrated than the nation itself.[4] Yet its regional strength is reflected in the success the Church has had in gaining full or partial provincial assistance for its elementary and secondary educational systems in all provinces except British Columbia and Manitoba (these two provinces together account for less than 5% of Canadian Catholics).[5] National activities, concerns, and interests are co-ordinated by the Ottawa-based Canadian Conference of Catholic Bishops. The Roman Catholic Church has dealings with about half the nation's population and has dominance in all regions except British Columbia, where it is matched by the United Church.

The United Church of Canada is the product of a merger in 1925 of three previous "companies" with British roots — the Methodists, the Congregationalists, and most of the Presbyterians. It is the largest Protestant company nationally and is in all regions except Quebec, serving almost two in ten Canadians. The denomination has come to be associated with theological diversity and an emphasis on moral issues and social action. As one lay leader puts it, "Like Canada itself, it tries to balance the urban and the rural, the east and the west, north and south to accommodate many points of view."[6] Seeing its two previous "Articles of Faith" of the 1920s and 1940s as outdated, the Church in 1977 established a Committee on Theology and Faith, "whose task is to stimulate the whole church to do its own theological thinking."[7] Its theological diversity and the effects of that diversity on occasion create tension between "liberals" and "conservatives" at the polar ends. Currently feuds are centred on such issues as theology, social action versus evangelism, inclusive language, and the ordination of homosexuals. A conservative movement within the church, the United Church Renewal Fellowship, has made some of this age-old division more explicit. Once described by John Webster Grant as being "as Canadian as ice hockey,"[8] the United Church is based in Toronto and is "Canadian-owned and operated."

The Anglican Church of Canada is a multinational corporation with "head offices" in England. Until 1955 it was known as the Church of England in Canada. Through World War II, most of its parish priests were still recruited from the British Isles, contributing to its image as "the English Church." The concept of a continuing tradition has been important to Anglicans. In one observer's words, "they did not come to build the New Jerusalem—they brought it with them."[9] The Canadian "division" now has complete autonomy, admitting women to the priesthood, for example, in advance of the Church of England, where the prospect continues to be controversial. The difference in the ties between Anglicans and England and Roman Catholics and Rome was suggested by the responses to the visits to Canada of Pope John Paul II in 1984 and the Archbishop of Canterbury, the Most Reverend Robert Runcie, in 1985. Whereas the Pope came to fanfare, large crowds, and major media attention, Runcie's visit was low-key, attracted mostly small gatherings, and received uneven media coverage. In contrast to the role of the Pope as the worldwide supreme pontiff,

TABLE 6.1.   **Share of the Religious Market, Nationally and Regionally**   *(In %s)*

	RC	UC	Ang	Cons	Luth	Pres	Jew	None	Other
Nationally	47	16	10	7	3	3	1	7	6
Atlantic	43	18	16	15	1	3	0	3	1
Quebec	88	2	2	1	0	1	2	2	2
Ontario	35	19	14	7	3	6	2	7	7
Prairies	30	25	9	9	7	3	1	9	7
BC	20	20	14	8	4	3	1	21	9

SOURCE: Derived from Statistics Canada, 1981 census.

the Archbishop of Canterbury as senior bishop in the Anglican communion is seen as the first among equals; he has no actual authority outside England. Just over 10% of Canadians are Anglicans. The Church is strongest in Ontario, British Columbia, and the Atlantic region.

The Conservative Protestants do not exist as an organization but rather as a number of small "companies" predominantly originating in other countries, notably the United States (e.g., Christian and Missionary Alliance, Nazarenes, Pentecostals) and Europe (e.g., Baptists, Mennonites, Salvation Army). Many of the Conservative groups are essentially "branch plants" of larger American denominations: they frequently look southward for direction and sustenance, educational institutions and materials, dynamic orators and congregational role models.[10] As was mentioned earlier, they have in common emphases upon the Believers' Church and the authority of Scripture. Co-operation and switching are fairly common. More than twenty groups and numerous individual congregations are members of an umbrella national organization known as the Evangelical Fellowship of Canada. Not to be confused with a denomination, this organization provides a forum for understanding, makes presentations to government, and deals with the media.[11] The Conservative Protestants collectively

TABLE 6.2. **Regional Distribution of Market Shares** *(In %s)*

	Atl	Que	Ont	Prair	BC
NATIONALLY	9	27	36	17	11
Roman Catholic	8	50	27	10	5
United Church	10	4	44	27	15
Anglican	15	5	48	16	16
Conservative	21	1	39	18	14
Lutheran	3	3	36	41	17
Presbyterian	8	4	64	13	11
Eastern Orthodox	1	20	46	16	7
Jewish	1	34	50	10	5
Hindu	3	10	60	14	13
Islamic	1	12	53	20	14
Buddhist	2	23	36	18	21

SOURCE: Derived from *Statistics Canada*, 1981 census.

embrace slightly less than one in ten Canadians; their greatest proportional representation is in the Atlantic region.

As noted earlier, these four major groupings, representing Canada's religious establishment, together serve about 80% of the entire population.

A sizable number of other "religious companies" operate within "the Canadian religious market." Most originated in Europe (e.g., Lutherans, Presbyterians, Greek and Eastern Orthodox, Jews, Unitarians), the United States (e.g., Christian Science, Mormons, Jehovah's Witnesses), and Asia (e.g., Hindus, Buddhists, Muslims). Like the larger dominant organizations, many are part of multinational and national operations. Canadian Jewry, for example, is served by essentially the same religious organizational structure as American Jewry; these in some instances are Canadian regions or branches of the American groups.[12]

These remaining "companies" hold down a relatively small portion of the religious market in Canada—together serving about 10% of the population, or 2.5 million people, who tend to be concentrated in Toronto and, in the case of Judaism, in Montreal (see TABLES 6.2 and 6.3.)

The major religious groups closely resemble each other with respect to the community-size distribution of their affiliates. Con-

TABLE 6.3. **Community-Size Distribution of Market Shares** *(In %s)*

	100T +	99-10	<10T	Totals
NATIONALLY	52	15	33	100
Roman Catholic	52	15	33	100
United Church	43	16	41	100
Anglican	51	15	34	100
Conservative	38	16	46	100
Lutheran	50	13	37	100
Presbyterian	53	16	31	100
Eastern Orthodox	60	9	31	100
Jewish	96	2	2	100
Hindu	88	7	5	100
Islamic	90	5	5	100
Buddhist	81	10	9	100

SOURCE: Derived from *Statistics Canada*, 1981 census.

servative Protestants (38%) and the United Church (43%) have a somewhat lower proportion of people in the larger cities than do other groups (see TABLE 6.3). All but 4% of Canada's Jews live in large metropolitan areas. Eastern Orthodox also tend to be slightly overrepresented in the larger cities.

As for age distribution, among the dominant groups, Roman Catholics and Conservative Protestants have the most youthful populations, followed by the United and Anglican Churches (see TABLE 6.4). Next come Lutherans, followed closely by Presbyterians. Jews and the Eastern Orthodox tend to have slightly older age structures than others, Hindus, Muslims, and Buddhists slightly younger.

These distributions reveal that Roman Catholics and Conservative Protestants, with younger affiliates, have the advantage of being able to add more members than others through the easiest pathway — birth. Conversely, groups like the Eastern Orthodox, Jews, and Presbyterians will be losing a greater proportion of affiliates through death at an earlier point than the others.

Given the relationship of age to commitment and involvement, the different age structures of the groups suggest significant possible trends. For example, older Presbyterians who represent one-third of the Church are more highly committed than younger ones and also are readier to support the church financially. Within

TABLE 6.4. **Age Composition of Market Shares** *(In %s)*

	<35	35-55	>55	Totals
NATIONALLY	59	23	18	100
Roman Catholic	61	23	16	100
United Church	54	23	23	100
Anglican	54	23	23	100
Conservative	61	21	18	100
Lutheran	51	26	23	100
Presbyterian	50	23	27	100
Eastern Orthodox	46	22	32	100
Jewish	50	21	29	100
Hindu	70	25	5	100
Islamic	70	24	6	100
Buddhist	64	22	14	100

SOURCE: Derived from *Statistics Canada*, 1981 census.

perhaps twenty years, most will be lost to the church. Clearly the Presbyterians have to brace themselves for such a reality. Similar deductions can be made for the other groups.

THE STABLE ESTABLISHMENT

S crutiny of the Canadian religious situation from the vantage point of a "market model" reveals a number of striking features.

First, the companies dominating the market are extremely stable. The nation is not made up of a wide variety of individual, isolated congregations or parishes struggling for personal survival, vulnerable to every new aggressive movement. Quite the opposite. A critical comment offered by a 21-year-old Saint John woman is actually very accurate: "Most religions are being run like big businesses." Canada's dominant religious groups have substantial resources. As national and multinational "corporations," they constitute formidable opposition to non-establishment competitors, including independent, single-outlet operations. Organizationally, the religious establishment appears to be in better shape than ever before to retain and even expand its market dominance.

This is not to say that the established companies do not have pockets of weakness regionally or locally. Religious groups vary considerably in their organizational structures. It is conceptually helpful, however, to think of them as having three levels — executive, clerical, and lay.[13] Organizationally, groups desire strong personnel at all three levels and smooth co-ordination between the three tiers.

In reality, of course, such goals are at best approximated. Initiatives at the executive level — such as a Papal encyclical on birth control or a United Church committee's report on the ordination of homosexuals — may, for instance, be applauded by the clergy and ignored by the laity.

Clergy may have mixed success in exerting influence in either direction. Roman Catholic priest Sean O'Sullivan recalls how, in 1982, when he was serving as the Toronto archdiocese's full-time

recruiter, he sometimes received the wrath of feminists supporting women's application for the priesthood. O'Sullivan notes that
"while they may have been aiming at me, their real argument was
with the Pope and two thousand years of Catholic tradition. As the
recruiting officer for future priests, I was in sales, not management."[14] And the laity may feel they have little power or, in some
settings — such as a Nazarene church deciding annually whether
or not to retain its minister — most of the power.

From the standpoint of performance, religious companies rely
heavily on volunteers, most of whom are elected by members
rather than hired by a professional staff. These "lay" volunteers
bring with them diverse levels of competence and expertise. Because
they are volunteers, for the most part they can't be disciplined for
poor performance. They can't be readily chastised or fired.

One solution is for the clergy or the executive to minimize
significant input and thereby minimize possible organizational
damage. The Roman Catholic Church historically has limited lay
involvement severely, a situation that is changing through the
combined impact of Vatican II and the lack of candidates for the
priesthood and religious orders. Protestant laity, says Harold
Fallding, have frequently been "roustabouts to whom practical
tasks are assigned if enough can be found for them; tasks like
looking after the finances, singing in the choir, organizing the
social evening or teaching in Sunday School." Denied more direct
and significant opportunities for ministry, he suggests, the laity
have been paralysed and in many instances have lost interest.[15]

Fallding's claim has recently received support from Ann Squire,
the first lay woman moderator of the United Church. In a press
conference after her election in 1986, Squire said, "Lay people
are not picking up their responsibility to minister and some ordained
ministers are making it difficult for them to do so."[16]

Highly involved Roman Catholic laity also indicate a desire to
carry out significant ministerial roles. Asked by the Canadian
Bishops what they think the role of the laity should be, 22% said
that they should have a role in decision-making, 18% wanted an
active part in the ministry of the Church, 17% indicated a desire to
support the clergy, and only 7% said they wanted a role in the
education of young people.[17]

Possible administrative and program deficiencies are not limited to the laity. At the clerical level, the one or more local full-time employees — usually a minister, priest, or rabbi — are not necessarily good personnel co-ordinators or business managers. Even though clergy consistently report that most of their time is taken up with administrative matters, seminary training seldom gives extensive attention to teaching these skills.[18] As a consequence, many trained clergy are faced with the difficulty of being prepared best for what they do least, and prepared worst for what they do most.

The net result is that many local "religious outlets" are "paper organizations," whose power is limited to the flow chart. Frequently they lack the organizational strength to be effective and successful businesses. My father, who as an accountant assumed the task of treasurer in three congregations, spanning more than twenty years, once commented to me that if local churches were ordinary secular businesses, many would fold. But aided by appeals that people should "give to God" along with "government subsidies" in the form of tax-free status, not a few poorly managed operations continue to survive. As the national treasurer of the Evangelical Lutheran Church in Canada, Ernest Kurbis, puts it,

> *The bottom line for a business is to have profits and pay dividends to shareholders. That's not what the church is about. [But when] you're asking people to make a money commitment you have to be responsible in how you account for and spend that money.*[19]

Many such lay and clerical shortcomings at the local level, however, are overcome at the executive level. International, national, and regional administrative staffs, funded collectively by the individual "outlets," are able to maintain the guise of organizational stability, sustain confidence, and perpetuate the religious group. While not without problems of their own, central office staffs can to varying degrees influence individual congregational programs, personnel, and, of course, the local group's sheer existence.

The result is that individual congregations and clergy come and go, but the dominant groups show signs of lasting forever.

COMPETITION FOR CONSUMERS

A second important feature of "the religious business" is that groups compete for consumers. As shown in Chapter 3, there is a high level of affiliational stability owing to factors including intergenerational transmission and the Canadian emphasis upon pluralism rather than the pursuit of truth. Consequently, the competition—particularly in the case of the larger groups—is not so much between groups as within them.

Roman Catholics minimize (although they do not eliminate) the competition issue by designating geographical areas as "parishes," each served by a building and staff. Mormons and Jews also deal with the problem by setting geographical boundaries.

Most of the remaining Protestant groups, however, compete for parishioners. Within groups, members typically criss-cross city areas in order to attend "the church of their choice." The result is that, in the long run, few churches survive as purely neighbourhood churches. Increasing numbers of large and impressive regional churches, strategically located on or near major transportation arteries, are becoming living testimonials to the nature of viable urban congregations. Rev. Ralph Rutledge, having put in place Metro Toronto's Queensway Cathedral, with its 4,000-seat facility and its weekly nationally televised service, has even greater intentions: "I do not see ours as just a community church," he said recently, but as a church that attempts "to reach beyond the borders of our community, even to the nation."[20]

In the Conservative Protestant grouping competition is particularly marked, both between and within denominations. Geographically mobile members frequently engage in the well-known practice of "church shopping," whereby they literally "try out" a number of Conservative Protestant settings before deciding where to attend. Subsequent switching to other Conservative churches in the face of discontent is also far from rare. My colleague and friend Benton Johnson of the University of Oregon, eyeing our Calgary findings documenting the high level of interchurch movement, summed it up this way: There is considerable "circulating of saints."

Here an interesting cultural paradox characterizes the Conservatives. On the one hand they defy much of modern culture in upholding traditional Christian beliefs and values. On the other hand, their church-shopping tendencies epitomize a consumer attitude towards religion. In looking for the "true" gospel, the "right" version of the Bible, "good" music, "Biblical preaching," "warm fellowship," and so on, the Conservative Protestant— like so many people in other religious groups — becomes a customer in search of a product.

The ministers and congregations under scrutiny also feel the competitive pressure. In the light of the relatively small size of the evangelical pool, Conservative Protestants — like Avis — need to "try harder" than the mainline groups if they want to attract "the initiated in transit."[21] Members are encouraged to "make visitors feel at home"; ministers are regarded as negligent if they do not find out who the visitors are and pay calls on them as soon as possible.

Competition for members means that religious groups, like other businesses, are forced to upgrade facilities, programs, and personnel. To varying degrees, they also have to promote their services and programs, primarily through newspaper advertising, door-to-door canvassing, and, to a lesser extent, radio and television programs and ads. And, as noted earlier, the competition is intensified by the fact that there is little respect for geography. If people want to go to a certain church, miles seem no great barrier, proximity no great advantage.

The reality of religious competition can be further seen in the techniques existing groups have used and can continue to use, even in a day of pluralism, to "cut out the competition."

As recently as the 1930s and 40s, the Roman Catholic Church in Quebec, say political scientists Sheilagh Milner and Henry Milner, made it "virtually impossible for an opposition [viewpoint] to develop, for no media would carry its message and all public forums of discussion were dominated by the clergy and lay people who articulated the philosophy it taught."[22] The renowned American sociologist Everett Hughes, who spent a short time at McGill University in the early 1940s, wrote that the Montreal daily, *Le Devoir*, was at that time "officiously" Catholic: "It loves to accuse English people of not respecting the

Catholic religion and of thereby wounding French Canadians."[23] Further, the enactment of the Padlock Law in 1937 literally provided for the padlocking of all premises used for "communist" purposes, with "the definition of communism left sufficiently vague so as to apply to almost any philosophy other than rightwing Catholicism."[24] The Milners assert that discontent was focused upon two scapegoats — the communists and the Jews. Parish priests, says Lita-Rose Betcherman, made use of fascist hate propaganda to update prejudices against Jews, with a 1937 parish newspaper containing the following:

> *All countries are unanimous in recognizing that we have no greater enemy than the Jews. They are the source of all great cataclysms. They participated in the French Revolution and the Russian Revolution. They are the most fervent leaders of Freemasonry, the promoters of discord, the agitators of strikes, and finally they are the propagandists of Communism.*[25]

But the Catholics have not exactly been the only monopoly-minded religious company. We have already noted how missionaries — both Protestant and Catholic — often obliterated Native religion and culture. In 1830, the Grand Orange Lodge of British North America, stocked primarily by Presbyterians and Anglicans, was founded in Brockville, Ontario. In the minds of the Orangemen, writes Pierre Berton, "the Church of Rome was a sinister and secret international conspiracy, bent on controlling the minds of men through the confessional." Violence was not uncommon. On July 12, 1843, men were killed in an attack on the Orange Hall in Kingston. In 1849, there were twelve deaths and numerous injuries in St. John's, Newfoundland.[26]

During the 1920s a strong spirit of anti-Catholicism swept over much of English-speaking Canada. In Saskatchewan, for example, many Protestants became upset over the question of separate, French-language, Roman Catholic schools. No less an infamous organization than the Ku Klux Klan made its appearance, led by the ex-Catholic, Irish-Canadian extremist, J.J. Maloney. In the winter of 1927-28, aided by two hours a week of air time on a

Saskatoon radio station, Maloney slandered the Catholics and was engaged in a major organizational campaign that gained an appreciable following.[27]

In Manitoba, Mennonite relations with the predominantly Protestant-led provincial government began to deteriorate around the turn of the century, some thirty years after their arrival in the province. The Manitoba School Attendance Act of 1916, in part reflecting World War I hostility towards Germany, made English the sole language of instruction and attendance compulsory for children seven to fourteen. When the Mennonites made their schools private, as permitted, these schools were condemned in 1918, forcing Mennonite children to attend public school; parents who refused were fined and sometimes even jailed.[28] The federal government also abolished automatic exemption of Mennonites from conscription. By the 1920s, some began to leave for Mexico and Paraguay.[29]

John Webster Grant comments that when the Jehovah's Witnesses were labelled as a subversive organization in 1940, "other denominations seemed more relieved by the elimination of a troublesome competitor than disturbed by possible implications for religious liberty."[30] In the 1940s, Jehovah's Witnesses in Quebec faced bitter attacks from the Roman Catholic Church and civil authorities. Historian Jim Penton writes,

> Priests preached bitter sermons about "these apostles of heresy" and sometimes suggested the use of a broom, stove, poker, or kettle of hot water on them when they called at Catholic homes. Catholic writers argued that they were the tools of communism, and . . . once again, policemen, public, officials, and above all, Premier Maurice Duplessis decided to suppress them through the most sweeping series of arrests ever carried out against any religious movement in Canadian history.[31]

Hutterites found themselves the objects of suspicion during World War II. In 1947, the Alberta legislature — dominated by Conservative Protestants — passed the Communal Property Act, which denied Hutterites and Doukhobors the right to establish agricultural colonies outside the terms of the act — a right not denied to any other citizens of the province. The act was not repealed until the 1970s.[32]

According to Anson Shupe and David Bromley, in the 1970s an anti-cult movement in the United States was involved in neutralizing the inroads and impact of new religious movements such as the Unification Church. The movement, backed by many established religious bodies, tried to discredit the Moonies and others by attacking their financial credibility along with their kidnapping and brainwashing techniques. Politicians and educators were lobbied, while the media was "fed" accounts of activities contributing to the image of the cults as strange and dangerous.[33] Similar "undercover" activities have taken place in Canada, too, reports new religion expert Irving Hexham, with university chaplains leading the way.[34]

And in 1983, in my home metropolis of Lethbridge, Alberta, a psychic fair was evicted from a major shopping mall two days into its four-day stand. A sizable local charismatic congregation charged that the things taking place were "of the devil" and proceeded to put pressure on the mall management, threatening to bring on a widespread boycott of the centre. The manager belatedly gave in; with apologies for any inconvenience, he sent the Ontario-based psychics on their way.

Pluralism notwithstanding, there are times when religion has been — and perhaps can still be — "a tough and dirty business."

MENU DIVERSIFICATION

A third important feature of the Canadian religion market has been the diversification of available beliefs and practices, programs and professional services. In *Megatrends* John Naisbitt makes the point that successful businesses will be ones that constantly change with the times. "When the business environment changes," he says, "a company or organization must reconceptualize its purpose in light of the changing world."[35] Railroads didn't, and became obsolete.

The same has been regarded as true of successful religious organizations. One of the dominant features of contemporary society is that such groups, like their secular counterparts, are having to contend with highly individualized patterns of consumption. This is the age of the specialty store, catering to extremely specific consumer demands. A casual walk through any major Canadian shopping centre provides the data. It is well known that all-purpose department stores are feeling the pinch; it is less and less easy to be "all things to all people."

The desire for religious fragments on the part of Canadians has put considerable pressure on religious organizations to diversify their offerings or lose business to more specialized religious organizations and secular interest groups. For the most part, they have bowed to consumer demand.

Over the course of the century, a population increasingly preferring religious fragments over religious commitment has found the suppliers responsive. Canada's dominant religious groups have taken a pluralistic view of religious belief and practice, leaving much up to the individual. Consequently, few beliefs and practices are regarded as normative. At the same time, the nation's religious organizations have gradually enlarged and diversified their program offerings, their "religious menus." Beyond conventional activities, the major groups now cater to virtually every interest of every individual. And if a program or committee does not exist to deal with one's interests or concerns, it can readily be created.

Thus it is that many a local Roman Catholic, Anglican, United, and Conservative Protestant church has activities ranging from home Bible and prayer groups, through rallies opposing American intervention in Central America and Henry Morgentaler's open abortion clinics, to the annual Hallowe'en Party and the early risers' aerobics class. As Fallding has put it, "It is probably not true to say that 'anything goes' — but almost anything does."[36]

Other religious groups have also been diversifying. The Jewish synagogue-centre, for example, functions to maintain Jewish identity. Consequently, the synagogue has become far more than only a place of worship. It is multi-functional, with staffs that program for a wide range of interests and age groups.[37] In the words of one observer, what we see is the continuing centrality of the synagogue in Jewish culture and community. Jews receive a range of services from a synagogue that functions more like a distribution centre that receives orders than as an authoritative base for dispensing them.[38]

Belief choices for Jews also seem to abound. Abraham Arnold writes:

> While some Jews cling to tradition, beliefs are reinterpreted to suit the times. Hence today, Jewish religious groupings range from Chassidism (Jewish mysticism) through traditional Orthodoxy, Reform and Conservative movements, to Jews who believe in religion without supernaturalism (Reconstructionist) and to secular Jews who still consider themselves free-thinkers.[39]

As in the business world, religious "companies" — by accident, providence, or otherwise — have not hesitated to borrow the attractive items from their competitors' menus. Social action, for example, has long been associated with the United Church. It is not a misguided stereotype. Hugh McCullum, editor of *The United Church Observer*, recalling some of the highlights of the 31st General Council in Sudbury in 1986, writes:

> And so the United Church continues to take a stand on uncomfortable issues. . . . South Africa and the Native apology were debated. Strong policies supporting a peace tax fund, opposing free trade, supporting refugees, emphasizing structural changes in the economy to benefit the poor and unemployed, seeking help for family farms in crisis, questioning low-flying NATO fighters in Labrador and for justice in Central America were approved.[40]

A former moderator, the Reverend Robert Smith, maintains that the United Church is better than most churches at evangelism, leading the way in evangelism through social action. "Where we stack up poorly," he acknowledges, "is in terms of transformation of individual lives." He says members of the church have minimized the fact that "accepting Jesus as Saviour is indeed a radical transformation of values and life." Christians, Smith maintains, need both to bring people back to Christ and to act on their faith.[41]

Conservative Protestants, in contrast, have been associated with an individual-centred religion, focusing on evangelism and personal morality. There are signs that the focus is broadening. Richard Coffin, general secretary of the Canadian Baptist Federation, recently commented: "We believe our elected officials on the whole need our collective thinking on all issues that affect the quality of life."[42] The Evangelical Fellowship of Canada's executive director, the Reverend Brian Stiller, said in 1986:

> *In the mid 70s, evangelicals woke up. We recognized that biblical principles no longer were the guidelines of society. . . . So what is taking place? Alarmed by the abdication of moral leadership by those we assumed to be trustworthy, evangelicals are taking on a new interest in Canadian issues.*[43]

EFC accordingly has been submitting briefs to the federal and provincial governments and various commissions, dealing with such issues as universal day care, sexual-orientation legislation, and pornography.[44]

Charismatic gifts and small Bible-study groups have become increasingly common among Roman Catholics and Anglicans, while prayer groups and the importance of regeneration have been among the emphases of the United Church Renewal Fellowship and the fledgling Anglican evangelical organization, Barnabas Ministries.[45]

The charismatic movement, stressing the importance of Christians' being empowered by the Holy Spirit, has Pentecostal roots, but, since the 1950s, has spilled over into mainline denominations. The movement's presence is fairly well known to Roman Catholic, United Church, and Anglican members. In the Anglican instance, for example, it is organized around "Anglican Renewal Ministries," which publishes a quarterly magazine, *Tongues of Fire*.[46] The "ARM," as it is called, states its purpose as contributing to *spiritual renewal among Christians both personally and corporately.* ARM *believes that God is re-awakening His Church to the realities of the historic Pentecost and empowering the contemporary church in a calling to joyous renewal in worship, biblical teaching, the ministry of all believers, and the equipping of the saints. . . .*

The organization stresses it is not a special interest group, but seeks to be of service to the Church.[47]

The surveys have found that 3% of Canadians indicate they are currently involved in the charismatic movement, with levels ranging from 7% for Conservative Protestants through 3% for Anglicans and Roman Catholics and under 1% for people with United Church ties; the number of Lutherans and Presbyterians in the sample is insufficient to provide reliable percentages. Past involvement levels are slightly higher, suggesting that participation in the movement has been transitory for many.

The official Roman Catholic and Anglican responses to the charismatic movement have been ones of tolerance and co-operation. As a result, conflict has been minimal. The Canadian Conference of Catholic Bishops, while warning of excesses and calling for channels of communication, declared in a message of April 1975:

This trend, even if recent, cannot be isolated from the Church. Within the Church and part of the Church, it serves as a new witness proclaiming that Pentecost continues. . . . many Christians have re-discovered a taste for prayer, the joy of belonging to Christ and a sense of fraternal community.[48]

The experience of the United Church Renewal Fellowship has been quite different. Founded in the mid-1960s, this theologically conservative movement aims to renew the United Church from within. The Fellowship has developed a national structure and has its own publication, *The Small Voice*. Its executive director, the Reverend John Tweedie, insists that the UCRF is not competing with the Church for funds; its budget in the 1986-87 year was about $200,000, compared with something around $250 million for the United Church.[49] The fellowship claims a membership of about 3,000 people out of a United Church membership of some 880,000 (.3%). The 1985 PROJECT CANADA survey found that a somewhat higher proportion of United Church affiliates — 3% — say they are currently "participating" in the Fellowship. They include an overrepresentation of the church's weekly attenders — 17%, or about 1 in 5 people.

United Church officials and laity at the national, regional, and local levels have been highly critical of the Fellowship. It is seen by many as disruptive and divisive—an effort by "fundamentalists" to set up a Church within the Church. One inactive United Church woman recently told Observer readers that she has been considering reactivating her membership after a period of uninvolvement. But "one thing that holds me back," she continues, "is the rise of the conservative, backward-looking and intolerant Renewal Fellowship. I am dismayed and, frankly, frightened by the program espoused by the UCRF."[50]

Reverend K.D. McKibbon, the Ottawa-area United Church minister who has been studying "Clergy Abuse" for the past decade, says there is a particularly high attrition rate among the fundamentalist-minded. "Evangelical and charismatic are unacceptable things to be in the United Church," says McKibbon, who describes himself personally as somewhat left of centre theologically. He maintains that in clergy disputes, ministers with such inclinations seldom win when, for whatever reason, church authorities are called in.[51]

To be sure, the Fellowship's conservative and outspoken position on sexual matters, inclusive language, theology, and the nature of the Scriptures, along with their attitudes towards others in the Church, have alienated many. The Reverend William Calderwood of Lethbridge, for example, wins few friends when he is quoted in the Observer as saying that the UCRF "is the only body which speaks for evangelicals in the church" and that the church "spends so much time engaged in action that it neglects its spiritual base."[52]

A break with the denomination could occur. Yet the Reverend Ralph Garbe, a member of the General Council Executive of the Church and a former UCRF chairman, says: "We care about the

United Church. . . . It's not our intention to split the church."[53] Such sentiments are echoed by the Reverend Harold Moddle of Toronto, who laments the tendency of the public press and the church's paper, the *Observer*, to dichotomize the United Church of Canada and the Renewal Fellowship. "We who are members of the Renewal Fellowship are as fully a part of the United Church as those who often attempt to speak on its behalf," he says. "Its position has always been a desire to support and strengthen the church."[54]

KEEPING THE CUSTOMERS

Despite difficulties such as those in the United Church, menu diversification has had the effect of allowing the country's religious groups to cater to a wider range of people. But it has done more than facilitate fragment selection. It has also served to keep membership stable.

This broadening and enlarging of religious offerings supports affiliational loyalty; it is increasingly unnecessary for the affiliates of the dominant groups to turn elsewhere for desired religious fragments. I recall from my teen years in Edmonton how some people who were upset with the McDougall United Church's rejection of the evangelical tendencies of the Reverend Hart Cantelon came over to the Braemar Baptist Church. In turn, the occasional Braemarite who wanted more of a "Holy Spirit emphasis" would move over to the Central Pentecostal Tabernacle. A social activist or two headed in the direction of Avonmore United.

Today's diversification makes such switching largely unnecessary. Roman Catholic, Anglican, United Church, or Conservative Protestant members now have the choice within their own denominations of being evangelical or agnostic, charismatic or formal, detached or involved, socially concerned or pietistic.

The failure of the alternatives — the Conservative Protestants, the new religions, invisible religion, and no religion — to recruit Canadians who appear to be "churchless" is therefore not surprising. All the major religious groups are capable of providing a wide range of content and functions. As a result, the vast majority of affiliated Canadians can readily make functional shifts within their own religious groups, without having to go elsewhere.

If an Anglican, for example, wants to be more deeply committed, he or she can become an evangelical Anglican, rather than defying conventionality and horrifying friends by "running off and joining the Baptists." The capacity of established groups to accommodate functional shifts has intensified affiliational stability.

In addition to individual adaptability, the growing tendency of the dominant Canadian religious groups to replace passive co-existence with active co-operation has made the advance of new religions even more difficult. Beyond the near-merger of the United and Anglican Churches in the late 1960s, the strong resolve for dialogue springing from Vatican II has contributed to increasing involvement by Protestants and Roman Catholics in a variety of joint ventures, ranging from worship and clergy associations through education and counselling to social protests and political lobbying.[55]

Because of menu enlargement and co-operation, switching rarely occurs. Menu diversification has served to intensify the affiliational stability that was already durable because of parent-offspring transmission. Even the "no religion" category is unattractive, since almost everyone requires some professional religious services in the course of a lifetime. Just as it is handy to have a good dentist or lawyer, so it is handy to have access to a minister or priest or rabbi.

The net result is that "the Canadian religious establishment" has become even more entrenched in recent years. What we have in this country is an extremely tight religion market. The service attendance drop-off in no sense means "things are up for grabs."

Academics like Stark and Bainbridge are misreading the Canadian religious scene when they suggest the country is ripe for the invasion of new religious movements.[56] Evangelistically minded church leaders, such as Atlantic Baptist executive Dr. Eugene Thompson and the Ontario Baptist minister Donald Hill, likewise make a serious error in equating irregular attendance with non-affiliation. Referring to recent Gallup polls, Thompson comments,

"Every Sunday there are 16,113,856 Canadians who do not attend any church. Canada is a mission field."[57] Hill, in a similar vein, writes:

If 32% are attending churches regularly, then 68% are not. This means close to 70% of our country's population is unchurched, 70% of 28 million people who are a fertile field for outreach and evangelism, close to 70% of any city, town, or village.[58]

The Canadian religion market is anything but open. The previously mentioned Canadian Baptist Federation's goal of growing to 200,000 members by the year 2000, for example, is out of touch with the reality of Canadian religion, given that these Baptists presently have approximately the same number as they did in 1910 (130,000). The lesson learned by the Presbyterians should not be ignored. That denomination embarked on a program to "double in the eighties." At the church's 112th General Assembly in London, Ontario, in June 1986, the retiring chairman of "The Committee on Church Growth to Double in the Eighties," Terry Ingram, reported that "it was manifestly clear that the church would not double in the eighties, though it appeared that the decline in membership had been almost halted."[59] The "double in the eighties" part of the title was dropped — the Presbyterians now have a "Committee on Church Growth."

The Presbyterians have simply learned the hard way what groups like the Conservative Protestants have been reluctant to acknowledge through failing to analyse critically who they are adding to their membership lists. The Canadian religious market is very tight. Fragment-minded consumers continue to identify with the historically dominant groups that are serving up religion à la carte across the country.

What is at issue is not so much group selection as menu selection. Canadians are still eating in the restaurants. But their menu choices have changed. Roman Catholics, for example, continue to dine out. What is disconcerting to many leaders and observers is that many Catholics are opting only for appetizers, salads, or desserts, rather than full-course meals. Even more upsetting to some people is that the minimum charge has been lifted—it is now permissible to skip the entrée page altogether.

THE SERVICING SUCCESS STORY

Canadians, then, are not looking for alternative religious expressions. On the contrary, the evidence supports the assertion that Canadians who want religion in their lives rely on fairly conventional organizational forms of Christianity.

To the extent that they look to the nation's religious groups for belief, practice, and professional-service fragments, they by and large are coming away satisfied. The diversification of the groups' programs and services seems to reflect in large part the varying concerns and interests of their different clienteles. Fragment offerings abound.

At the beginning of the chapter I suggested that religious groups themselves have played a major role in the great Canadian attendance decline. In providing Canadians with fragments, they have responded to a cultural demand for a specialized contribution. By being so graciously compliant, the groups have essentially served up religion in whatever form consumers want. They have not provided a religion based on what religion is, but a religion based on what the market will bear.

The result is that service attendance is just another fragment to be drawn on when customers find it convenient to do so. Ironically, religious groups are losing active attenders not because they are failing, but because they are succeeding. In my study of Toronto Anglicans, I asked inactive Anglicans pointedly if there was anything the Church could do to bring them back. The most frequent response—offered by more than 30%—was simply "no." They, along with actives, had acknowledged that the Church had usually been there whenever they had sought help. In fact, some indicated that the Church had been there even when they hadn't particularly sought help! In the light of their generally favourable views of the Church and its role in their lives, the response was puzzling at first.

Upon more reflection, the response began to make sense. If the inactives wanted to attend services more frequently, I guess they would. But from the cold standpoint of a "cost-benefit" analysis, most of the inactives were already getting an acceptable fragment return from the Church. The question "What would it take to bring you back?" was therefore fairly meaningless to many inactives; they are content with things pretty much the way they are. It is perhaps analogous to asking people, "What would it take to get you to eat five meals a day?" and having them answer, "I don't want to eat any more than three."

Gordon Turner, the secretary of evangelism for the United Church of Canada, has been studying what he calls "religious dropouts" for a number of years. In one project, he conducted in-depth interviews with twenty-five family units. Turner did not find *any* who stressed loss of confidence in the Church or theological conflict as reasons for leaving. In only three cases did people fault the Church for inadequate ministry; another two acknowledged crisis of faith; a further two mentioned conflict with the minister or a church member.

However, nine of the twenty-five cited changes in their lifestyles, related to increases in affluence and leisure time, along with vocational and marital changes. The remaining nine indicated the church wasn't meeting their personal needs — with a consumer outlook prevalent. One family stopped attending after their daughter was confirmed, stating, "There didn't seem to be any point. We didn't need to [come] any more." Their children in turn said, "Sure, we'll come back to church when we have kids and they need Sunday School." Turner says that when they were pressed a bit further, they admitted, "Yes, we'll probably leave too when they're out of Sunday School."[60]

Canadians opting for religious fragments are finding willing accomplices in the churches. A central question is whether or not they should. If it is true that the gods call for religion to be a system of meaning that addresses all of life, then their representatives are "selling them out" by dismantling religion and offering it as a piecemeal consumer item.

I am not trying to say that such fragmentation of religion is intentional and planned; I suspect that it has taken place largely unconsciously, as leaders and others try to relate religion to culture. In some ways, the "conscious vs. unconscious" question is academic; motives fail to alter the end result of a specialized style of religion.

Much of the reason that religious groups get caught up in supplying fragments is that they are in such strong demand—unlike a faith that speaks to all of one's life. The demand is anything but accidental. Fragments "work."

7
WHY FRAGMENTS WORK

On a hot summer afternoon in July 1981, he climbed into the pulpit and began to speak to some twenty thousand people in McMahon Stadium in Calgary. I was among them. Now greying and showing some of the wear of a lifetime of mass evangelism, Billy Graham proceeded with vigour and conviction to stress one of his central themes:

> *If you want lasting peace,*
> *lasting joy,*
> *lasting hope,*
> *then you need Jesus Christ!*

In a pastoral counsellor's office a few years before sat an attractive young woman. She looked anxious and tense as she opened her explanation of why she had come for help with these words: "My problems began the day I became a Christian."[1] Her enjoyment of partying, drinking, and sex had been curtailed by the norms of her new-found church. Occasionally she would have a relapse. Consequently she found herself unable to enjoy either life.

A real-estate salesman quit his job; he was unable to resolve the tension between being under pressure to sell in order to make a living and being totally honest about the houses he was trying to sell. A mechanic whose religious commitment was deepening found himself beginning to question some of the billing practices at work. A ministerial student thanked his friend for the lavish dinner, only to feel extremely uneasy when advised — with a wink by the expense-acccount user — to remember that "we talked about business if the tax people should ever ask." The Member of Parliament was well aware that what the caucus had decided was politically wise. But he struggled to decide what to do with his sense of what was ethically appropriate.[2]

And so it goes. The person who tries to live out faith in everyday life can be excused for at least asking Billy Graham to clarify his claim. Allowing religion to inform all of life is not without its problems. Therein lies a clue to why Canadians are increasingly opting for fragments over commitment.

THE SOCIAL AND CULTURAL SOURCES

Sociologically, the popularity of religion à la carte is not particularly surprising. Behaviour and ideas do not exist in a vacuum. They are part of culture and are largely a product of culture. Religious fragment adoption is merely a reflection of social and cultural developments characterizing not only Canada but also much of the contemporary western world.

What is happening therefore needs to be understood in the context of the changing nature of modern industrial and post-industrial societies. Fortunately, we are able to draw upon some very penetrating work.

One of the earliest and most illuminating analyses of the impact of industrialization on societies was provided by the French sociologist Emile Durkheim around the turn of the century.[3] Durkheim observed that as societies become more advanced they come to be characterized by increasing specialization. At the individual level, there is pronounced division of labour — people tend to become specialists. At the institutional level, the spheres of social life — politics, economics, education, religion, and so on — also become more specialized.

Such is the nature of life in present-day Canada. Ours is a country of specialized occupations and specialized institutions. Generalists may be admired, but they are virtually extinct. Successful individuals and successful organizations are those who do very little very well.

ROLE SPECIALIZATION AND COMMITMENT

The personal and social consequences of such developments are clear. Living in larger and larger cities, we relate to other people in very specialized ways. In our occupations, for example, we act different, feel different, and are different from when we play our additional roles of husband or wife, parent, friend, community leader, consumer, and parishioner. There are major role adjustments to be made as one moves from businessman to grocery buyer to Little League coach to United Church elder. Specialized settings call forth specialized roles.

Obviously people in all ages have had to play a variety of roles. In a stereotypical primitive society, an adult male might simultaneously be a husband, father, hunter, friend. But the roles, say the likes of Durkheim, were played out in settings characterized by a high level of consensus about how the world worked, what things were important, and what gods were valued. The occupational division of labour also was not particularly complex. Further, people were known on an individual basis.

In highly developed societies like our own, large cities, large corporations, and a highly specialized economy add up to a situation in which our connection with other people is largely a function of the roles we play, not of who we are. Most people don't get the chance (or perhaps even have the inclination) to get to know us. We tend to be known by our occupation, or as the parent of our children, or as a customer or parishioner.

Life is not the same as it was in the past. People before us may have done a variety of things, but they did not begin to experience the multiplicity of specialized and impersonal role performances common to our day.

One problem is that we have what sociologists dub "role conflict" — maintaining some continuity of self as we play our diverse roles. It is sometimes difficult, for example, to be the same person in work and consumer situations that we think we are in home and leisure settings. The job frequently calls for ethics and behaviour quite different from those we subscribe to in church on a Sunday morning.

Historically, religion has been seen as an overarching system of meaning that ideally informs all of life. Christianity, for example, calls followers to live out the faith in every facet of their lives.

In view of this role conflict, it is therefore not surprising that many Canadians find that commitment creates problems. Commitment complicates things by calling for a level of role consistency that is very difficult to achieve. Business ethics are frequently incompatible with religious ethics. Sexual inclinations are commonly in conflict with religious expectations. People very often are not particularly responsive to the "nice guy" approach. Many frustrated people have, somewhat defensively, protested that religion is simply not relevant to life as they know it — a simple way of saying that what it frequently enjoins in belief and behaviour is inappropriate to or dissonant with the roles one plays.

Fragments, on the other hand, seem to work. For example, retaining belief in God means that one can still have recourse to prayer. Continuing to believe in life after death gives one a measure of hope in the face of bereavement. The use of religious fragments permits one to retain some central elements of belief and practice without requiring a high level of role consistency. Commitment does not resolve the problem of role conflict; fragment adoption does.

Harold Fallding sums up the style of fragment choice in discussing its relative nature, its dependence on context:

> What was right for another time and place is not necessarily right for now. What is right for another person is not necessarily right for me. What was right for me last time is not necessarily right for now. It all depends on the situation.[4]

Many critics will be quick to argue that role consistency is essential to good mental health. Fallding is among them. He writes:

Perhaps [relativism] is also too much infected by the sickness it is supposed to help. For its atomizing of personal biography and human history into a series of situations neglects the distinctively religious vision of all situations cohering in a total situation in which . . . we must strive to locate ourselves.[5]

The criticism may be too severe. Social psychologists readily recognize that most of us at the best of times know only a precarious level of role consistency. Peter Berger, for example, has pointed out that

a sociological view of personality . . . challenges radically one of the fondest presuppositions about the self—its continuity. Looked at sociologically, the self is no longer a solid, given entity that moves from one situation to another. It is rather a process, continuously created and re-created in each social situation that one enters, held together by the slender thread of memory.[6]

Meaning systems may contribute to role consistency and hence to an integration of self. But there are other paths to integration.[7] In modern societies such as our own, there is good reason to believe that many individuals approximate integration, not so much through role consistency as through the pursuit of general biographical goals. To express it another way, they gain a sense of personal integration by giving their energies and role performances to the things they value, such as wellbeing and success.

In responding to a complex, specialized world, the tendency seems to be one of trying to find integration in self rather than in existence as a whole. Canadians, frequently sensing the choice between having a fragmented self or a fragmented world, tend to choose the latter. Such a choice represents a radical departure from historical Judeo-Christian thinking, whereby the individual finds oneness through being linked to a larger reality that gains its unity from God.

In short, for many people, fragments may, ironically, be highly conducive to integrated role performances. Life is much happier for some Roman Catholics when they can attend Mass every week yet reject the Church's position on birth control as unacceptable and based on questionable authority (e.g., "I don't think the Pope is always right in everything he says"). Some Conservative Protestants are relieved to be able to drink socially despite the widespread evangelical position of abstinence, using the rationale of showing moderation and being individually "led by the Spirit." Employers and employees in all religious groupings have a weight taken off their shoulders when they distinguish between what they would like to do ideally and what the competitive world of economic life, and their very job requirements, actually calls them to do.

Commitment, on the other hand, at the very least poses problems for role integration. Faith has to be applied to the Roman Catholic's sex life, to the Conservative Protestant's social life, to everyone's work life. Such an application frequently leads to tension and stress. As a result, given a choice, the majority of Canadians are rejecting religious commitment and drawing upon religious fragments.

INSTITUTIONAL SPECIALIZATION AND AUTHORITY

Beyond the individual level, highly advanced societies experience a high degree of institutional specialization. Primitive societies are integrated by homogeneity. Economic and religious spheres, for example, are fused to the point where analytic distinctions between the two are meaningless.[8] The gods are readily summoned when there is a need for rain, and invited later to the feast celebrating the harvest.

In medieval Europe, the Church exerted considerable influence over all of life—political, economic, educational, and social. The extent of such overlap in that period and others was deplored centuries later by Karl Marx:

The social principles of Christianity justified the slavery of Antiquity, glorified the serfdom of the Middle Ages, and equally knew, when necessary, how to defend the oppression of the proletariat. . . . The social principles of Christianity transfer . . . all infamies to heaven and thus justify the further existence of those infamies on earth.[9]

But as societies move towards and beyond industrialization, the various spheres of human life and their institutions, like individuals' roles, become increasingly specialized; in the jargon of the sociologist, they become highly differentiated. Religion's role, for example, becomes more and more specific. Further, it ceases to have significant authority over other realms.

The relatively recent industrialization of Quebec briefly alluded to earlier serves as a graphic contemporary example. Religion, embodied in the Roman Catholic Church, once had authority in virtually all spheres of life. Up to the middle part of this century, the Quebec Catholic parish was the unit around which communal life revolved. The parish priest presided over social life. In the words of Léon Gérin, he was "the most powerful bond of parish life . . . the natural protector and representative of the habitant."[10] Marcel Rioux writes that the priest exercised extreme control. He cites early observers who "do not recommend to the unvirtuous that they come here," and who say that priests "are not content to examine the deeds of men [but also] want to pry into their very thoughts."[11] So thorough was the Church's control of the community, says Jean-Charles Falardeau, that the habitant "was never able to play, at any time, an active role in the life or in the administration of his community."[12]

Jean Chrétien, in his memoir *Straight From the Heart*, maintains that the Church and the Quebec government were extensively intertwined through the era of Premier Maurice Duplessis. Chrétien argues that the Church benefited from Quebeckers' continuing to be poor, rural, and uneducated — that it instilled a mentality of grim resolution, obedience, and gratitude. Says Chrétien,

Even as late as 1960 I had a fight with my parish priest, who suggested in his weekly newsletter that we owed our alle-

giance to the Union Nationale because it had given us a tennis court. It was as scandalous then as in my grand-father's day for a feisty young lawyer to tell a priest to mind his own damn business during an election. [13]

However, from around 1960, coinciding with the conscious effort to modernize the province, the Church saw its spheres of influence diminish. Jean-Paul Rouleau notes that "by losing the majority of its schools, hospitals, and welfare institutions, the Church was deprived of valuable means of action in society." [14] Today, in groping for presence and involvement, it can make declarations and presentations. It can still "speak" to all of life. But now it is only one voice among those of many interest groups. Its current unique role in the life of the province may well be limited primarily to administering the Eucharist and performing rites of passage.

But the factors transforming Quebec society are no different from those operating upon the rest of Canada and much of the modern world. Industrialization and post-industrialization have placed strict limits on the areas of life over which religion has authority. That process has come to be called secularization.

SELECTIVE CONSUMPTION

As institutions have become more clearly and narrowly defined, a large number of organizations have come into being to service these spheres.

For example, sharper definition of the political domain has produced political parties that compete for votes, and interest groups that compete for preferential legislation. The educational realm has a number of options — the public system, separate systems, private systems. The moral, humanitarian sphere has a seemingly countless array of interest groups dealing with issues including world peace, nuclear disarmament, the environment, racial equality, poverty, mental health, driving safety, smoking, drug abuse, pornography, abortion, and capital punishment — to name only a few. The religious sector likewise is now occupied by a wide range of established groups, along with a large number of would-be competitors.

There seem to be an unlimited number of organizations that compete for consumer dollars. The emergence of a world economy, characterized by international corporations competing for world markets, has dramatically increased the variety of available products, as well as accelerating the sheer pace of technological innovation. We hardly had time to breathe as recorded sound moved from 78s to 45s to 8-tracks to cassettes to compact discs. But if you buy today's disc player, you will find yourself with an outdated version within a year.

The choices are many, the marketing strategies diverse and intense. Variety is imposed upon us whether we want it or not. If we do not already have "a need" for products ranging from matches to mental health, match-makers and psychiatrists — or their promotional designates — will try to instil the desire.

Canadians, like people in other highly advanced countries, obviously only have so much time, money, and energy. The PROJECT CANADA surveys have shown that the three foremost personal concerns of late-twentieth-century Canadians are money, time, and health.[15]

The result? Selective consumption. Precisely because of the wide array of societal offerings available to us on the one hand, and our limited ability to partake on the other, we have become highly selective.

It can be seen everywhere. Television series are literally here today and gone tomorrow in accordance with our whims as monitored by the Nielsen ratings. Endless numbers of products come and go, with manufacturers using mass advertising both to create and to supply markets. In the end, the life span of products and services is dictated by consumer response.

Other institutions gain no exemption from such selective consumption. Educators are under unprecedented pressure to provide good education, and to provide it quickly; otherwise parents and students will turn elsewhere. Politicians are only election away from oblivion. Even interest groups have a precarious life-span. People form more and more groups to deal with increasingly specific concerns — alcohol abuse organizations are too general for "Mothers Against Drunk Drivers," anti-crime organizations too vague for "Victims of Violence."

For some time now, religion has been getting similar treatment. But religious leaders have been slow to catch on. Because they have been preoccupied with attendance, they have given excessive attention and energy to the issue of people's making a regular appearance in their buildings. Such a view is myopic.

Canadians continue to be consumers of religion. However, as with the rest of life, they are very selective about what they choose. Some opt for overall commitment and face the role conflicts; more opt for a choice of fragments. When it comes to organizational involvement, some choose active participation; more choose to be marginal.

But the overwhelming majority nonetheless are in the market for religion. There is not a strong demand on their side for commitment and weekly attendance. Selective, consumption-oriented Canadians are more typically looking to religious organizations to provide fragments of belief, practice, and professional service. They still shop in the religion marketplace. But they are no longer buying the same things.

THE SUPERNATURAL MARKETPLACE

People are sometimes surprised that supernatural ideas and practices continue to thrive in a modern, rationally oriented society like ours. Personally, I am equally surprised that they are so puzzled.

Since the birth of modern science, people have readily supplemented scientific explanations with supernatural, "non-naturalistic" ones. Indeed, it might be more accurate to say that historically the pattern has been the other way around: people have supplemented supernatural explanations with scientific ones.

One reason individuals turn to non-science is that some questions simply cannot be answered scientifically. Science, for all it can do, is limited to the empirical realm, to that which can be perceived by the senses. Consequently, the question of the existence of God, for example, cannot be addressed—let alone answered— by science.

In addition, supernatural explanations are sometimes drawn upon because scientific explanations are not yet available. Durkheim, for example, said that we are impatient with science and "rush ahead to complete it prematurely."[16] Here "the gods" become the famous "gods of the gaps." We dream we meet a certain person; later the same day we, indeed, do. We fumble for explanations. If science comes up short, we look to alternatives.

Consequently, when we arrive in the world, we find that religion and a large number of other supernaturally based explanatory frameworks are offered by the culture. They tend to be "legitimized" as optional supplements to science and compete for our adoption.

As Luckmann has observed, individuals "may select from a variety of themes," with the "selection based on consumer preference."[17] While Christianity obviously dominates the Canadian supernatural market, advocates of other religions and complementary supernatural systems—such as astrology—work hard to publicize and deliver their products, and hence experience market gains.

The result is a market that is potentially robust and changing. Irving Hexham and his associates at the University of Calgary note that the new religious offerings, for example, are constantly changing. The mid-1960s featured TM (Transcendental Meditation), the early 1970s the Divine Light Mission, the mid-1970s the Unification Church, the early 1980s Rajneeshism.[18]

In short, the presence of a wide variety of supernatural expressions in Canada as we approach the year 2000 is neither new nor surprising. Science and the supernatural continue to co-exist.

In the tight Canadian market, offerings such as astrology and ESP appear to thrive because they enjoy the status of what some have called "consumer cults." Such fragments are easily absorbed by Canadians who have already responded in much the same way to Christianity. Bryan Wilson writes that modern societies offer

a supermarket of faiths, received, jazzed-up, homespun, restored, imported and exotic. But all of them co-exist because the wider society is so secular, because they are relatively unimportant consumer items.[19]

Proponents of the consumer cults perhaps can most accurately be seen as operating "fragment outlets," rather than providing replacements for the old religions. When W.E. Mann looked at cults in Alberta in the 1930s and 1940s, he found that while cults never did have very large formal followings, their centres "serviced the population, distributing books and magazines in numbers far exceeding their memberships."[20] Little seems to have changed over the century.

In supplementing science with the supernatural, the tendency of the Canadian majority is to select a variety of items from a cosmopolitan menu. Religious and other supernatural fragments, however, seem much more popular than the all-inclusive, consistency-demanding meaning systems, old or new.

THE FRAGMENT SUCCESS STORY

As was discussed above, the inclination to prefer fragments of belief, practice, and professional services is rooted in important changes associated with the industrialization of Canada. Canadians are faced with the demand to play many roles that often call for very different performances. Religious commitment frequently only adds to role conflict. On the other hand, the choice of religious fragments helps them avoid conflict.

Faced with a wide variety of choices in every sphere of life, they become selective consumers. Religion is not exempt from this process. It, too, is drawn upon carefully by Canadians for whom time and financial concerns are paramount. For most, selective participation takes the place of wholesale involvement.

But the people of this country are in no sense abandoning the supernatural. On the contrary, they give every indication of readily embracing a wide range of supernatural practices, in the course of supplementing scientific explanations. They choose fragments, not because there are no system options available, but rather because they are more conducive to life in our present age.

Fragments are thriving. Consumers are wanting them and religious companies are obliging. But the gods are becoming increasingly silent in Canadian life. The reason is simple. Religion has always claimed to bring something from beyond to culture. The gods, so believers have claimed, have spoken to us about life and death. However, when religion is drawn upon in accordance with the whims of customers, the gods are dismantled. They are custom-made according to individual taste. Rather than looking to them for direction, we direct them, as if we were ventriloquists and they our dummies.

When religion becomes nothing more than a consumer item, the customer is in charge. The gods, relegated to an à la carte role, have little to say about everyday life. In Canada, the stability of religious affiliation is matched by the poverty of religious significance.

8

RELIGION AS
A CONSUMER ITEM

I
t's not that no one's trying. In their final report at the
conclusion of the 1985 Synod in Rome evaluating the
state of the Church twenty years after Vatican II, the
Roman Catholic Bishops wrote,

All the laity must perform their roles in the Church in their
daily occupations such as the family, the workplace, secular
activities, and leisure time, so as to permeate and transform
the world with the light and life of Christ. [1]

Pope John Paul II told 50,000 Argentinians in April 1987 that
faith is to be lived out in everyday life. "You are not called to live
in segregation, in isolation," he said. "You are fathers and mothers, workers, intellectuals, professionals or students." [2] The
Evangelical Fellowship of Canada asserted in a 1986 brief to the
Canadian government that

people's religious beliefs have shaped and do shape the life
patterns of many Canadians — social as well as individual,
communal as well as personal, public as well as private,
Monday as well as Sunday (or Saturday or Friday), weekday
as well as Christmas or Chanukah. [3]

Leaders from every other major and minor religious organization
in the country could be cited just as readily. In theory, virtually

everyone would agree with a young Regina man who told me on a phone-in show, "We're not offering a product; we're not offering some kind of merchandise. We're offering an entire way of life."[4]

But it simply isn't happening. Religion — relegated to a consumer item and uninvited into many and perhaps most spheres — is having a limited impact on Canadian lives. Even in the case of people who claim they are committed, the tendency to compartmentalize faith frequently means that their lives are little different from those of other consumers of fragments. Religion's impact is consequently specific and limited, rather than general and comprehensive.

Religion's lack of significance in everyday life is readily apparent to most Canadians. In 1980, the PROJECT CANADA survey asked the nation to assess how important a number of characteristics are in "predicting how a person thinks and acts." Only about 20% said that they thought religion was a very important determinant, compared with almost 50% for education and 30% for occupation (see TABLE 8.1). Moreover, only 29% of the religiously committed cited religion as a salient factor.

It's not just that Canadians in general don't think religion is particularly important in influencing how people function. Individuals who are religiously active also question the impact they

TABLE 8.1. **Perceived Importance of Select Characteristics by Religious Commitment**

% Viewing as "Very Important"

	National	Committed	Uncommitted
Their educational level	47	47	47
Their occupation	31	34	29
Their age	22	24	21
Their income	22	24	21
Their religion	18	29	9
Size of community they live in	13	15	12
Their nationality	13	16	11
Their astrological sign	2	1	2

SOURCE: PROJECT CAN80.

have in a secular society. Highly involved Roman Catholics participating in the Bishops' recently completed national lay survey were asked, "As you see it, how much influence would you say that YOUR OWN FAITH has on . . . people?" More than 50% responded that their faith has a high level of influence on their families, but the figures dropped to about 15% for friends and work colleagues, to a low of 2% for politicians and the business community (see TABLE 8.2).

And it's not just that Canadians in general do not view religion as a key factor in influencing thought and behaviour, and that active members have a limited impact on their world. A key reason for this apparent lack of influence on life is that religion is not comprehensively influencing the lives of even the committed.

Findings from the detailed 1985 study of the Toronto Anglican diocese are instructive here. Even in the case of the Toronto-area Anglicans who see themselves as committed Christians, compartmentalization is widespread.[5] The Church has significance for the personal faith and family life of the committed, but its importance tends to diminish as its members participate in the broader, everyday world of Canadian society. The report noted that it is difficult to find signs of a unique "Anglican factor" in areas such as value formation and the perception of problems, in views of people and in social, economic, and political attitudes.

Perhaps what is most surprising — and for some people most disturbing — is that active Anglicans readily acknowledge that the

TABLE 8.2. **Perceived Impact of One's Faith on Others: Roman Catholics**

% Indicating "A Lot of Influence"

My family	55
The school of my children	20
My neighbours and friends	16
My colleagues at work	15
My employers	9
People who organize leisure	4
Politicians	2
Business people	2

SOURCE: LAY PEOPLE'S SURVEY, CCCB, 1986.

Church has decreasing influence in their lives as they move beyond personal faith and family life through social attitudes, work, and leisure, to their political views. For example, 61% of active Anglicans say the Church has significance with respect to their personal faith. But the figures drop to 39% for the Church's role in child-raising, 20% for social issues, 13% for leisure activities, and to a mere 4% for political views (see TABLE 8.3).

Religion à la carte does not stop at the church steps or touch only the occasional attender. It has invaded the sanctuaries, the education departments, the boardrooms, and the regional and national councils. Religion à la carte is everywhere.

SEXUALITY

NON-MARITAL SEX AND HOMOSEXUALITY If there is one area in which religion and contemporary culture tend to have different official postures, it is sexuality. Christianity and Judaism

TABLE 8.3. **Areas of Personal Life the Church Is Seen as Significantly Influencing: Toronto Diocese Anglicans**

% Indicating "Very" Significant

"At present, in which areas of YOUR LIFE do you feel the Church plays a significant role?"

	N	Actives (1158)	Inactives (562)
Your personal faith		61	30
Your living life generally		46	17
Raising your children		39	16
Your marriage/relationship		34	12
How you relate to others		25	9
Your views of social issues		20	11
Your choice of friends		17	7
Your performance at work		14	2
Your leisure activities		13	1
Your political views		4	2

SOURCE: Derived from *Anglitrends*, 1986:75.

historically have disapproved of sexual relations outside marriage, along with homosexuality.

The Roman Catholic Church continues to be explicit in its stance on these and other sexually related issues. In March 1987, a new forty-page document appeared, written by a Vatican committee and approved by Pope John Paul II. It carried the formidable title, *Instruction on Respect for Human Life in Its Origin and on the Dignity of Procreation*. The document condemned all forms of test-tube fertilization, surrogate motherhood, and experimentation on living embryos, declaring that the human body cannot be treated as a "mere complex of tissues and organs." While condoning prenatal diagnosis, it warned that such a procedure "is gravely opposed to the moral law when it is done with the thought of possibly inducing an abortion depending upon the results."[6]

The Catholic Church's position on sex outside marriage, expressed in the encyclical *Humanae Vitae* and other statements, is clear:

> *Relationships of sexual intimacy are reserved to marriage, because only then is the inseparable connection secured — which God wants. . . . Therefore, sexual relations outside the context of marriage constitute a grave disorder, because they are reserved to a reality which does not yet exist.*[7]

As for homosexuality, the Catholic Church's position is that it defies the moral order and is "a problem" that "must be received with understanding . . . in the hope of overcoming their personal difficulties and social mal-adaptation."[8]

Many Conservative Protestants hold similar views on non-marital sex and homosexuality. The positions of the other major Protestant groups have been far less unequivocal. The exception within the United Church is the United Church Renewal Fellowship. In late 1985, UCRF, claiming Biblical authority, voiced its disapproval of non-marital sex.[9]

The problem some groups are facing can be illustrated by looking at the Presbyterians, a denomination that tends to disapprove of homosexuality. In July 1986, "The Presbyterian Gay Alliance" came out of the closet, unveiling itself to Michael McAteer and *The Toronto Star*. Comprising seven members or adherents of the Presbyterian Church in Canada, the Alliance expressed its intention, when requested, to provide information concerning homosexuality and homophobia and to support other Presbyterian homosexual members and adherents.[10] Such "moral minorities" are not easy to deal with, neither theologically nor from the standpoint of simultaneously appeasing "moral majorities." And there is little doubt that the majority of Canadians have clear-cut ideas when it comes to both non-marital sex and homosexuality.

The surveys reveal that only about two in ten Canadians regard premarital sex as wrong (see TABLE 8.4). The majority appear to think that its rightness or wrongness depends not on some kind of moral law, but rather on how it affects those involved. As one

TABLE 8.4. **Sexual Attitudes by Religious Group**
% Indicating "Always Wrong" or
*"Almost Always Wrong"**

	N	Nat (1201)	RCOQ (236)	RCQ (244)	UC (187)	Ang (144)	Cons (74)	Luth (59)	Pres (79)	Oth (118)	None (122)
A man or a		22	24	17	20	18	61	27	27	31	5
woman having											
sex relations	C	39	32	30	35	34	77	47	48	45	na
before	U	10	9	8	12	8	17	10	9	21	na
marriage											
A married person		81	90	66	88	80	96	86	86	84	64
having sex relations	C	91	96	75	93	93	99	93	97	89	na
with someone other	U	73	80	60	86	73	87	79	78	80	na
than the marriage											
partner											
Two adults of		70	83	69	68	67	89	85	68	72	44
the same sex											
having sex	C	84	86	81	79	87	95	90	88	80	na
relations	U	60	77	61	61	55	71	76	57	66	na

SOURCE: PROJECT CAN85.

* The remainder indicated "sometimes wrong" or "not wrong at all." The Ns are the same in subsequent tables for these groups.

NOTE: C = Committed (self-described). U = Uncommitted (the remainder). In this and further tables in this chapter, full data for the committed and uncommitted are included only when the difference between them is at least 10% nationally. Otherwise, no significant difference is being assumed. na = Not applicable.

42-year-old Cornwall, Ontario, woman puts it, ''Premarital sex is wrong if people feel guilty.'' Only a minority would agree with a Regina man in his early thirties who maintains that Canadians have become ''like animals, cohabiting with whoever happens to be available.'' Those who disapprove of premarital sex include almost 40% of those who view themselves as religiously committed, compared with only about 10% of those who do not claim to be devout.

The majority of Roman Catholics defy the Vatican's position: approximately 80% of all Catholics and 70% of those who say they are committed Catholics do not disapprove of premarital sex. Disagreement with the Papal stand is slightly higher in Quebec than elsewhere. Further, some 40% of Conservative Protestants — including more than 20% of those who are committed — also hesitate to condemn sex outside of marriage, feeling it is wrong only sometimes or is not wrong at all. About one in four Lutherans, Presbyterians, and Religious Others do not endorse premarital sex; about one in five United and Anglican respondents disapprove. Predictably, opposition is higher among the committed in each of these last four categories but is still characteristic of only a minority of the committed.

Extramarital sexual relations receive the disapproval of some 80% of Canadians, including 91% of those claiming to be religiously committed (see TABLE 8.4). Such a sentiment seems to be closely tied to the value people give the family generally and durable relationships more specifically. The sexual revolution has altered attitudes to premarital sex but done little to change attitudes to extramarital sex.

Quebec, however, on the heels of reaction to traditional institutions, including religion, sexuality, and the family, currently appears to have more lenient views. While Protestants along with Roman Catholics outside Quebec—especially the committed among them— are almost unanimous in taking a negative position, three in ten Catholics in Quebec say that what the Church regards as adultery is only sometimes wrong or is not wrong at all. The Quebec Catholics who give tacit approval to extramarital sex include an astonishingly high 25% of those who claim to be committed. Whether this reflects a temporary backlash or a continuing attitude and lifestyle remains to be seen.

Homosexuality has been the subject of considerable controversy in the United and Anglican Churches, particularly with respect to the ordination of homosexuals. In 1979, the Anglican House of Bishops declared that homosexuals could be ordained, provided they agree to abstain from homosexual acts.[11]

Yet the 1986 study of what is seemingly one of the more progressive dioceses in the country—Toronto—found that a minority of only about 40% of active and inactive Anglicans agree that homosexuals should be allowed to be ordained. Some of the comments in the report, *Anglitrends*, are illuminating.[12] One active Anglican from a rural community states simply that "no homosexuality whatsoever should be permitted in any aspects of church life." Another active Anglican in Toronto, a 54-year-old man, explains his apprehension this way:

> *I feel homosexuals are somewhat more prone to sexually exploit a trusting relationship than heterosexuals. This gives me concern, wherever they have contact with vulnerable people, especially under the age of 21. It would be very worrying where there was only one priest in the parish. If he were an assistant, under the direction of a senior who knew about it, it could be acceptable.*

Another active from a small town, also in his early fifties, is among those willing to accept the ordination of homosexuals, with the key qualification of abstinence:

> *I agree with the current Anglican position that homosexuals who agree to remain celibate should be allowed to be ordained. Practising homosexuals should not be allowed to be ordained.*

But one woman doesn't mince her words about a possible health dimension: "Because of AIDS I may never be comfortable again receiving Communion."

Her fears are not isolated. In early 1987, growing fears among Nova Scotia Anglicans that AIDS could be transmitted by using common Communion chalices prompted clergy to offer parishioners the option of participating without drinking wine. Even though no one had contracted the disease in that manner, Bishop G. Russell Hatton said the concern had become real for many. One study carried out by an Ontario doctor, David Gould, and presented in February 1987 to the Canadian House of Bishops in Toronto, concluded that it would not be impossible to transmit AIDS by a Communion cup, but that the risk is low.[13]

The issue of the ordination of homosexuals may well be one of the most divisive issues the United Church has ever faced. In 1984, when the issue dominated the Church's General Council, *The United Church Observer* received more than two thousand letters on the subject. The possibility has particularly raised the ire of the United Church Renewal Fellowship. Despite the efforts of some within the Church to have a decision on the matter deferred until the 1992 Council, because of the fear of a possible denominational split, its resolution lies with the August 1988 General Council in Victoria.[14]

Despite the controversy at the executive and ministerial levels, the laity of the United and Anglican Churches differ little from other Canadians in disapproving of homosexual relations to the tune of about 70% (see TABLE 8.4). Opposition is slightly higher among Conservative Protestants (nine in ten) and Lutherans and Roman Catholics outside Quebec (eight in ten). Further, seven in ten Catholics in Quebec express disapproval of homosexuality —a level similar to that of the remaining groups. Here, as with premarital and extramarital sex, opposition increases with commitment.

SEX-RELATED RIGHTS   Religious groups, as we have seen, endorse human rights in a diverse world generally and a pluralistic Canada specifically. When the rights involve moral issues, some obvious confusion and ambivalence emerge at the executive, clerical, and lay levels.

In Canada, it is clear that moral pluralism—the moral mosaic— has won out. Whatever their personal preferences, Canadians are very reluctant to impose their morality on others through law.

This can readily be seen in our findings concerning teenagers and birth-control information, the rights of homosexuals, and the availability of legal abortion.

Canadians, whether religiously committed or not, are overwhelmingly in favour of making birth-control information available to teenagers who want it. Indicative of the pervasiveness of this view is the comment of a 78-year-old woman in a small southern Ontario town: "I think the Ten Commandments should be taught, but rather than having unwanted children, birth-control information should be given." A Toronto man, 41, is dogmatic: "Birth-control information should be available whether they want it or not."[15] There is no significant variation by commitment, and only minor variations by religious group (see TABLE 8.5). Roman Catholics and Conservative Protestants, despite the official positions of their Churches on premarital sex, nonetheless join others in showing little inclination to withhold birth-control information from young people.

Even though some 80% of the nation feel that homosexuality is wrong, almost the same proportion say homosexuals are entitled

TABLE 8.5. **Attitudes Towards Other Select Sexual Issues by Religious Group** *(% Agreeing)*

		Nat (1201)	RCOQ (236)	RCQ (244)	UC (187)	Ang (144)	Cons (74)	Luth (59)	Pres (79)	Oth (118)	None (122)
	N										
Birth-control information should be available to teenagers who want it		91	88	88	92	98	92	97	98	88	97
Homosexuals are		76	78	75	75	86	54	73	63	69	87
entitled to	C	70	79	66	72	85	46	63	55	66	na
the same rights as other Canadians	U	81	76	80	76	87	74	86	67	72	na
There should		38	39	29	37	39	62	36	40	50	27
be laws forbidding	C	52	52	37	53	47	77	55	56	56	na
the distribution of pornography to ALL ages	U	28	16	24	29	33	23	17	27	46	na

SOURCE: PROJECT CAN85. NOTE: C = Committed. U = Uncommitted. na = Not applicable.

to the same rights as other Canadians. The committed tend to be somewhat less tolerant, especially in the case of Quebec Roman Catholics, Conservative Protestants, Lutherans, and Presbyterians.

While the Conservative Protestants are slightly less likely than others to sanction homosexual rights, a majority of 54% nonetheless say they should be accorded. Illustrative of their "anti-homosexuality/pro-rights" position is the following statement, offered by their largest national organization:

> *The Evangelical Fellowship of Canada affirms the rights of all Canadians, including homosexuals, to share in the privileges of a free and democratic society. We uphold the view that the Scriptures teach that homosexual practice is unacceptable. At the same time, we call on all Christians to affirm justice and equality to all people.*[16]

Concerning the distribution of pornographic materials, some 40% of Canadians favour a ban for all ages, including a leading 62% of Conservative Protestants. Here there is a strong difference between committed and uncommitted (52% versus 28%); the religiously committed in every group exceed the proportion of the uncommitted in wanting the ban. A Lutheran from Ottawa who regards himself as a committed Christian maintains that "laws should be made to make it very unprofitable." A Church of Christ minister from Ontario says, "I feel adults have to be free to choose their manner of living. Yet I believe pornography is a serious problem, especially for some who are unstable anyway." A Halifax woman of 23, who is an infrequent church attender, comments, "I feel that it is an infringement on my rights as an individual when someone else tries to tell me who I can read or what movies I can see, etc."

In the case of abortion, the tendencies of religious groups to be either pro-life or pro-choice are fairly well known. The Pentecostal Assemblies of Canada, for example, opposes abortion under any circumstances, including pregnancy resulting from rape:

> *The consequences of a rape are very traumatic and devastating for the victim . . . she must be given special care and support. However, we maintain that the unborn child result-*

ing from such a crime is entitled to life. We do not believe that the innocent unborn child should be killed for the crime of his or her father.[17]

The surveys reveal that approximately nine in ten Canadians maintain a pregnant woman should have the option of a legal abortion in situations involving her health, a serious birth defect, and rape (see TABLE 8.6). Roman Catholics — who are told by the Canadian Conference of Catholic Bishops that abortion is an "abominable crime" and a "mistaken solution"[18] — nonetheless show only a slightly lower tendency than others to favour its availability. Conservative Protestants differ only slightly from the prevailing sentiments. In each of these three situations, the religiously committed are less inclined than the uncommitted to be in favour; nevertheless, a majority of the committed in every group believe that legal abortion should be available.

Attitudes towards abortion are quite different, however, when some other situations are posed. For example, the approving proportion drops to about five in ten when the main issues are poverty or unwanted pregnancies of single or married women (see TABLE 8.7). About four in ten Canadians are in favour of "abortion on demand."

In each of these last situations, the committed in every religious group are considerably less likely to approve of abortion. At the same time, it is very interesting to observe that there is a pronounced tendency for the attitudes of the uncommitted to follow the same pattern of agreement as those of the committed — suggesting that sheer affiliation with their respective religious groups is "making a difference."

Overall, Catholics outside Quebec strongly resemble Conservative Protestants in their attitudes on abortion; the two groups are followed closely by Quebec Catholics. The other Protestant groups tend to be somewhat more liberal, while the religious Nones are by far the most supportive of the legal availability of abortion.

Contrary to the impression that many get from media coverage, we are not a country divided down the middle, with the pro-abortion team squaring off at mid-field against the pro-lifers.

TABLE 8.6.   **Attitudes Towards Abortion by Religious Group** % "Yes"

"Do you think it should be possible for a pregnant woman to obtain a LEGAL abortion if:"

		Nat	RCOQ	RCQ	UC	Ang	Cons	Luth	Pres	Oth	None
N		(1201)	(236)	(244)	(187)	(144)	(74)	(59)	(79)	(118)	(122)
Her own health is seriously endangered by the pregnancy		93	87	91	99	87	83	98	100	90	98
	C	88	81	88	98	95	78	92	100	88	na
	U	96	96	93	99	98	97	100	100	92	na
She became pregnant as a result of rape		87	73	89	94	95	70	95	96	89	96
	C	78	64	84	93	91	63	87	93	82	na
	U	94	88	93	94	97	89	97	98	94	na
There is a strong chance of a serious defect in the baby		86	73	90	95	95	67	88	92	79	96
	C	76	62	87	93	95	58	77	82	67	na
	U	94	94	92	96	95	90	100	100	84	na
She is not married but does not want to marry the man		48	31	40	62	59	24	55	47	46	74
	C	29	20	25	51	47	16	45	22	27	na
	U	62	52	50	68	66	44	69	60	60	na
The family has a very low income and cannot afford more children		52	34	45	63	69	25	60	54	48	83
	C	34	23	28	55	60	17	50	38	31	na
	U	65	54	55	66	74	49	72	64	63	na
She is married and does not want to have any more children		46	26	37	54	58	24	54	56	50	79
	C	28	14	23	49	48	17	41	34	33	na
	U	59	47	47	57	65	42	66	69	62	na
She simply wants an abortion		38	20	28	48	47	21	48+	35+	41	69
	C	20	11	15	37	31	13	33	25	23	na
	U	51	38	37	53	57	42	56	43	54	na

SOURCE: PROJECT CAN85. NOTE: C = Committed, U = Uncommitted. na = Not applicable.

Canadians overwhelmingly sanction the availability of legal abortion under certain circumstances. The split — about forty for and sixty against — is over legal availability under any circumstances. Some sample comments from women show that at that point the struggle is intense. A 33-year-old Atlantic region mother of five children who is a Roman Catholic says, "The child should be born and placed for adoption if the mother cannot face looking after it." A young United Church mother from Regina with three children comments that "it is not an option I personally would choose, but I don't have the right to make that choice for anyone else." A single, 29-year-old Hull technician and part-time student who describes herself as a non-practising Catholic takes the position, "Laws on abortion were made by men. I believe a woman should have legal control over her own body." And from a 39-year-old rural Manitoba mother of three, a non-attending United Church affiliate, comes this straightforward assessment:

A woman's body should belong to herself, not the government. There will never be a man qualified by personal experience on the subject; therefore, men should butt out. And I would never let a church tell me what to do.

In the light of people's tendency at least to specify situations in which legal abortion is appropriate, it is noteworthy that the mainline groups, especially the United Church and the Anglicans, have been slow to speak out decisively. Reflecting on the Church's silence concerning Henry Morgentaler, *The United Church Observer* has put the predicament this way: "Feeling the pulse of the constituency and worried about a possible backlash against its abortion policy, [the Church] has been relatively cautious about entering the fray." Its policy since 1980 affirms the sanctity of human life, while stating that a woman, in consultation with her physician, "has the right to make a choice to obtain an abortion."[19] These findings on rights pertaining to moral issues document the extent to which our culture, for better or worse, has succeeded in instilling the ideal of moral pluralism. Nothing is true; everything is a viewpoint. What is true for me cannot be imposed on you.

What this means is that any religious group—Roman Catholic, Conservative Protestant, Mormon, or whatever—that advocates a particular moral position does so in a cultural context that neutralizes the impact of its claims. Their statements are declared viewpoints and added like tiles to the moral mosaic. Bryan Wilson, the renowned Oxford sociologist, pointedly comments that

> *the very fact that religion becomes an optional matter, the fact that there is freedom of religion, tolerance, and choice, is an indication that religion is apparently of little direct consequence to the functioning of the social order.*[20]

When it comes to sexuality, the country's religious groups are frequently both ignored and stripped of any unique claim to authority by the committed and the uncommitted alike. In the case of most Protestants and Jews, the tendency towards the selective interpretation of sexual norms in part may reflect organizational structure. Official hierarchies seldom have authority over individual conscience.

The Roman Catholic case is very different. The Pope and the Bishops are authoritative. Despite Rome's explicit pronouncements on sexuality, however, a significant commentary on the power of fragmentation is the ready and frequent defiance of Vatican positions by Roman Catholics. The same week in 1987 in which the Church released its statement condemning test-tube fertilization, for example, the Trois-Rivières parents of an eighteen-month-old test-tube baby, Benjamin-Pierre Bousquet, openly disagreed. The mother, Madeleine Bousquet, said that she was convinced she was doing the right thing and that there was nothing wrong with such a means of having children. Rites are important, even if Church authority is rejected: Benjamin-Pierre was baptized, and his mother said the next child would be, too.[21]

THE INCREASINGLY SMALL VOICE

Tom Harpur, the noted Toronto religion writer, comments in his recent book, *For Christ's Sake*, that he finds it "odd that the churches . . . have always seemed almost obsessed with sex and sexual matters when Jesus himself had so little to say on the topic."[22]

Sociologically, maybe it isn't so odd. Few areas in life are more immediate and more personal. It calls out for definition. Societies like ours offer few definitions of sex. There is a lot of information about sex, about the so-called whats and hows. But beyond directives simply to enjoy sex as an end in itself — words that seem incredibly hollow in the light of the personal relationships involved in sexual experience — there are few authoritative sources.

Religion, because to its claim to supernatural, revealed authority, speaks with a special voice. What the survey findings show is that fewer and fewer Canadians are being influenced by that voice.

When religion moves outside the relatively narrow realm of sexuality, it has even more difficulty being heard and heeded. This is the age of the information explosion. As observers such as Naisbitt have described so well, education, science, and technology have combined forces to provide us with an unprecedented amount of information.[23] That information can be processed and transmitted as never before. The personal computer I am using to write and amend these words glistens arrogantly, overshadowing its ten-year-old predecessor in the corner of the room — a once state-of-the art Selectric typewriter that is now a seldom-used relic. We are being deluged with information and are increasingly drawing our incomes from processing and disseminating it.

In the midst of ideas unlimited, the words of the former president of the Saskatoon Lutheran Seminary, William Hordern, are penetrating: if religion is to have a unique voice in the modern age, he says, it has to be able "to tell the world something that the world is not already telling itself."[24] Former United Church of Canada moderator Robert Smith calls for precisely such a voice, borrowing the words of the anti-apartheid leader Allan Boesak: "Contradicting the present is the central evangelical task in our time."[25]

However, Bryan Wilson is blunt in his assessment of the inability of church leaders in England, for example, to provide that voice:

Religion no longer explains the world, much less the cosmos, and its explanations of social phenomena are utterly ignored; indeed, when Catholic or Anglican archbishops today wish to pronounce on social affairs they rely neither on revelation nor on holy writ. They set up commissions, often with considerable reliance on the advice of sociologists.[26]

In Canada as well, one has difficulty finding much evidence that affiliates hear some unique voice from the nation's religious bodies. Their positions tend to bear an uncanny resemblance to those of the culture. Echoes are interesting to listen to, but they don't exactly say anything new.

VALUES

R eligious organizations stress values such as love and family life, honesty and hard work; so does everyone else. Religion teaches compassion and respect for other people, regardless of race or nationality; so does everyone else. As a result, when we probe the values of Canadians, we find virtually no differences between religious groups or between those who profess to be committed and those who do not.

Some 57% of those who regard themselves as devout think values in Canada have been changing for the worse, and the sentiment is shared by 52% of those who do not regard themselves as religiously committed. People in both these categories give similar levels of endorsement to values such as happiness and family life, friendship and success (see TABLE 8.7).

In fact, the only characteristics valued by an appreciably higher number of the committed than the non-committed are acceptance by God and, to a lesser extent, family life.

Both between and within religious groups, differences are fairly minor. Conservative Protestants, whether committed or not, are slightly less likely than others to value a comfortable life and more likely than others to value acceptance by God. Roman Catholics in Quebec, historically disadvantaged, are more inclined than other Canadians to value success and recognition.

Further, the committed and the uncommitted differ little in the importance they give to values known to social psychologists as instrumental or goal-like traits (see TABLE 8.8).[27] Virtually every-

TABLE 8.7.   Terminal, "End-State" Values by Religious Group   % *Viewing as "Very Important"*

		Nat (1201)	RCOQ (236)	RCQ (244)	UC (187)	Ang (144)	Cons (74)	Luth (39)	Pres (37)	Oth (118)	None (122)
	N										
Happiness		90	94	90	87	86	87	93	83	95	87
Freedom		89	90	79	91	92	91	98	90	89	94
Family Life		84	89	81	85	84	91	86	88	88	68
	C	91	90	90	92	89	95	96	91	96	na
	U	79	86	75	81	81	79	79	86	83	na
Friendship		83	84	83	84	86	82	79	91	79	80
Being loved		84	89	84	83	85	90	76	89	80	72
Privacy		76	76	77	77	76	68	69	84	76	75
A comfortable life		66	73	65	66	66	54	69	58	68	64
Acceptance by God		45	63	42	37	40	83	41	55	46	6
	C	77	77	68	73	70	94	90	88	74	na
	U	22	38	25	21	16	53	9	31	26	na
Recognition		34	31	66	13	30	16	25	27	33	28
Excitement		23	28	20	18	18	11	33	17	23	37

SOURCE: PROJECT CAN85. NOTE: C = Committed, U = Uncommitted. na = Not applicable.

TABLE 8.8.   **Instrumental Values by Religious Group**
% Viewing as "Very Important"

		Nat (1201)	RCOQ (236)	RCQ (244)	UC (187)	Ang (144)	Cons (74)	Luth (39)	Pres (37)	Oth (118)	None (122)
	N										
Honesty		96	97	94	96	98	97	97	95	97	96
Reliability		88	85	90	88	91	94	88	83	85	89
Cleanliness		75	77	81	72	72	77	75	77	74	64
Forgiveness		75	81	63	78	74	95	77	78	80	61
	C	83	85	74	79	81	98	93	91	87	na
	U	68	75	56	77	69	88	67	68	75	na
Politeness		69	72	74	65	67	67	67	82	74	54
	C	75	74	74	73	74	72	76	94	90	na
	U	65	68	73	60	62	53	61	75	70	na
Success		67	72	77	54	67	57	74	75	71	56
Working hard		66	68	73	57	64	71	74	73	74	51
Intelligence		61	60	70	50	56	64	64	60	61	66
Imagination		41	36	49	33	36	27	49	54	48	51

SOURCE: PROJECT CAN85. NOTE: C = Committed, U = Uncommitted. na = Not applicable.

body sees honesty and reliability as important, which is particularly interesting in the light of a recent Gallup finding that two in three Canadians think honesty — along with morals — is deteriorating in this country.[28]

The traditional middle-class virtues of cleanliness, politeness, success, and hard work are endorsed as highly important by some 65% to 75% of both the committed and others. A slightly lower proportion place a high value on intelligence. The trait given the lowest endorsement of all is imagination (41%).

Perhaps it is an interesting and, indeed, pathetic, commentary on our society that the dawn of the information age finds us placing more importance on traits like success and industriousness than it does on having a good mind and being creative. The fears of some that we may end up mass-producing knowledge but mass-reducing understanding—creating modern societies long on the "what" but short on "the why" — may well be warranted. What these findings reveal is that Canada's religious groups are not succeeding in instilling such centrally human values as intelligence and imagination. In fact, some are not doing very well at all.

Only in the cases of forgiveness and politeness is there a noticeable difference between the committed and others. Yet here again the magnitude is fairly small, indicating that these values are hardly held exclusively by the devout. These values, like most of the others, are pervasive. Among Canada's 15- to 19-year-olds, most of whom are religious consumers, 67% see forgiveness as very important, while 65% say the same of politeness. The figures for teenagers drop to 63% for intelligence, and a mere 41% for imagination.[29]

Between groups, differences are slight. Forgiveness is valued somewhat less by Quebec Catholics and somewhat more by Conservative Protestants. Those with United Church ties are marginally less likely than others to place a high value on success, hard work, and intelligence. Presbyterians slightly exceed others in the importance they give to politeness and imagination, while Conservative Protestants tend to maximize the importance of forgiveness while minimizing the value of imagination.

Despite these minor variations, the overall picture is one of value convergence. Peter Berger's comment in the 1960s concerning American Christians seems applicable to the religiously committed in contemporary Canada: "[They] hold the same values as everyone else, but with more emphatic solemnity."[30] More recently he has suggested that values are "antiseptically free of religious referents," with the contents reflecting secular humanism.[31]

The movement from commitment to consumption appears to be making a limited difference in the realm of values. Religion may contribute to the holding of values. But it is very clear that Canadian society does not lack for alternative, secular contributors. In Quebec, for example, the decline in the role of the Church in life, says Jean-Paul Rouleau, did not mean the abandonment of values, but rather a movement from the dominance of religious sources to the dominance of secular sources. When the Québécois became a city dweller, he says, change occurred subtly:

Values lived up to then in the religious mode, such as charity and love for one's neighbour, became secular, and fundamental values such as liberty, universal equality, and social justice acquired a quasi-sacred aura. [32]

The surveys indicate that the values offered by religion and culture will be very similar in the twenty-first century. The person in the pew and the person with little religious involvement will find themselves thinking much the same when it comes to values. If there is any crisis in values, a need to call for greater emphasis upon traits like reflection and creativity, religion is providing little leadership and having little impact.

SOCIAL CONCERNS

Experts who study social problems tell us that there are probably three dominant sources of our views on what constitutes a serious issue. The first is experience — we encounter the problem first-hand. Because we are unemployed, are burglarized, or encounter pollution, we assume everyone else has these problems as well. The second source is information — we are told a particular issue is a problem and therefore assume it is. We may have had limited or no personal experience with drug abuse, spouse-beating, or AIDS. But if the media say something's a problem, it must be so. The third source is our values. In the light of our believing that some principles or traits are important, certain conditions and behaviours are causes for concern. As a result, poverty, the threat of nuclear war, suicide, prostitution, and any number of other issues may be viewed as serious problems.

If religion is more than just a cultural mirror, then it is interesting for the social scientist to examine whether or not religion can go beyond experience and media influence and, on its own, "spot" some issues everyone else doesn't see just as readily. In short, does religion provide some leadership in detecting social problems, or does it merely take its orders from culture?

The 1985 *PROJECT CANADA* survey found that the country's foremost concerns were unemployment and the economy. A number of other issues, of course, were also viewed as requiring attention. An examination of the perceptions of the committed and the uncommitted, however, reveals that there is little difference in what people in the two categories regard as serious problems. Both are equally likely to "spot" such issues as unemployment and the economy, child abuse, pollution, crime, and poverty (see TABLE 8.9). Only in the limited areas of drugs and divorce do the committed show greater concern than the uncommitted.

To compare groups, Quebec Roman Catholics tend to be proportionately somewhat more concerned about almost every issue, Lutherans the least troubled. But among themselves, Quebec's committed depart little from others. Anglicans and Presbyterians are somewhat more inclined than people from other groups to view the economy as a problem area. Conservative Protestants

TABLE 8.9. **Social Concerns by Religious Group**
% Viewing as "Very Serious"

		Nat (1201)	RCOQ (236)	RCQ (244)	UC (187)	Ang (144)	Cons (74)	Luth (39)	Pres (37)	Oth (118)	None (122)
	N										
Unemployment		78	80	83	78	78	68	69	76	79	77
The economy		57	52	57	60	66	48	52	66	58	58
Child abuse		51	52	63	42	48	44	38	63	53	42
Pollution		51	43	66	47	51	40	39	45	41	61
Crime		48	52	56	46	41	42	36	54	51	40
Drugs		47	52	57	44	44	49	33	51	46	28
	C	54	52	63	55	45	48	43	66	58	na
	U	42	52	52	39	44	51	27	41	39	na
Poverty		37	37	47	33	35	28	22	39	35	38
Divorce		20	22	26	13	16	36	10	26	28	17
	C	26	23	29	22	28	42	20	35	34	na
	U	15	11	8	14	18	22	19	13	22	na

SOURCE: **PROJECT CAN85.** NOTE: C = Committed, U = Uncommitted.
na = Not applicable.

are consistently less troubled than others about social issues, with the exception of drugs and divorce. The religious Nones show less concern than others about the same two subjects. United Church affiliates show no greater concern overall about social issues, despite the denomination's strong emphasis on social involvement. This apparent discrepancy between the executive and lay levels may help to account for some of the charges of estrangement between "Toronto" and "the grass roots."

These findings suggest that, in Canada, the sense of what is socially urgent is not, for most people, uniquely informed by religion. Religious consumers and the religiously committed perceive issues in pretty much the same way. To the extent that this is the case, religion runs the risk of being accused of simply parroting the culture, failing to be socially perceptive and pronouncing judgement when judgement is called for. A 51-year-old Vancouver man expresses concern that our society, whether because of government, media, or social ineptness, concentrates on far too many minor issues: "We wrap ourselves up in debates over some jerk named Keegstra, or constitutional wording, or Ann Landers' sex survey, and ignore significant world matters."

Assuming there is some truth in what he says, the question arises whether religion has the capacity to rise above experiential and media definitions of social problems and attempt to redirect society's attention when redirection is necessary. Our findings indicate that such a call for refocusing is either not being made or not being heard. Jean Chrétien has observed that "the media have more impact by deciding what is news than in their editorials."[33] Judging from the responses of their clientele, religious leaders are neither deciding what's news nor having their editorials taken seriously.

PERSONAL CONCERNS

Religion is more than beliefs, practices, experience, and knowledge. Historically, it has also been a resource. It has had a supernatural component, God; it has also had a social component in the form of a community of believers. The result is that the committed have claimed spiritual and social support as they live out their lives.

When religion is reduced to consumption fragments, it is unlikely to be able to function as such a resource. The supernatural component is fragmented: a relationship with the Divine is reduced to an occasional prayer; the social component is fragmented: participation in a community is replaced by attendance at an occasional service.

The survey findings support this argument. When they focus upon their personal lives, five in ten Canadians express concern about money and time — they don't seem to have enough of either (see TABLE 8.10). Health is the third most widely expressed personal concern — an issue for more than three in ten people.

After these "big three concerns" come a number of other issues, including lack of recognition, loneliness, boredom, job, aging, looks, sexual life, children, and feelings of inferiority.

However, virtually all these concerns are felt equally by the committed and the uncommitted. At the same time, there are some noteworthy variations for Catholics and Conservative Protestants.

TABLE 8.10.   **Select Personal Concerns by Religious Group**   % Indicating "A Great Deal" or "Quite a Bit"

"How often do these common problems bother you?"

	Nat (1201)	RCOQ (236)	RCQ (244)	UC (187)	Ang (144)	Cons (74)	Luth (39)	Pres (37)	Oth (118)	None (122)
Money	48	48	66	37	46	32	43	41	44	46
Time	47	39	55	44	43	41	55	43	48	52
Health	34	29	63	25	29	22	22	20	32	20
Lone-liness	27	21	51	18	23	9	18	32	29	18
Looks	23	22	45	15	16	9	23	19	13	15
Getting older	22	15	37	15	18	13	25	20	22	24
Sexual life	22	18	41	18	15	10	23	25	15	16

SOURCE: PROJECT CAN85.

As with social issues, Quebec Roman Catholics — committed and otherwise — are more concerned than others with almost everything. Perhaps this reflects disposition; undoubtedly it also reflects their perception of the country and their personal lives as seen through the eyes of a province that has been undergoing radical change. Very significantly, the 1984 national survey of Canadian teenagers, including almost a thousand young people in Quebec, found no consistent differences between Quebec teens and others. A measure of equilibrium seems to be on the horizon.[34]

Conservative Protestants across the nation show the same pattern on the personal level as on the social level — the tendency to express the least concern with just about everything. What might have been interpreted as indifference rooted in an "otherworldly" outlook in the instance of social issues now takes on an alternative interpretation: Conservatives may well believe that faith reduces anxiety about both social and personal problems; things are "not so bad" at either level, if they can know, for example, "that God is in control of all of life." As we saw earlier, Conservative Protestants are considerably more inclined than others both to endorse a traditional type of Christianity and to be highly involved in their own groups. Their emphasis upon one's relationship to God may combine with group participation to provide resources for living that are unusual in our day. We will have the opportunity of examining this possibility further shortly.

Looking at the nation as a whole, we find that in the areas of sexuality, values, and social and personal concerns, there are some differences by religious group and religious commitment. They tend, however, to be fairly minor and primarily associated with the Roman Catholics and Conservative Protestants. As discussed at the beginning of the chapter, it is significant that both groups are explicit in admonishing their members to apply faith to all of life. Both stress traditional theological views and further take positions in the area of personal morality — notably sexuality — that place them in opposition to dominant Canadian opinion. The Conservatives further stress a very personal faith in which God is immanently present, personally and socially. Our findings reflect such Catholic and Conservative emphases.

What seems to be apparent is that when religion is presented as something that is intended to address all of life, it at least has the potential to influence some aspects of life. When reduced to consumer-oriented fragments, however, it predictably has a significant influence on the values and concerns of relatively few Canadians.

Maybe we have been asking too much. Sexuality, one might argue, has formidable hedonistic proponents. Non-marital sex, for example, is glamorized by the media, sanctioned by friends, desired by the individual. It is a noteworthy commentary on "who decides what is sexually appropriate" when the fear of AIDS easily outstrips religion in modifying sexual practice. One might further assert that values and concerns are learned like the alphabet as one grows up in our culture.

Perhaps we have been looking in the wrong areas. Maybe the place to look if we want to see the impact of religion is in interpersonal relations — tolerance, compassion, and the like. And if we want to observe religion's influence on the individual, maybe we need to go beyond what concerns average people to an examination of how they respond to their problems — the extent of their happiness and satisfaction, for example. After all, haven't the committed maintained all along that religion promotes social and individual enrichment?

9

RELIGION AND
QUALITY OF LIFE

I t seemed as if life had come full circle. There at the national prayer breakfast in Ottawa in April of 1987, Coretta Scott King, with calm intensity, was telling a gathering of four hundred people, among them Prime Minister Brian Mulroney and John Turner, that "Canada needs strong moral leaders. That should start with the highest offices of the country, Mr. Prime Minister and Mr. Head of the Opposition, down through all levels of government." As I watched and listened, my mind drifted back to a scene in a church in Louisville, Kentucky, almost twenty years ago, where I had sat in the first row and listened to the poetic and passionate oration of her husband, Martin Luther King Jr., one month before his assassination.

People like the Kings have had little doubt that religion can — indeed *must* — enrich life at the social and individual levels. There has nonetheless been considerable speculation about how religion affects relationships and personal wellbeing. Some obviously think religion makes people happier and more compassionate. Others disagree, and can readily cite examples of their favourite hypocrites.

Systematic research, however, has been carried out only relatively recently, almost all of it American in origin.[1] One of the first empirical attempts to examine the relationship between religious commitment and compassion was carried out by Clifford

Kirkpatrick in 1949. Using a sample of Minnesota students and other adults, Kirkpatrick found that religiously committed people were actually somewhat less humanitarian in their outlook than others.[2]

Some twenty years later, two important U.S. studies offered support for Kirkpatrick's findings. The Berkeley researchers Rodney Stark and Charles Glock conducted what has come to be regarded as a classic pioneering study of American religion. They contended that a traditional style of Christian commitment was negatively associated with social concern for Protestants but not for Roman Catholics. The reason for the difference, they suggested, was the tendency of Protestants to believe that social problems could be solved through God's changing of individuals.[3] A Methodist evangelist I heard in a country church in Indiana one Sunday night a number of years ago zealously put it this way: "If you want to get the slums out of the cities, you have to first get the slums out of the people!"

In the second study, Milton Rokeach, a social psychologist who taught for some time at the University of Western Ontario, observed that religious commitment among American adults was negatively related to social compassion for Protestants but not for Roman Catholics. He concluded that "the results seem compatible with the hypothesis that religious values serve more as standards for condemning others . . . than as standards to judge oneself by or to guide one's own conduct."[4]

These findings have not gone unchallenged. Studies involving certain American groups (e.g., Mennonite college students)[5] and certain localities (e.g., a southwestern American city)[6] have found a positive relationship — that, in fact, compassion has increased with religious commitment.

Considerable research has also been carried out on another facet of interpersonal relations of particular interest to many Canadians — racial prejudice. Two American scholars, Richard Gorsuch and Daniel Aleshire, reviewed all the studies published on the topic up to the mid-1970s and found that the marginal church member showed more prejudice than either the inactive or the most active members. Their conclusion: "The highly committed religious person is—along with the nonreligious person—one of the least prejudiced members of our society.''[7]

They did add, however, that the precise role of organized religion in influencing prejudice is unclear. We have yet to see sophisticated studies that measure the impact of churches on individuals over time.

We know virtually nothing about the relationship between religion and interpersonal relations in Canada. The research has not been done. But given our country's emphasis on the pluralistic ideal, one would expect to find a fairly high level of tolerance and acceptance of each other, at least in attitudes. The question is, does religion enhance such favourable intergroup attitudes?

VIEWS OF OTHER CANADIANS

In Canada, there is little difference between the committed and the uncommitted in the way they regard and relate to other people. Both categories hold cautious but generally favourable views of others. About one in two feel that it is difficult today to know whom one can count on, but most nonetheless maintain that people either are basically good (68%) or simply vary (30%). Only about 1% think that people are ''basically bad'' (see TABLE 9.1). A 40-year-old Charlottetown man seems to sum up the sentiments of many when he says, ''I feel that most Canadians are good, well-meaning people.'' A Montreal woman of 38 says, ''I personally believe that we should appeal to what is best in a person's heart. Every human being should be respected.''

Contrary to stereotypes, the committed in every major religious group are as positive about people as everyone else. Differences between and within groups are trivial. Even among committed Conservative Protestants, many of whom inherit a theological view stressing the sinful, depraved nature of humanity, only about 8% take the ''basically bad'' position.

DEVIANTS Nor does commitment appear to make Canadians either more or less comfortable with people who are ''different.'' Like the population as a whole, seven in ten of the religiously

TABLE 9.1. **General Views of People by Religious Group**
(In %s)

PROJECT CAN85:	Nat	RCOQ	RCQ	UC	Ang	Cons	Luth	Pres	Oth	None
These days a person doesn't really know who can be counted on	55	59	53	59	48	57	67	47	61	46

PROJECT CAN80:	Nat	RCOQ	RCQ	UC	Ang	Cons	Luth	Pres	Oth	None
PEOPLE are . . .										
• basically good and usually try to be fair	35	41	17	48	39	35	61	31	32	36
• basically good but have to look out for themselves	33	36	33	33	36	38	25	31	30	24
• not basically anything; they simply are all different	30	22	47	17	23	21	14	35	34	39
• basically bad	1	0	0	1	0	1	2	0	2	1
• other	1	1	3	1	2	5	0	3	2	0

SOURCES: PROJECT CAN85 and PROJECT CAN80.

committed say they think they would be uneasy in the presence of a drug addict, an ex-convict, or a former mental patient; five in ten say the same of alcoholics (see TABLE 9.2). A slightly higher proportion of the committed than of the uncommitted, however, say they would feel uncomfortable with drug users or male or female homosexuals. Uneasiness with these categories of people tends to be lowest among Quebec Roman Catholics. Other group variations are not consistent but seem to depend upon the type of "deviance" involved.

Religious commitment is *not* associated with a greater tolerance of people who are different; in the cases of drug use and homosexuality, the opposite appears to be true.

TABLE 9.2.   **Extent of Interpersonal Tension With Select Categories of People by Religious Group**
% Indicating "A Bit Uneasy" or "Very Uneasy"

"Please put yourself in the situation of just having met a person and the ONLY thing you know about them is ONE of the following. What do you think your IMMEDIATE reaction would be?"

		Nat (1201)	RCOQ (236)	RCQ (244)	UC (187)	Ang (144)	Cons (74)	Luth (59)	Pres (79)	Oth (118)	None (122)
	N										
A drug addict		76	87	53	89	86	77	80	84	75	69
An ex-convict		73	83	51	83	73	79	93	83	79	65
A former mental patient		70	80	57	79	73	70	86	76	68	57
A drug user		66	73	48	81	73	72	69	78	66	46
	C	73	78	55	83	78	75	63	80	70	na
	U	60	64	43	80	70	63	75	74	63	na
A male homosexual		62	75	53	72	60	74	56	64	60	36
	C	69	75	59	74	62	82	62	79	60	na
	U	56	74	49	70	59	48	54	57	59	na
A female homosexual		61	74	50	72	66	73	70	68	63	28
	C	72	79	62	73	67	79	79	74	77	na
	U	53	65	43	71	65	57	54	61	52	na
An alcoholic		52	57	42	59	58	56	55	61	56	42

SOURCE: PROJECT CAN85. NOTE: C = Committed, U = Uncommitted. na = Not applicable.

LOYALTIES   Much has been written about the inability of Canada and Canadians to develop a clear sense of identity. Andrew Malcolm, in his recent analysis of the country, writes that Americans are surprised to discover that the country "still suffers anguish over its national identity."[8] He cites Northrop Frye's observation:

American students have been conditioned from infancy to think of themselves as citizens of one of the world's great powers. Canadians are conditioned from infancy to think of themselves as citizens of a country of uncertain identity, a confusing past, and a hazardous future.[9]

This lack of a clear identity is also frequently equated with a lack of nationalistic feeling. The assertion is commonly made that Canadians are more loyal to their countries of origin than to Canada. In the words of one 58-year-old St. John's man, "I am perturbed about the so-called Canadian mosaic and ethnic groups' identity. We need more Canadian Identity."

The national surveys have found that a minority of 30% of Canadians place a high value on their cultural heritages (see TABLE 9.3). On the other hand, a majority of 66% indicate that being Canadian is very important to them. Further, those who value their national backgrounds are far more likely than others also to place importance on being Canadian.[10] Culturally speaking, the "pro-past, anti-present" stereotype is simply inaccurate. As one 76-year-old New Canadian living in Toronto expresses it:

I am immigrant (Latvian). Now I am proud Canadian. My sons (3) finished Canadian universities, married Canadian girls. I have 5 grandchildren. They don't speak Latvian. They will be true Canadians, what else.

Illustrative of other pro-Canadian sentiments is the comment of an Edmonton woman that "Canada is not perfect but it is the best there is"; a St. Catharines newspaper printer who says, "In spite of what some people think, this is still the best country in the world"; and a Scarborough, Ontario, 54-year-old who proclaims,

As a Canadian who travels abroad with my wife, especially to Europe, we feel we have the best country in the world and that Canadians are well-liked. Most people think of Canada as a great country. We should be proud.

While his comments might sound a little too exuberant for some Canadian ears, he is not out of touch with the Canadian nationalistic reality. For all the publicity given our ho-hum attitude towards our country, the 1985 PROJECT CANADA survey has found that, given the choice of living in any country in the world, some 90% of us say we would choose to live in Canada.

As for religion, national-group background tends to be somewhat less frequently valued by Protestants than Catholics. Roman Catholics in Quebec are the most likely to place importance on national background. However, they are only somewhat less likely than others to value being Canadians. One 21-year-old Montrealer sums up his sentiments this way: "I am very proud of being Canadian, Québécois, and above all, French Canadian." Few religious Nones (11%) place a high value on their national backgrounds, and the proportion giving importance to being a Canadian (44%) is considerably below that of other categories.

Both as an aggregate and within groups, the committed are marginally more likely than others to place a high value on both their national-group background and being Canadian. Commitment, national heritage, and nationalism frequently seem to go hand in hand.

POLICIES   As is widely known, the two pivotal government policies guiding intergroup relations in Canada are bilingualism and multiculturalism. Bilingualism represents the recognition that two dominant linguistic groups exist within the country. With the passing of the Official Languages Act, the ideal of two official languages has been enshrined. Multiculturalism represents the official response to the Canadian reality of a large number of cultural groups living amidst a majority of people with British or French backgrounds. It is essentially a pluralistic solution taking on a "mosaic" form, stressing mutual respect and acceptance of cultural differences. This policy stands in contrast to the assimilationist, "melting pot" ideal that is frequently associated with the United States.[11]

While noting some concerns, theologian Gregory Baum comments that "from a theological viewpoint the human attitude expressed in multiculturalism is a cause for rejoicing." The less dominant groups in a country, he says, should never be made to feel badly about their ethnic or racial background, since God has created different peoples and different traditions. Baum maintains that Canada's social organization and citizens "should help minority peoples to say 'yes' to themselves and rejoice in their heritage."[12]

The surveys, however, have found that Canada's religiously committed are no more likely, nor any less likely, to support these two key government policies. The differences that do exist by religious affiliation are attributable primarily to region.

Bilingualism has not been readily accepted. The endorsement level has increased very slowly, from 49% in 1975 to 55% in 1980 to 57% in 1985. It receives its strongest support in Quebec and hence from Roman Catholics there. The surveys have uncovered the usual complaints from the rest of the country that "French is being stuffed down my throat" and that "the government is ruining the economy by forcing us to learn French." It has also found signs that Quebec is willing to tolerate some of the resistance. A Montreal woman who is a retired teacher maintains that "the day will come when all will understand that bilingualism is a necessity and an asset to our intellectual abilities."

A similar majority of just under 60% endorse the mosaic model over the melting pot (see TABLE 9.3). A 28-year-old mechanic in northern Manitoba defines a Canadian citizen as

> one who comes from all walks of life, nationality, race, creed, colour, religion. That's what made Canada in the first place and that's what makes Canada today.

Some, like a 44-year-old administrator in a small Ontario town, have reservations about the multicultural ideal: "Other cultures bring a rich heritage to Canada but they also can bring vicious racial hate and prejudice which easily erupts into violence. This tends to make me favour the melting pot." Still others, of course, are not ambivalent about their rejection of multiculturalism. A Liverpool, Nova Scotia, man, for example, comments,

> If people from other countries had any respect for Canada or the Canadian people surrounding them, they would forget about their culture. All they want is the good life they are having — at Canada's expense.

But here, as with bilingualism, religious commitment makes no difference in one's choice. The minor variations by religious affiliation seem to be associated with whether or not one's religious grouping has a minority or dominant status. A pro-mosaic outlook is somewhat higher among religious Others and Conservative Protestants, and slightly lower among Anglicans and those with United Church ties (see TABLE 9.3).

Attitudes towards these two central intergroup policies are seemingly not being informed by religion. If Canada's religious groups believe the concepts are meritorious, they are having limited success in convincing their parishioners. Religion is missing among the key determinants of Canadian attitudes towards these two policies.

CULTURAL MAJORITIES AND MINORITIES   The country's religious groups have tended to have strong national background correlates. The United, Anglican, Presbyterian, and Conserva-

TABLE 9.3.   **Nationalistic and Intergroup Policy Attitudes by Religious Group**   *(In %s)**

		Nat (1201)	RCOQ (236)	RCQ (244)	UC (187)	Ang (144)	Cons (74)	Luth (39)	Pres (37)	Oth (118)	None (122)
	N										
National Group Background:		30	33	48	20	24	28	25	31	30	11
Very important	C	36	36	49	33	27	31	26	29	37	na
	U	25	27	46	13	21	19	24	33	25	na
Being Canadian:		66	76	55	74	71	71	73	68	66	44
Very important	C	74	79	68	81	73	72	90	56	68	na
	U	60	71	47	71	69	68	62	77	65	na
Bilingualism: favour		57	54	90	34	51	40	38*	41*	51	62
Mosaic model: favour		56	57	59	51	48	64	52	59	65	56

SOURCE: PROJECT CAN85. * Includes 1980 cases: Ns 59 & 79 respectively.
NOTE: C = Committed, U = Uncommitted. na = Not applicable.

tive Protestant Churches have been heavily British; Roman Catholics have most commonly been of French, Irish, and Italian origin; Lutherans have most frequently had German, Scandinavian, and British roots. The term "Mennonite" has so blurred culture and religion that the moderator of the Canadian Conference of Mennonite Brethren Churches has recently suggested the denomination needs to delete the term from its name.[13] The association of the Netherlands with the Christian Reformed denomination is summed up in the comment of a typist entering a directory of members: "One good thing about this job is that you know you're halfway through when you get to the V's!"[14]

These national group ties make the question of religion's impact on the reduction of prejudice all the more interesting. The nation's most numerically prominent religion, Christianity, has stressed the oneness of all people. The Apostle Paul wrote that "there is neither Jew nor Greek . . . for you are all one in Christ Jesus."[15] Adults sing the hymn, "In Christ There Is No East or West." Many of us as children sang the chorus, "Red and yellow, black and white, all are precious in his sight." Such a religion, if it rises above culture, summons its followers to accept and care for all people.

Association   The *PROJECT CANADA* surveys have found that Canada's religiously committed and uncommitted do not differ significantly in their willingness to associate with members of other cultural and religious groups. Beyond association, however, some attitudinal differences have been uncovered.

Intermarriage   Gallup polls have shown that approval of racial intermarriage has increased steadily since at least the 1960s.[16] The *PROJECT CANADA* surveys reveal that opposition now stands at about 25% for Whites marrying Blacks and East Indians or Pakistanis, around 20% for White-Oriental marriages, and some 15% for Whites marrying Native Indians (see TABLE 9.4).

The surveys also show that a majority of the religiously committed approve of racial intermarriage; disapproval is nonetheless more frequent among the committed than the uncommitted, on the

TABLE 9.4.   **Attitudes Towards Racial Intermarriage by Religious Group**   % *Approving*

		Nat (1201)	RCOQ (236)	RCQ (244)	UC (187)	Ang (144)	Cons (74)	Luth (39)	Pres (37)	Oth (118)	None (122)
	N										
White-Native Indian		84	84	87	83	82	74	84	74	83	94
	C	79	84	81	77	80	69	79	78	73	na
	U	88	84	91	86	84	87	87	72	91	na
White-Oriental		79	77	79	75	76	69	78	76	80	94
	C	71	78	66	61	76	65	74	72	71	na
	U	84	76	88	83	76	81	79	78	86	na
White-Black		73	69	74	67	70	66	67	70	77	90
	C	65	70	59	58	69	60	63	66	69	na
	U	78	66	83	72	71	81	68	73	82	na
White-East Ind/Pak		73	72	75	66	71	66	65	70	75	87
	C	67	75	61	58	68	61	63	72	67	na
	U	77	66	85	71	73	81	66	69	80	na

SOURCE: PROJECT CAN85. NOTE: C = Committed. U = Uncommitted. na = Not applicable.

average about ten percentage points higher. Still, the variations are many. For example, one active Roman Catholic woman in Toronto says, ''I think intermarriage is a good thing in the long run if the people involved can accept each other's culture.'' Yet another Catholic, an infrequent attender in Summerside, Prince Edward Island, is not so sure:

> *The children suffer in these marriages, very few other race partners' families accept the other race member, so it only adds a serious problem to our high divorce society.*

Opposition to racial intermarriage is slightly higher among Conservative Protestants than among others. The Nones are the most favourably disposed.

In the case of religious intermarriage, there is slightly more opposition to Protestants and Roman Catholics marrying Jews (about 15%) than to Protestants and Catholics marrying one another (about 10%; see TABLE 9.5). Opposition to both kinds of

TABLE 9.5.   **Attitudes Towards Religious Intermarriage by**
Religious Group   *% Approving*

		Nat (1201)	RCOQ (236)	RCQ (244)	UC (187)	Ang (144)	Cons (74)	Luth (39)	Pres (37)	Oth (118)	None (122)
	N										
Protestant-		89	91	86	91	91	72	97	89	90	98
Roman	C	85	90	79	87	90	70	97	78	84	na
Catholic	U	93	93	91	93	91	78	96	94	93	na
Protestant-		84	86	81	88	88	71	86	79	79	94
Jew	C	79	87	72	81	87	70	86	58	71	na
	U	88	84	87	91	89	74	86	89	85	na
Roman		83	81	80	87	89	70	84	67	78	94
Catholic-	C	76	80	69	81	90	68	82	52	69	na
Jew	U	88	83	86	90	89	74	86	75	85	na

SOURCE: PROJECT CAN85. NOTE: C = Committed. U = Uncommitted. na = Not applicable.

intermarriage is slightly more common among Conservative Protestants, committed Presbyterians, and Quebec Catholics. Otherwise, the amount of disapproval varies little.

What seems to be reflected here is religious and cultural affinity. Protestants and Catholics feel slightly more at ease with one another than they do with Jews; Jews, for the same reason, are likewise undoubtedly somewhat more likely to approve of Jews marrying Jews than of Jews marrying Gentiles. As one 51-year-old Jewish businessman in Halifax puts it, "I think marriage is problematic enough without bringing race, religion, or ethnic differences to the table." The same principle, I think, accounts for the somewhat lower levels of endorsement of religious intermarriage on the part of Catholics in Quebec and Conservative Protestants; age may be a factor in the Presbyterian case.

Intergroup Strain   We asked Canadians how comfortable they think they would feel when finding themselves in a situation in which the only thing they know about a person is his or her race. "What," we asked, "do you think your *immediate* reaction would be?" More than 80% say they think they would feel "at ease" in the presence of most cultural minorities (see TABLE 9.6). Uneasiness, to the extent it is acknowledged at all, is higher when people are around East Indians and Pakistanis (17%) than in the presence of Blacks, Native Indians, Orientals, or Jews (about 10%). The

TABLE 9.6.   **Extent of Interpersonal Tension With Cultural Minorities by Religious Group***
% Indicating "A Bit Uneasy" or "Very Uneasy"**

	Nat (1201)	RCOQ (236)	RCQ (244)	UC (187)	Ang (144)	Cons (74)	Luth (39)	Pres (37)	Oth (118)	None (122)
N										
An East Indian/ Pakistani	17	18	15	21	22	12	14	20	16	14
A Black	12	12	15	12	13	12	12	5	10	5
A Canadian Indian	10	9	13	9	8	10	9	0	10	8
An Oriental	9	9	13	8	7	9	9	4	7	5
A Jew	8	8	12	9	5	5	12	3	9	3

SOURCE: PROJECT CAN85.
 *Members of these groups excluded in respective computations.
**For the wording of the question, see TABLE 9.2.

religiously committed are neither any more nor any less comfortable than others when encountering individuals from cultural minorities.

Some small variations do exist by religious group. Roman Catholics in Quebec, for example, show a very slight tendency to be more uncomfortable with a number of cultural groups than do other Canadians. The religious Nones claim to feel the least ill at ease.

As for attitudes towards other religious groups, the 1975 *PROJECT CANADA* survey asked Canadians to imagine that, for some reason, they could not attend their own group's service. "How comfortable," we asked, "would you be attending the services" of other groups? One's comfort level at another's worship service does not mean, of course, that a person is necessarily negative or hostile towards a given group. The question does, however, tap the level of affinity one feels.

The most popular alternatives were the United and Anglican Churches (57%), followed by the Baptists and Lutherans (around 40%); see TABLE 9.7. Next came the Roman Catholics (34%), Pentecostals, Unitarians, and Jews (about 20%), and finally the Jehovah's Witnesses and Mormons (10%). Roman Catholics in

TABLE 9.7.   **Sense of Being Comfortable at Services of Other Groups by Religious Group**
% *"Very Comfortable"* or *"Comfortable"*

with: N	Nat (1195)	RCOQ (224)	RCQ (257)	UC (210)	Ang (143)	Cons (67)	Luth (33)	Pres (53)	Jew (23)	Oth (185)
United Church	57	24	63	—	92	72	68	91	17	56
Anglican	57	35	69	81	—	50	45	61	10	50
Baptist	45	20	35	62	71	82	35	77	6	45
Lutheran	40	15	38	54	65	45	—	59	10	40
Roman Catholic	34	—	—	22	45	22	28	35	29	56
Pentecostal	24	13	30	27	25	54	12	20	6	26
Unitarian	20	10	23	25	24	18	14	23	19	22
Jewish	19	18	25	13	23	17	14	7	—	8
Jehovah's Witnesses	10	14	10	6	9	6	6	4	1	20
Mormon	10	4	15	10	8	10	14	3	2	21

SOURCE: PROJECT CAN75.

NOTE: Affiliates not included in computation of national total for their group; Baptists and Pentecostals not incuded in Conservative Protestant %s in their respective instances. The number of Jews in the sample is obviously too small to permit stable percentaging; it is included here for interest value.

Quebec express more affinity with other groups than their counterparts across the country—Catholics generally tend to feel their greatest rapport with Anglicans. Other "number one" preferences: the United Church, Anglicans; Anglicans, the United Church; Conservative Protestants, Lutherans; and Presybterians, the United Church. The small sample of Jews shows little worship affinity, about the same as what Gentiles show towards Jewish services (about 20%).

For some Canadians, the possibility of worshipping in other group settings creates little problem. A pilot in Ottawa, an Anglican, expresses an appreciation for all religions: "While I consider myself to be a Christian, I respect the other religions despite what they might call or refer to as 'their God.' They're one and the same." But a 74-year-old Toronto woman is among those with quite different feelings: "If I were unable to attend my own, Roman Catholic church," she says, "I would not be interested in attending any other."

Someone might well ask, "Why the national affinity with a sectarian-like group like the Baptists (45%) over the Roman Catholics (34%)?" Baptists are associated in most minds with a strict morality, — "no dancing, no drinking, no fun" — a stereotype that has been magnified by U.S. Baptists. But the majority of Canadian Baptists have British rather than American roots. Even as recently as the early 1970s, almost 75% were of British origin; this compares with 85% of Anglicans, 79% of United Church affiliates, and 85% of Presbyterians.[17] Historical problems notwithstanding, the current affinity levels between members of these groups is therefore quite predictable.

These overall findings on intergroup relations provide some good news for religious leaders: the religiously committed, contrary to widespread stereotyping, are no more negative or bigoted than other people. We have heard much about fundamentalist Prairie teacher Jim Keegstra; we have heard very little about Roman Catholic Prairie teacher Allan Melanchuk. The latter became concerned in 1983 about racism and intolerance in Saskatchewan and has been designing and evaluating curricula aimed at reducing prejudice. In 1987 he won a national award for his efforts.[18]

The point is that, on balance, the religiously committed fare no worse than others when it comes to how they respond to other people. But, at the same time, the committed do not give evidence of being any more positive and tolerant. Functioning beside secular sources of concern and acceptance, religion does not produce a greater "pro-human" effect.

SOCIAL ATTITUDES

The late Tommy Douglas related how, when he was a Baptist minister in Weyburn, Saskatchewan, in 1935, his flirtation with politics was his ticket out of the ministry:

I received a visit from the superintendent of the Baptist Church in western Canada. He made it clear that if I didn't stay out of politics he'd see to it that I never obtained another Baptist congregation. I replied, "You've just given the CCF a candidate."[19]

Times seem to have changed, dramatically. According to Stewart Crysdale, the United, Anglican, and Presbyterian Churches have been social-reform-minded since the early part of this century, with the United Church carrying on the social-concern emphases of its Congregational, Methodist, and Presbyterian antecedents.[20] We have seen that Conservative Protestants are taking a greater interest in social issues. The Roman Catholics — in keeping with Rome's call for the Church to "denounce every form of poverty and oppression, and everywhere defend and promote the fundamental and inalienable rights of the human person"[21] — have been making a number of statements through the Canadian Conference of Catholic Bishops.

This is a day in which the Catholic Bishops, led by Remi DeRoo of Victoria, tell the Canadian government what's wrong with the economy; when the aboriginal right to self-government is endorsed in a statement called, "A New Covenant" issued by the nation's Roman Catholic, United, Evangelical Lutheran, Presbyterian, Mennonite, and Quaker Churches;[22] when Canadian Churches find it essential to give attention to the problems of Latin America; when nuclear arms and nuclear war have to be addressed; when Church of England envoy Terry Waite puts his life on the line in the course of negotiating the freedom of hostages in the Middle East; when Black Anglican bishop Desmond Tutu wins a Nobel Peace Prize for leading the crusade against apartheid in South Africa.

Donald Sjoberg, the president of the Evangelical Lutheran Church in Canada, who himself has marched with placards in demonstrations, seems to express the dominant mood of religious leaders when he says that the Church must speak out on issues in which the hurts of society are most invisible.[23]

Gregory Baum notes that, since the late 1960s, Canadian Churches have been both particularly vocal and increasingly ecumenical in addressing social justice. For Protestants, Baum maintains, this emphasis has tended to represent the return to "an earlier tradition, the social gospel''; for Catholics, ''it has meant the emergence of new, prophetic Catholicism, closely linked to the world-wide social justice movement in the Church.''[24]

It is not at all apparent, however, that such activity at the leadership level is significantly influencing, or necessarily endorsed by, the religious laity. This day of religious social activity is also a day when no less than 48% of Canadians maintain that ''ministers should stick to religion and not concern themselves with social, economic, and political issues''! Among the nation's 15- to 19-year-olds, the figure is virtually identical — 50%.[25]

And the ''stick to religion'' attitude has some surprising advocates and non-advocates. Those holding such a position range from a high of about 60% of Roman Catholics in Quebec, along with Lutherans, through about 55% of religious Others and Nones, 47% of United Church affiliates, and about 40% of Roman Catholics outside Quebec, to a low of some 35% of Anglicans, Conservative Protestants, and Presbyterians. Social-change-minded Quebec Catholics tend to want the Church to continue to stay out of the spheres from which it has recently been evicted. Religious Nones, contrary to a stereotype that they are critical of the Church for its lack of social concern, are not necessarily wanting religious groups to ''take their heads out of the clouds'' and speak to everyday concerns. United Church affiliates do not lead the league in calling for the Church to address social issues. Conservative Protestants, in emphasizing that religion should deal with all of life, do not — as many people think — tend to support the viewpoint of this Port Coquitlam, British Columbia, Jehovah's Witness:

> *Ministers as private citizens should be permitted to speak out on anything they want. However, if done on behalf of churches, they should recognize their peculiar calling, namely to preach the gospel, not clothing it in a particular political statement.*

While religious organizations at the executive and clerical levels frequently pursue social causes in a high-profile manner, the evidence suggests that the interest and support of the laity are suspect. It should come as no shock that, oriented as they are towards fragments and services, religious affiliates are not particularly caught up in "the non-fragment" activities of religious leaders, especially when those leaders appear to be stepping out of their domain of competence and worth. For all the activity in the social realm, the survey findings suggest the impact on à la carte consumers is extremely light.

POLITICS, GOVERNMENT, LAW   The widely recognized tendency of Roman Catholics and new immigrants to prefer the Liberal Party and for Protestants and Nones to line up with the Conservatives and NDP[26] are corroborated by the *PROJECT CANADA* surveys (see TABLE 9.8). Contrary to what many people think, this pattern is not merely because the strength of the Liberal Party in Quebec tips the national scales. Roman Catholics in every region tend to favour the Liberal Party over others federally. Protestants in every region identify, on the other hand, with the Conservative and New Democratic Parties. The obvious question is why?

Along with a political science colleague at the University of Lethbridge, Peter McCormick, I set out to try to answer this unresolved question using historical, survey, and cross-cultural data. What we found is that the Canadian pattern is far from unique. In countries in which Catholics have been socially disadvantaged, such as the United States, England, Australia, and New Zealand, they have tended to identify with liberal-oriented parties advocating alterations in the status quo. In European countries where they have not been disadvantaged, they have been inclined to associate with conservative parties. For Protestants, the same tendencies have prevailed: when in an advantaged position, they have leaned towards conservative parties; when not, they have been attracted to the liberal ones.

The "lingering link" of religion with party preference in Canada appears therefore to reflect relationships that had their roots in the socially disadvantaged position of Roman Catholics and the socially advantaged position of Protestants. With the passage of time and the movement towards social equality, some people switch parties, but most stay, inheriting their party preference from their parents and grandparents. Ironically, this occurs despite the fact that the two major parties themselves have attained such a high

TABLE 9.8.   **Federal Party Preference and Perceived Political Orientation by Religious Group**   *(In %s)*

	N	Nat (1201)	RCOQ (236)	RCQ (244)	UC (187)	Ang (144)	Cons (74)	Luth (59)	Pres (79)	Oth (118)	None (122)
Party Preference											
Liberal		39	53	60	23	31	23	41	45	36	29
Conservative		35	27	20	47	48	56	32	25	32	30
NDP		18	14	8	23	18	12	22	22	24	27
	C	12	11	6	21	15	11	18	28	14	na
	U	21	20	10	24	19	16	28	20	31	na
Other		8	6	12	7	3	9	5	8	8	14
Perceived Orientation											
Liberal		25	27	28	12	24	15	26	27	25	47
Moderate, middle road		57	56	64	62	56	54	52	48	57	42
Conservative		18	17	8	26	20	31	22	25	18	11

SOURCE: PROJECT CAN85. C = Committed, U = Uncommitted. na = Not applicable.

degree of ideological convergence that they have become virtually indistinguishable from each other.[27] Consistent with such an argument is the tendency of people who are less committed religiously to be more inclined than the committed to identify with a newer political party, namely the NDP (see TABLE 9.8).

Largely inherited, federal political affiliation commonly appears to join religious affiliation, national heritage, and Canadian nationality as a major source of identity for a good many people.

When it comes to one's political outlook, versus party preference, there are no significant differences in how the committed and the uncommitted see their political positions (see TABLE 9.8). There are, however, some variations by group. Most group adherents see themselves as "middle of the road," although religious Nones show liberal, and Conservative Protestants conservative, political self-image tendencies.

Political scientist John Redekop, who is also the national moderator of the Mennonite Brethren Church, suggests that this tendency of Protestant Conservatives to see themselves as politically conservative can get them into political trouble. He notes that "Conservative Christians and conservative politicians both like the label 'conservative,' but their conservatism is not cut of common cloth." North American Christians who gravitate towards conservative politicians like Reagan or Mulroney frequently come away disillusioned, says Redekop, reluctantly acknowledging "that Reagan and Mulroney never really were in the conservative Christian camp—they only talked that way." He concludes, "The agenda of partisan politics generally turns out not to be the agenda of the church. The sooner that conservative Christians accept that fact, the less frustrated they will be."[28]

THE SYSTEM Canadians, including the religious Nones, exhibit no such consistent "liberal-conservative" patterns in their attitudes towards a variety of social issues. For starters, they hold very similar views regarding our political and economic system, the prospects for social mobility, input into government, and Communism as a form of government (see TABLE 9.9).

Some variations by religious group do exist on specific items: Quebec Catholics are far more likely than others to believe that upward movement is possible; Conservative Protestants are the most leery of Communism, religious Nones the least. But differences in social attitudes by commitment exist only in the case of the endorsement of the political and economic system. The committed are no more likely than the uncommitted to believe in upward social mobility or the possibility that individuals can influence government. For example, an uncommitted 41-year-old Lutheran in a small Alberta community says,

In Canada anyone has the opportunity to become what they want, provided they are willing to put in the work and effort required. About the only thing keeping anyone back is their own attitude. Times may be tough, but not impossible.

A 37-year-old United Church salesman in Kelowna, who is also uncommitted, is wary about the chances for upward movement: "It's not as true as a few years ago," he says. "Now it is easier to see that it is beneficial not to work quite so hard." But a Roman

TABLE 9.9. **Attitudes Towards the System by Religious Group** % *Agreeing*

	N	Nat (1201)	RCOQ (236)	RCQ (244)	UC (187)	Ang (144)	Cons (74)	Luth (59)	Pres (79)	Oth (118)	None (122)
The political & economic		53	51	52	57	54	58	59	62	50	55
system we have in this	C	61	57	54	67	69	65	63	70	69	na
country is about the best there is	U	48	40	51	52	44	36	48	57	36	na
Anyone who works hard will rise to the top		49	49	79	32	38	43	43	47	44	46
People like me don't have any say about what the government does		49	52	47	52	44	45	54	57	53	43
Communism is the worst kind of government		38	46	43	32	35	53	39	39	31	22

SOURCE: PROJECT CAN85. NOTE: C = Committed, U = Uncommitted. na = Not applicable.

Catholic nurse in St. Catharines who describes herself as a committed Christian is even more skeptical:

> *It is not true that everybody that works hard will rise to the top. A lot of people never make it even though they are very capable because it has always been who you know in the right places.*

LAW-RELATED ISSUES Religious groups historically have given considerable official emphasis to justice and mercy. Despite such emphases, Canadians who claim to be religiously committed are neither more likely than others to be critical of the equity of law enforcement, nor less likely to think court treatment of criminals should be more severe (see TABLE 9.10).

TABLE 9.10.   **Attitudes Towards Law-Related Issues by Religious Group**   *% Agreeing*

	N	Nat (1201)	RCOQ (236)	RCQ (244)	UC (187)	Ang (144)	Cons (74)	Luth (59)	Pres (79)	Oth (118)	None (122)
Law enforcement is applied evenly to all those who break the law		27	18	52	18	20	19	21	30	22	30
In general, the courts do not deal harshly enough with criminals		83	88	81	88	84	87	69	89	83	67
The death penalty should be exercised in some instances		83	85	83	87	91	88	81	91	79	64
The use of		31	25	26	32	28	18	39	25	39	49
marijuana	C	18	18	10	19	23	8	33	18	27	na
should be	U	40	40	36	36	33	45	48	30	47	na
legalized											

SOURCE: PROJECT CAN85. NOTE: C = Committed, U = Uncommitted. na = Not applicable.

Further, at a time when the restoration of capital punishment has come to a free vote in the House of Commons, all the nation's major religious groups stand in opposition to the death penalty. The United Church, for example, has agreed since 1956 that capital punishment is "contrary to the spirit and teaching of Christ."[29] In early 1987, well-known Toronto United Church minister and former moderator, Bruce McLeod, was named co-chairman of the National Coalition Against the Return of the Death Penalty.[30] The Anglican House of Bishops reaffirmed the position the Church has formally had since 1958, in asserting in early 1987 that "Canadians cannot be content with an answer that responds to violence with even more violence."[31] Around the same time, the Canadian Conference of Catholic Bishops, officially opposed to the death penalty since 1965, issued a statement,

A Spiral of Violence, indicating their ongoing disapproval.[32] Conservative Protestants are more organizationally diffuse and unable to express one position. McMaster theology professor Clark Pinnock, a Baptist, states, "I believe that the state has the God-given right to condemn to death criminals guilty of certain heinous acts"; John Redekop, a Mennonite, responds that "Christians should urge governments not to practise capital punishment."[33]

The laity, however, either are not listening or are ignoring what they hear. Nationally, some 83% of Canadians favour the use of the death penalty in at least some instances. Support ranges from about 90% to 80% for people affiliated with the nation's dominant religious groups.[34] It drops off to 64% for individuals who claim no religious affiliation. Very significantly, there is no difference between those who claim to be religiously committed and those who do not.

Of the law-related areas probed by the surveys, differences in attitudes by religious commitment have been found only in the case of the legalization of marijuana use. Here Conservative Protestants (82%) lead the opposition, with religious Nones (49%) the most supportive of legislation in favour of its use.

When it comes to the law, it seems ironic that religion's substantive impact is chemical rather than social. It may be a case of Rome burning while the devout are blowing out candles.

WAR   The arms race and the possibility of a nuclear holocaust have put the issue of war on the minds of people all over the world. The 1985 *PROJECT CANADA* survey found that some 40% of Canadians regard the threat of nuclear war as a "very serious" problem; this compares with 48% of the country's 15- to 19-year-olds.[35] The country's religious groups have been concerned about the issue of war as the flip side of their concern with world peace.

Only about one in five adults think that war is ever justified as a means of settling disputes, with Conservative Protestants and Nones exhibiting marginally higher levels of pacifism than others (see TABLE 9.11). As for the possibility of nuclear war, about one in two people believe it will occur, with the expectation marginally higher among Quebec Roman Catholics and Nones. The

TABLE 9.11.   **Attitudes Towards War and Social Compassion by Religious Group**   *% Agreeing*

	Nat (1201)	RCOQ (236)	RCQ (244)	UC (187)	Ang (144)	Cons (74)	Luth (59)	Pres (79)	Oth (118)	None (122)
N										
WAR										
War is justified when other ways of settling international disputes fail	20	21	28	18	17	13	20	23	23	13
A nuclear war will occur	47	42	61	39	36	43	43+	48+	46	57
If a nuclear war does take place, it will mark the end of human life on earth	38	41	38	35	30	37	36+	34+	49	37
SOCIAL COMPASSION										
People who cannot afford it have a right to medical care	97	97	94	96	99	99	97	96	98	96
People who are poor have a right to an income adequate to live on	90	92	94	88	87	90	85	86	88	90

SOURCE: PROJECT CAN85.

inclination to think that nuclear war will mark the end of human life on earth differs little from group to group, although it is slightly higher among religious Others, who typically have Middle East and Asian cultural roots.

Despite the importance of the issue of war and the attention it is being given by religious organizations, there is no evidence that Canadians who are committed to or associated with these groups are coming away with views that set them aside from other people. The religious and the non-religious see war and its effects in much the same way.

SOCIAL COMPASSION   It is very clear that, in theory at least, humanitarianism is "in." Fund-raising drives for charity receive the endorsement of everyone from the NHL star to the business community and from the civic group to the local disc jockey. People like Terry Fox, Steve Fonyo, and Rick Hansen have become nationally and internationally applauded celebrities.

In Canada, almost everyone feels that people who cannot afford it have a right to medical care (see TABLE 9.11). And some nine in ten maintain that people have a right to incomes adequate to live on, although many do add that people should be willing to work. Significantly, however, there is no difference in compassion levels between the committed and the uncommitted. Also, there are only minor variations among affiliates of the various religious groups.

These findings indicate that basic social compassion is pervasive in Canada. It is exhibited by the religious, but is also equally characteristic of the uncommitted.

EDUCATION   During the past few years, the issue of public funding for Roman Catholic schools has been hotly contested in Ontario. The courts have finally ruled that the provincial government has not acted inappropriately in providing funding for Catholic education. In other parts of the country, notably Alberta, other religious groups have maintained that they, too, have a right to operate their own schools, with and without the assistance of the public purse.

The national surveys make it clear that public funding of private religious education is supported by Roman Catholics but not by others. Some 70% of Catholics say governments should provide funding for Roman Catholic schools, including about 80% of those who are committed. In contrast, fewer than one-third of non-Catholics agree (see TABLE 9.12). The dissenters are frequently vociferous. A 69-year-old Presbyterian in Hamilton, for example, says:

> *I disagree entirely with any separate school funding. There should only be a public school system that is sufficient for anyone. And if someone wants to be educated in religion or otherwise, then surely that is why we have churches. Schools are for education.*

A college instructor in a small Ontario community who claims no religious affiliation offers similar sentiments: "I strongly feel that we should have only one school system — *public*. Why do we insist on emphasizing our differences instead of our similarities?"

For their part, Roman Catholics obviously regard their case as a special one, warranting unique consideration. Only about 30% of Catholics think government funding should be available to *all* religious groups that want to establish schools. About 30% of Conservatives and religious Others also concur, considerably above the 10% level for the remaining groups.

One of the infrequent differences between the committed and the uncommitted is over the issue of prayers in public schools. Only about 25% of the committed are opposed to school prayers, compared with around 65% of the uncommitted. The latter category includes a 21-year-old in rural Saskatchewan, who comments, "Religion should be taught at home and church, not at school." Opposition is lowest among Conservative Protestants, Presbyterians, and Roman Catholics. It is predictably highest among the religious Nones.

GENDER ROLES   Religion has commonly been seen as contributing to the perpetuation of traditional role expectations of men

TABLE 9.12.   Attitudes Towards Education by Religious Group   % Agreeing

		Nat (1201)	RCOQ (236)	RCQ (244)	UC (187)	Ang (144)	Cons (74)	Luth (59)	Pres (79)	Oth (118)	None (122)
	N										
Government funding should be provided for Roman Catholic schools		47	73	68	27	25	32	26+	30+	41	34
	C	57	79	83	29	25	37	40	33	43	na
	U	39	63	58	26	25	21	18	27	39	na
Government funding should be provided for all religious groups wishing to establish private schools		23	35	29	10	12	30	7+	15+	33	11
	C	29	41	33	8	14	29	10	29	33	na
	U	18	22	27	11	11	33	5	6	33	na
Because not all Canadians have the same religious beliefs, it would be better not to have prayers said in public schools		44	34	31	51	49	22	38	39	50	79
	C	26	27	21	34	29	16	20	18	36	na
	U	57	48	38	60	62	40	54	54	60	na

source: PROJECT CAN85. note: C = Committed, U = Uncommitted. na = Not applicable.

and women. A group like the Roman Catholic Church has further been accused of sexual discrimination because of its refusal to admit women to the priesthood. Some, such as the Anglican and United Churches, have actively attempted to rid their organizations of any semblance of sexism, including the expansion of terminology in referring to God and Faith.

The finding that the committed do not hold significantly different views from the uncommitted on the role of women may therefore come as a surprise to many. The devout, nationally and within these religious groups, are no more likely than other Canadians to oppose married women's having paid jobs, being involved in public life, or receiving pay equal to men's (see TABLE 9.13). A divorced United Church woman in Barrie, Ontario, who regards herself as a committed Christian, articulately offers the following viewpoint:

> *I seem to be constantly pulled between the new and the old values. In a positive way we may be the lucky ones. It is necessary for most of us to go into the work place. We have to take care of ourselves, we are stimulated by the business world, we associate with many different groups of people. Naturally we still long for some of the old familiar values, but one must be realistic and try to adapt.*

There are, however, some minor affiliational differences. Roman Catholics in Quebec are slightly more likely than others to be opposed to married women's being employed and participating in politics. Lutherans are less wary than others of married women's having paid jobs, but a bit more guarded when it comes to public life. Religious Nones are the least likely to be opposed to such roles for women.

These findings on attitudes towards the system, law, war, compassion, education, and gender roles add further support to the assertion that religion in Canada is saying little to culture that culture is not already saying to itself. In very few instances do we find signs that religion speaks with a unique voice and is having a unique impact. When religion is relegated to the status of a consumer item, it clearly transforms few lives.

TABLE 9.13.   **Attitudes Towards Gender Roles by Religious Group**   *% Agreeing*

	Nat (1201)	RCOQ (236)	RCQ (244)	UC (187)	Ang (144)	Cons (74)	Luth (59)	Pres (79)	Oth (118)	None (122)
N										
Married women should not be employed if their husbands are capable of supporting them	23	20	31	27	20	23	14	25	23	8
Women should take care of running their homes and leave running the country up to the men	11	12	15	8	10	7	17	14	14	4
Women who do the same work as men should receive the same pay	96	97	94	96	98	98	95	94	96	97

SOURCE: PROJECT CAN85.

A PERSONAL COST-BENEFIT ANALYSIS

B illy Graham is not alone in claiming that religion *uniquely* enriches one's life. The Canadian Conference of Catholic Bishops stated in a recent publication that "only in communion with the living God do we find true fulfillment and real happiness."[36] Interestingly, even those two outspoken critics of religion — Karl Marx and Sigmund Freud — both essentially conceded that religion contributed to positive personal characteristics such as happiness, satisfaction, and hope. Their widely known criticisms of religion rested in their belief that such qualities were based on illusion rather than reality. Their "concessions," however, were largely speculative. The truth of the matter is that they may have been too generous! Religion's relationship to wellbeing has not been definitively demonstrated.[37]

The research findings on religion and wellbeing to date have been contradictory. Rokeach, summing up a number of his studies, wrote,

We have found that people with formal religious affiliation are more anxious [than others]. Believers, compared with non-believers, complain more often of working under great tension, sleeping fitfully, and similar symptoms.[38]

Other researchers, however, have consistently found a negative relationship between religious commitment and feelings of despair.[39] Further, rural immigrants and immigrants involved in sectarian groups have been found to have received gratifying social ties, improved self-images, and hope in the face of economic deprivation.[40] A Connecticut study of some one thousand adults found that church affiliation and mental health were positively related, a finding corroborated in California.[41] A recent comprehensive analysis of American national data spanning 1972 to 1982 by Arthur St. George and Patrick McNamara has revealed that religious commitment is not a good predictor of wellbeing for Whites, but it is for Blacks—the majority of whom are Conservative Protestants (mainly Baptists). The two researchers suggest this reflects "a genuine ethnic or racial effect with deep roots in

Black American history'' that shows little sign of diminishing ''as Blacks improve their socioeconomic status in American society.''[42]

Why the contradictory conclusions? One reason is that quality of life is not an easy concept to tap. We can fairly readily examine some of the so-called ''objective'' correlates of commitment and non-commitment — income, marital status, number of close friends, and so on. But when probing quality of life, we have no guarantee that we are actually getting accurate indicators of how well people are living — materially, relationally, totally.

I am convinced that when all is said and done one of the best methods of exploring the quality of individuals' lives is simply to ask them. Otherwise, we run the risk of pompously telling people what they are really like and ignoring what they tell us they are like.

Relying on what people tell us about the quality of their lives is not without its strengths. A basic social psychological truism is the ''Thomas theorem'' posited by American social psychologist W.I. Thomas earlier in this century: ''If we define things as real, they are real in their consequences.''[43] To use the example of happiness, the important issue is not whether people, in our opinion, have reason to be happy; the more important issue is whether they themselves think they are happy. In the well-worn saying, as one thinks, so one is.

WELLBEING Let's look first at the overall national picture. When we ask Canadians point-blank how happy they consider themselves to be, we find that three in ten describe themselves as ''very happy,'' and another six in ten as ''pretty happy''; only one in ten say that they are ''not very happy.'' It is interesting to note that the current 92% ''happiness'' total is slightly higher than the 86% the polls were finding in the alleged ''Happy Days'' of the late 1950s and early 1960s.[44] Contrary to rumour, we do not appear to be getting any less happy as time jets on.

As for marital happiness, five in ten people claim they have ''very happy'' marriages, with a further four in ten describing them as ''pretty happy''; a mere one in ten say their marriages are ''not too happy.'' In the early 1950s and again in the early 1970s,

Gallup polls found that a similar proportion —nine in ten Canadians — described their marriages as successful.[45]

Financially, three in ten Canadians say that their present financial situation leaves them "pretty well satisfied," and four in ten are "more or less satisfied." Another two in ten say that they are "not very satisfied," with just one in ten "not satisfied at all." The 74% who are essentially satisfied compares with 68% found by the polls around 1960.[46]

As for trends, about five in ten people say they are happier now than they were around 1980, and the same proportion report the same positive change for their marriages. Four in ten tell us they are more enthusiastic about life than they were coming into the 1980s; almost four in ten say the same about their financial outlook. In each of these instances, most others report that things have not changed; smaller proportions indicate things have become worse.

As Maclean's magazine put it in the light of their own late 1985 national poll, "Canada continues to be a remarkably contented and confident land."[47] Comparative research shows that we fare as well as or better than most countries with respect to happiness and satisfaction with life.

What about the role of religion in all this? The PROJECT CANADA surveys have found that those people who are religiously committed are neither more nor less likely than other people to claim to be happy or satisfied (see TABLE 9.14).

The differences that do exist are related to specific group affiliations rather than to commitment. Conservative Protestants, for example, are slightly more inclined than others to say they are "very happy." Roman Catholics are marginally less likely to describe their marriages in the same terms. Religious Nones, in part reflecting their comparative youth, score relatively high on happiness and relatively low on financial satisfaction.

United Church, Anglican, and Presbyterian affiliates—perhaps exhibiting a legacy of "British reserve" — are the least likely to report increases in wellbeing over time.

The important finding here is not that religion makes no difference in people's lives. Many Canadians are undoubtedly happier

TABLE 9.14. Levels of Perceived Wellbeing by Religious Group *(In %s)*

	Nat (1201)	RCOQ (236)	RCQ (244)	UC (187)	Ang (144)	Cons (74)	Luth (59)	Pres (79)	Oth (118)	None (122)
N										
General Happiness "Very Happy"	26	22	30	24	26	37	40	36	21	25
Marital Happiness "Very Happy"	48	46	44	51	52	53	49	51	42	63
Financial Satisfaction "Pretty well satisfied"	27	22	29	28	30	32	36	30	30	15
Increase In: Happiness	45	49	46	34	36	46	48	38	46	59
Marital enjoyment	45	48	49	39	35	43	53	42	36	59
Enthusiasm for life	42	44	48	36	35	46	43	44	43	47
Financial outlook	36	36	40	31	34	40	41	28	33	42

SOURCE: PROJECT CAN85.

and more satisfied because of their faith. The significant finding is that religious commitment—in fact, religious affiliation—is not generally associated with a higher level of personal wellbeing than are non-commitment and non-affiliation. The conclusion of St. George and McNamara seems applicable to Canada: "Most Americans take their cues from the surrounding nonreligious culture which offers them alternative means for achieving a sense of well-being."[48]

Happiness and satisfaction have a number of important sources. Religion, seemingly, is only one of them.

Some of the committed are concerned about this lack of joy. Edmonton writer Paul De Groot discloses that The Fellowship of Merry Christians was born in Michigan in 1986, dedicated to the principle that humour, joy, and faith go together. The group's publication notes, "The opinions expressed in this newsletter are not always those of the editors or of God." One member comments that "in this super-serious age of ours, we've gotten away from celebrating life and the joyfulness of the Christian message." He sees humour as a serious tool for promoting peace and reconciliation in the world.[49] I am reminded of former United Church moderator Clarke MacDonald's critique of some social activists: "They don't seem to pray enough, for or with each other. And they lack a sense of humour."[50]

GENERAL SOURCES Canadians report that their foremost sources of enjoyment are relational. Family life in general and friendship, children, and marriage more specifically are cited by some two in three as bringing them "a great deal" of enjoyment (see TABLE 9.15). Music is next. Among the nation's teenagers, friendship is first, music is second; enjoyment of parents fails to make the 50% level (46% for mothers, 39% for fathers). Church life is cited as the source of "a great deal" of enjoyment by only 16% of adults and just 8% of teenagers.[51] An interesting commentary on the relatively low ranking of religious-group involvement is the survey finding that a greater proportion of Canadians—20%—say they are receiving a high level of enjoyment from their pets!

TABLE 9.15.   **Select Sources of Enjoyment by Religious Group**
% Indicating They Receive "A Great Deal" of Enjoyment

From:		Nat (1201)	RCOQ (236)	RCQ (244)	UC (187)	Ang (144)	Cons (74)	Luth (39)	Pres (79)	Oth (118)	None (122)
Family life generally		65	69	63	68	68	71	67	61	65	51
	C	74	71	75	67	81	78	71	86	82	na
	U	58	66	55	68	60	53	64	46	51	na
Music		48	48	48	49	47	43	38	61	46	52
House/apartment		47	53	58	41	42	39	42	49	47	32
	C	54	54	66	47	47	41	47	51	66	na
	U	41	50	52	37	39	35	39	48	34	na
Job		39	36	45	35	41	43	50	43	42	28
Sports		23	23	26	22	24	24	31	22	23	14
Church/synagogue life		16	19	12	12	13	49	15	24	21	0
	C	31	25	24	27	23	61	31	49	39	na
	U	4	6	3	3	5	12	1	3	5	na
Household work		10	13	18	7	7	6	8	12	10	0

SOURCE: PROJECT CAN85. NOTE: C = Committed, U = Uncommitted. na = Not applicable.

When sources of happiness are examined by religious group and commitment, very few and very small differences are found. The committed more frequently than the uncommitted cite family life, their house or apartment, and church life. The minor differences among groups include the slightly greater tendency of Roman Catholics to cite home-related sources of enjoyment — one's house or apartment and one's household duties.

LEISURE ACTIVITIES   It is virtually impossible to distinguish between the committed and the uncommitted on leisure-time activities. People in both categories claim approximately the same levels of TV viewing, reading, going out, participation in sports, and the like (see TABLE 9.16). Further, for most, religious-group involvement is not a substitute for secular-group involvement: the committed and the uncommitted show similar levels of club memberships.

Leisure differences emerge only in the areas of smoking and drinking. People who are religiously committed are more likely than the uncommitted to refrain from either or both, with Conservative Protestants more likely than others to refrain from alcohol (see TABLE 9.16). Yet even among Conservatives the selective application of "official faith" seems evident. Although many of these evangelical groups still disapprove of alcohol, more than six in ten Conservative Protestants indicate that they use alcohol at least occasionally, including five in ten who say they are committed Christians.

In short, the findings indicate that Canadians, whether religiously committed or not, report very similar levels of wellbeing and similar sources of gratification. The major source difference for the committed is the Church.

THE BOTTOM LINE

Our findings concerning sexuality and social and personal concerns have now been corroborated further in our examination of intergroup relations, social attitudes, and personal wellbeing. Religion in Canada shows little sign of having either a

TABLE 9.16. **Select Leisure Activites by Religious Group** *(In %s)*

	Nat (1201)	RCOQ (236)	RCQ (244)	UC (187)	Ang (144)	Cons (74)	Luth (39)	Pres (79)	Oth (118)	None (122)
ACTIVITIES: "Very Often"										
Watch/listen to news	70	70	62	76	75	70	72	69	72	71
Read books	53	46	51	50	54	60	43	72	57	62
Watch television	54	57	65	52	51	42	61	55	45	42
Go out to dinner	23	24	31	18	22	20	18	25	22	22
Work out	20	19	26	13	18	17	13	19	17	27
Participate in sports	16	17	18	16	19	5	11	23	15	18
Watch videos	12	13	17	9	14	3	7	18	11	10
Dance	9	11	10	10	10	2	1	10	10	8
Go out to a lounge/bar	7	8	5	5	8	1	5	8	6	14
Go to a movie	6	3	8	1	7	2	1	12	7	16
ORGANIZATIONAL INVOLVEMENT										
Member of private club	28	33	31	25	22	32	14	20	28	25
Member of service club	26	29	29	26	21	30	17	31	18	17
SMOKE: "Never"	61	56	59	63	63	81	64	81	61	53
C	69	60	65	75	65	89	85	89	65	na
U	56	49	55	56	62	59	52	75	58	na
DRINK: "Never"	13	12	12	12	12	37	12	14	16	5
C	19	11	17	21	17	46	21	16	24	na
U	9	14	8	8	10	15	7	12	8	na

SOURCE: PROJECT CAN85. NOTE: C = Committed, U = Uncommitted. na = Not applicable.

unique voice or a unique influence. Canadians who are religiously committed construct reality in much the same manner as others. They relate with neither more nor less compassion. They experience a level of wellbeing that is neither higher nor lower than other people's.

The discrepancy between the ideal and the real, the official and the unofficial, is summarized by Gregory Baum. The survey findings show that what he says about Roman Catholics is applicable well beyond the Catholic community:

> Gone are the days when Catholics simply followed the directives given them by their bishops. In the area of social justice, Catholics have never shown a strong inclination to follow the Catholic tradition. In that area Catholics on the whole tend to follow the political and social ideals mediated to them by their culture. . . . Catholics who have had . . . a religious experience that reveals the emancipatory thrust of the Gospel are a minority.[52]

But then again, when religion is adopted in fragments, by many of the committed as well as the uncommitted, it can be expected to do no more. The world's great religions,including Christianity, have never claimed that one's outlook on life is transformed by the holding of an isolated belief, engaging in an occasional prayer, or having a rite performed by a religious professional. When culture tells religion that it is no longer required as a life-informing phenomenon, and when religious leaders unconsciously and consciously acquiesce by dismantling the gods, all that is left is culture.

What has been taking place in Canada is not unique to our country. Before examining in the Conclusion what the immediate future holds and looking at the implications of the fragmentation of the gods for the country, individuals, and religion, it is worthwhile to look beyond our boundaries and locate ourselves in cross-cultural perspective.

10

BEYOND THE GREAT WHITE NORTH

T
he social and cultural sources of the fragmentation of the gods are having a dramatic impact upon religion in other parts of the world as well as in Canada. Highly developed societies such as the United States and England have likewise known the reality of role and institutional specialization. The developing countries of Latin America are also beginning to feel specialization's influence. There are both similarities and differences between Canada and these societies.

WE ARE NOT LIKE THE AMERICANS

E
arlier, in what seems like almost another life, I was a budding Baptist minister. I never proceeded to ordination, since I planned to go on to graduate school and frankly didn't know what the future held. I recall sitting at a gathering of Calgary ministers during the late 1960s, hearing a Florida group proclaiming the wonders of a program called "Evangelism Explosion." The program, featuring certain so-called "spiritual laws," was virtually guaranteed to work, and the ministers were excited. Being also, at the time, an embryonic sociologist, who had spent three years in the evangelically receptive southern U.S., I whispered to a young American colleague, "But don't you think things are different

up here — that Canadians will not be as receptive to this approach as Americans?" To my surprise, he looked at me with a strained look on his face and replied, "That's sociology — don't you believe in the Holy Spirit?"

I'm not convinced that things have changed all that much. I was sitting across from a Baptist minister at a luncheon in Lethbridge recently. He had just come back from a training session at the Department of Church Growth at Fuller Theological Seminary in California. This department was founded by the missions scholar Donald McGavran and his protégé, C. Peter Wagner. It attempts to bring together missions theology and social-scientific research to promote church growth. It has fostered other church-growth organizations and the church-growth movement more generally. When I — graciously, I think — asked the minister if the staff there takes into account possible Canadian-American cultural differences, he looked at me reflectively and replied, "Well, not too much — one or two of them do a bit."

It is not my intention to discuss in any detail here the fine points of differences between life in Canada and the United States. Writers such as Andrew Malcolm (*The Canadians*) and Pierre Berton (*Why We Act Like Canadians*) have recently provided us with superb comparisons of the two cultures. Nor do I want to go into the intricacies of the differences between various groups in the two countries. Fortunately, Kenneth Westhues (Roman Catholicism), Harold Fallding (mainline Protestantism), Harry Hiller (Conservative Protestantism), and Stuart Schoenfeld (Judaism) have already made those important contributions.[1]

What I want to stress is that history has produced two very different religious marketplaces. Canada is neither a replica nor an underdeveloped version of its southern neighbour. We both have continuing markets for the supernatural, and we are both opting primarily for fragments. But the rules and the companies are different.

THE MARKET   I have already argued that life experience and the limitations of science create a market for supernatural explanations. The question is not, "*Will* people believe and practise?"

but rather, "*What* will they believe and practise?" The United States — generally regarded as the world's most advanced nation — shows no signs of a diminished interest in the supernatural.

RELIGIOUS FRAGMENTS The extensive religion surveys carried out by the Gallup organization[2] reveal that Americans readily endorse the central traditional beliefs concerning the existence of God (95%), the divinity of Jesus (70%), and life after death (71%). Some 87% say they pray at least sometimes, while 72% recognize the Bible as "the Word of God" (37% endorse the view that it is to be taken literally). As for weekly service attendance, Americans have what many regard as a world-leading level of about 40%. The figure for Catholics is 51%, for Protestants 39% — in both cases about ten percentage points above their Canadian counterparts.

But the signs of fragment adoption are readily evident. Despite the way in which they view the Bible, only 15% say they read it daily (24% never). They, like us, stumble on fairly simple knowledge questions: fewer than half know who delivered the Sermon on the Mount (42%) or the names of the four gospels (46%). While 40% of all Americans claim to be "born again," just 56% say religion is "very important" in their lives, a noteworthy drop from 75% in 1952.

Further, all is far from well on the attendance front. The current Catholic level of 51% represents a significant drop from 74% in 1958; the Protestant figure in the same year was 44%. Fewer than one in two Americans are regular attenders. The regional variations are notable, with attendance being far higher in the predominantly Baptist South than in the East and Midwest, and lowest in the West.

Like Canadians, Americans readily "buy" less conventional ideas and practices at the supernatural shopping market. More than two in ten think they have seen a ghost or spirit; six in ten report ESP or *déjà vu* experiences; more than 20% believe astrological predictions are correct.[3] The ability of Americans to combine the conventional and the unconventional was suggested to me on a recent trip to Nashville, the headquarters of the nation's largest denomination, the Southern Baptist Convention. In its Saturday issue, the local newspaper's church page included the daily horoscope offerings, along with Ann Landers' column!

No one has compiled American survey data on religion like George Gallup Jr. Drawing upon fifty years of research, Gallup recently made the following observations about the current religious scene. Catholics who in the 1960s might have left the Church today "feel they can disagree on [various] issues and still be part of the Church."[4] Even so, the 1978 study, *The Unchurched American*, has revealed that for many Protestants and Catholics, believing has become divorced from belonging.[5] According to his own scale, Gallup rates the commitment of only about one in ten Americans as high, four in ten as moderate, and five in ten as low.[6] He further depicts a consumer type of faith:

> *While high levels of religious belief and activity are found in U.S. society, there is ample evidence of a self-centered kind of faith . . . stated in terms of "it makes me feel good." . . . The religious-motivated behavior . . . is more often in the nature of a passive "live and let live" philosophy than in the nature of selfless and heroic action on behalf of others.*[7]

Religion has come to have a highly specialized place in American society. Robert Bellah and his associates note in *Habits of the Heart* that "diversity of practice has been seen as legitimate because religion is perceived as a matter of individual choice"; there is, however, "the implicit qualification that the practices themselves accord with public decorum and the adherents abide by the moral standards of the community."[8] The fragmented gods of Canada are no strangers to the U.S.

THE RULES   But the rules of the religious marketplace are different. In Canada, a pluralistic ideal means that religious groups are expected to co-exist for servicing. In the United States, the pursuit of truth means that religious groups are allowed to compete for truth.

Our countries' respective evolutions are well known. Canada grew out of the union of French and English colonies and has spent most of its history simply trying to consolidate "the two solitudes." In Westhues' words, "Canada cannot be understood as an attempt to embody a theory of society, but only as an effort to achieve working agreements among diverse parties with conflicting theories of society."[9] In contrast to the Americans, "we did not separate violently from Europe," Pierre Berton reminds us, "but cut our ties cautiously in the Canadian manner — so cautiously, so imperceptibly that none of us is quite sure we actually achieved our independence."[10] Our religious groups did not compete for truth but serviced the immigrants in the French and English expressions to which they had grown accustomed, aided in whole or in part by public funds.

Americans, on the other hand, made their dramatic break with England and set out to establish a distinctive nation. Their "charter myth" included the belief that the country had been founded by God to give leadership to the world. The key to its development was the creation of a milieu of liberty, an environment in which individuals could have freedom of expression and the freedom to pursue truth.

The constitutional guarantee of religious freedom accordingly separated Church and State, giving individuals the opportunity to explore and proclaim truth as they understood it. As with the other sectors of American life — the economy, education, and politics, for example — the religion market was technically "up for grabs."

Thus it is that the American religion market is, and has always been, a dynamic one, characterized by aggressive, persistent claims to truth, a style quite foreign and frankly rather repugnant to pluralistically minded Canadians. Compared with Americans, quips Berton, "we are not good salesmen and we are not good showmen."[11] We are also slow to recognize national heroes and to be very positive about anything. As one survey respondent, a 25-year-old food inspector in Edmonton, playfully expressed it,

After reviewing my answers, I find I am an unreligious, chauvinistic bigot with a dismal view of everything around me, plus I hate my job. I guess in Canada that may be considered normal.

In sharp contrast, religion in the U.S., reflecting "the American style," is marketed with the flair and aggressiveness of a "hot" commercial commodity. Perhaps this is why emerging Canadian "religious superstars" like the Foursquare evangelist Aimee Semple Macpherson and the youthful Charles Templeton migrated to the more open and richer American market, not unlike entertainers such as Anne Murray and Paul Anka.

Further, variations on the normative Judeo-Christian theme are welcome in the U.S. The American obsession with pursuing and disseminating truth legitimizes "new and improved" truth claims. A natural outcome of this free-enterprise emphasis in a rewarding environment is religious innovation. In the mid-1970s, there were 223 distinct religious bodies in the U.S., compared with only 63 in Canada.[12]

There is also little doubt that American soil has been the base for a large number of new religious movements which, as noted earlier, have spread to Canada and many other parts of the world.[13] From a market-model point of view, what is being reflected is not only a greater American receptivity to new religions but also a competitive and lucrative milieu in which religion — primarily within Judeo-Christian limits — is a robust and potentially profitable product, financially and otherwise.

The search for truth produces a lively market. Pluralism, insisting as it does on respect for diversity, either kills the ability to make market inroads or dulls the inclination.

THE COMPANIES The U.S. media, based in New York and California, depict the nation's religious scene in terms I doubt the average American is able to recognize. A Canadian, therefore, can be excused for misreading what's happening stateside. The scene portrayed is one in which Catholics, Episcopalians, and Jews are dominant, with mysterious cults in California and sectarian fundamentalist preachers in pockets of the rural South. The media consequently act amazed to find evangelical, Conservative Protestant churches growing and interpret this development as another indicator of the country's swing to the right.

In reality, U.S. Conservative Protestants, primarily in the form of Baptists, constitute the largest Protestant grouping (more than 20%; see TABLE 10.1). Moreover, they have had this status since about 1950. Before that time, they were exceeded in numbers only by the Methodists, now the second-largest Protestant denomination (9%). Lutherans (7%) stand third, followed by Episcopalians (3%), and Presbyterians and United Church of Christ (2% each).

Together, Protestants account for 57% of the population. Roman Catholics are the largest single grouping (28%); one in four Americans are Catholic, compared with one in two Canadians. Jews make up 2% of the U.S. population.

These findings show that four "religious companies" — the Roman Catholics, Baptists, Methodists, and Lutherans — hold down 64% or almost two-thirds of the American religious market. It is true that these groupings are not organizationally homogeneous. The Baptists, for example, have typically had more than twenty separate bodies listed in *The Yearbook*.[14]

TABLE 10.1. **Religious Affiliation of Americans: 1947-84**
(In %s)

	1947	1957	1967	1976	1984
ROMAN CATHOLIC	20	26	25	27	28
PROTESTANT	69	66	67	61	57
Baptist	**	**	21	21	20
Methodist	**	**	14	11	9
Lutheran	**	**	7	7	7
Presbyterian	**	**	6	5	2
Episcopalian	**	**	3	3	3
Other	**	**	16	14	16
JEWISH	5	3	3	2	2
OTHER	1	1	3	4	4
NONE	6	3	2	6	9

SOURCE: Derived from *The Gallup Report*, May 1985.
NOTE: Because of rounding, some percentage columns do not equal 100.

Nevertheless, from the standpoint of sheer affiliation, these have been the dominant religious denominations now for some time. The U.S. market may be open to "religious entrepreneurs" and indeed appears to have been a hotbed of religious innovation. Yet the market is clearly monopolized by four main companies.

It is important to keep in mind in making Canadian-American comparisons that the dominant companies are different in the two countries. Most striking is the strength of the Conservative Protestants in the U.S. — more than 20%, compared with 7% in Canada.

Consequently, there is little basis for assuming that because a program "works" in the U.S. it will "work" in Canada. In the case of Conservative Protestants, for example, the difference in numbers has important implications for possibilities of growth. In Canada, as in other societies where they constitute a numerical minority, expansion is very difficult, especially if the other dominant religious groups provide an evangelical menu offering of their own. The only path to significant proportional growth is "the tough path" of proselytization; birth and immigration — much easier means of numerical expansion — do not produce sufficient numbers of new members to alter the evangelicals' percentage.

In the United States, on the other hand, the numerical prominence — indeed, dominance — of evangelicals means that considerable growth occurs through birth and retention. Proselytization is consequently neither particularly common nor necessary. In Canada it is a necessity, though it is a path less travelled; in the U.S. it is an unneeded luxury.

Incidentally, despite the highly publicized claims of accelerated evangelical church growth during the post-1960 period, the largest evangelical grouping, the Baptists, did not increase its proportional share of the U.S. population (see TABLE 10.1). In sheer numbers, Southern Baptists claimed to have experienced a net gain of two million people. However, in doing so, the denomination was simply keeping up with the general increase in the U.S. population, while many other denominations lost ground.

The increased profile of American Conservative Protestants

does not reflect the penetration of an unchurched society by an evangelical minority, but rather the increased social and political stridency of what has historically been a religious majority. As Gary Wills has pointed out, "There has been no religious revival because there is nothing to revive."[15]

Canadians taking their cues from the United States in trying to understand current religious developments or plan effective programs have mistaken a window for a mirror.

MAYBE A LITTLE LIKE THE ENGLISH

When we travel across the Atlantic to England, we will probably find more familiar religious turf. After spending a few days in London and the south, we could take British Rail through Oxford and the Midlands to Liverpool, go still farther north to Newcastle, and then begin our journey back to London, crossing the plush green hills of Yorkshire, stopping briefly at Lincoln and Cambridge.

England's religious setting is similar to ours in that a market for the supernatural exists, fragment adoption abounds, and the rules of the competition are fairly similar. We differ significantly, however, when it comes to our respective religious companies.

THE MARKET England has historically been characterized by a pervasive interest in the supernatural. In addition to the visible role played by Christianity over the centuries, interest in magic, superstitition, spiritualism, and psychic phenomena has been high. The world's first professional psychical organization, for example, was the British Society for Psychical Research, founded in the late nineteenth century. Recent survey research has documented extensive continuing interest in "the world beyond."

RELIGIOUS FRAGMENTS The English exhibit a wide range of supernatural beliefs and practices. Belief in God or a Supreme Being is high (72%), while belief in the divinity of Jesus and heaven is held by about half the population.[16] Close to one in three people say they engage in daily private prayer,[17] and claims of religious experiences are very common.[18] A University of Leeds researcher, Robert Towler, further reports that "folk religion," characterized by a wide variety of heterogeneous beliefs and practices, is widespread. [19]

As noted, the English have not lacked an interest in less conventional phenomena either. David Hay and Ann Morisy have reported widespread claims of paranormal and ecstatic experiences.[20] Other surveys have found that one in six continue to believe in ghosts, while one in ten assert belief in reincarnation.[21] In the words of London School of Economics sociologist David Martin, the English are not suffering from "any atrophy of the capacity for belief."[22]

It is also very clear, however, that fragment adoption rather than commitment has been widespread. Only one in four describe their religious beliefs as very important to them.[23] The smorgasbord-like combinations of beliefs and practices are described by researchers who examined a London borough:

> *Of the doubters, agnostics and atheists, over a quarter say they pray on occasions to the God whose existence they doubt. . . . Of those who say they believe in a Deity, one in five are definite in their assertion that they do not believe in life after death; one half say they never go to church. . . . Of those who attend Church of England services regularly or intermittently, one-quarter do not believe in an after-life — on the other hand, one-fifth of those who don't go to church at all do believe.[24]*

Martin comments that English culture, far from being secular, "wobbles between a partially absorbed Christianity" and a strange mixture of values like fate and luck.[25]

Fragment adoption is also evident in weekly service attendance. Levels have declined from 36% in 1851 to a current level of about 10%.[26] The general pattern has been for attendance to be lower in the larger cities and among the working classes. In Liverpool, for example, the drop has been from 70% in 1831 to about 30% in 1891, 20% in 1934, to a current level of under 10%.[27] Attendance is, however, higher than the national level for Roman Catholics (close to 40%), and Nonconformist groups (some 25%).[28]

Yet the country has come to be characterized by many a majestic cathedral, standing as a deserted monument to some reality of yesterday. That reality, like the dinosaur, seems to have vanished mysteriously into history.

English churches, like their North American counterparts, have found themselves dealing with a selectively minded clientele. Donald Reeves, Rector of St. James' Anglican Church, Piccadilly, maintains that "religion is just another commodity to be consumed," regarded "on the same level as playing golf or washing the car or belonging to Rotary."[29]

The churches, faced with this downturn in attendance, have sought to make changes, to update and upgrade. David Jenkins, the Church of England's Bishop of Durham, became a household name when he declared on the eve of his consecration that he had grave doubts about the virgin birth and Jesus' resurrection. The magnitude of the negative reaction spoke volumes about the Church's theological diversity. One commentator suggests that a major dilemma for the Church of England has become one of continuing "to appeal to a broad range of believers without appearing hopelessly contradictory."[30]

People like Andrew Walker, the Russian Orthodox director of the C.S. Lewis Centre and honorary fellow of King's College, London, decries the consumer-tailored state of contemporary religion:

> *Christianity is now on sale in multiform shapes and sizes. Competing in the open market with other religions, there is a bewildering yet broad choice of "real" and "best" Christianities for anyone who wants to buy. No doubt someone will soon publish "The Consumer Guide to God" so that people can pop in and out of churches with the same ease and comfort as they visit their favourite restaurants.*[31]

The religious fragments so common to Canada and the United States are everywhere in England.

THE RULES AND THE COMPANIES From the year 1531, when Henry VIII defied the Pope and declared himself the head of the Church of England, "the Anglicans" have enjoyed the monopoly that goes along with being a state religion. However, following a century and a half of severe persecution, religious freedom, officially at least, came into being with the passage of the Toleration Act in 1689. People who declined to qualify as Anglicans by subscribing to the Thirty-Nine Articles but who were willing to swear allegiance to the monarchy *and* reject the authority of the Pope *and* no longer call on Mary and the Saints were given the label of "Dissenters" and were allowed to live and worship as they otherwise saw fit.[32] The Roman Catholic hierarchy was not restored in England until 1850.

The Church of England has been and continues to be the official state church. British sovereigns are the supreme governors of the Church and in turn are crowned at their coronation services by the Archbishop of Canterbury (the Primate of All England and leader of the worldwide Anglican communion). The senior Bishops are entitled to sit as members in the House of Lords. Clergy, however, are not paid by the state unless in its employ.[33]

For three hundred years, other non-Catholic religious groups have been allowed to compete for whatever part of the market they find it possible to garner. The market results have never been in doubt. Aligned with the state, in 1900 the Church of England was the Church with which almost seven in ten people in Britain claimed affiliation. Today it continues to be the choice of some six in ten (see TABLE 10.2). Roman Catholics and religious Nones

TABLE 10.2.   **Religious Affiliation of the British: 1900, 1970, 1980***   *(In %s)*

	1900	1970	1980
Anglicans	66	57	57
Other Protestants	25	18	16
Roman Catholics	6	14	14
Other	1	3	4
None	2	8	9

SOURCE: Derived from Barrett, 1983:699.
*These figures are for Great Britain (i.e., England, Scotland, Wales, and Northern Ireland).

have increased during this century, while other Protestant groups, "the Nonconformists" of old, have along with the Anglicans experienced a drop of nine percentage points.

This historical move in the direction of semi-pluralism has created a market mood not dissimilar to Canada's. Groups primarily service their own; they do not aggressively raid each others' ranks. Further, the proportional market shares of Anglicans and Roman Catholics are essentially reversed in the two countries (10% and 46% respectively in Canada). Attempts to shuffle policies and programs back and forth across the Atlantic obviously need to be sensitive to these large differences in market share. As noted with Canadian-American program transfer efforts, what "works" on one side may be a flop on the other.

My reading and my experience of having lived in England lead me to point out that the tendency towards a fairly stable religious market is not attributable only to semi-pluralism. Its sources also include dominant cultural traits. I am thinking specifically of reserve and non-aggressive competitiveness. We have already examined the hype that is associated with Americans' promotion of the religions of their choice. Such emphases are foreign — and, I would suggest, unacceptable — to most of the English. Everything's relative, and compared with people there, we Canadians *are* good salesmen and showmen! Little wonder Americans seem strangely flamboyant and "showbiz-like" on England's side of the Atlantic.

The attendance drop-off in England has been much greater than that experienced, at least to date, in Canada. Nevertheless, as in our country, sheer religious affiliation has power in England. It continues to be related to a strong demand for rites of passage.[34] In addition, it carries with it emotional weight. Reeves writes that "we are not just a nation of lazy agnostics or cool rationalists. There are many who have jettisoned the dogma but cherish the music or admire the buildings inspired by faith. . . ."[35]

Affiliation, while usually falling short of commitment, may also be commonly associated with endorsement, making defection unlikely. Edward Bailey, for example, maintains that people who appear to have unclear personal faiths nonetheless frequently affirm "Christianity" itself. When they make reference to terms like "Christ," "God," or "the Church," they may be clumsy theologically. But the more important thing for them is that these terms stand for this "Christianity" to which they subscribe.[36] Carrying an affiliational name-tag may be indicative of one's general endorsement of Christianity as seen through the eyes of one's group.

Our examination of two other highly developed societies, the United States and England, reveals that interest in supernatural phenomena persists. Beliefs and practices are everywhere. Yet the nature of modern life in all three societies, with its emphasis upon role and institutional specialization, has limited the influence of religion. At the personal level, people are opting for fragments. At the social level, religious groups are typically relegated to the role of interest groups.

Canadians do not differ from Americans in either their inclination to embrace the supernatural or their tendency to adopt religious fragments. What is different is that we live in a society that values pluralism over competition and has a religious market dominated not by Conservative Protestants but by Roman Catholics and denominations of British descent.

When we compare ourselves with the English, we find that they, too, embrace the supernatural, primarily in fragment form. They also have a stability fostered by a belated religious pluralism. But the religious market knows the legacy of giving one company a major advantage for a long time. The fact that there are opposite proportions of Anglicans and Roman Catholics has important additional implications for how the markets operate in the two countries.

SOME WILL FOLLOW IN OUR FOOTSTEPS

What about the religious situation in developing countries? Do the patterns characterizing Canada, the United States, and England offer us any insight as to what is to be expected? I think they do.

THE MARKET   My position, of course, is that a market for the supernatural exists wherever there are people, because of the limits of science and our impatience with it. The interest in the supernatural that has characterized developing societies in the past will continue as they evolve in the direction of modern societies. The question is, *"Who* will provide *what?"*

RELIGIOUS FRAGMENTS   It is not inevitable that the "what" will be isolated beliefs, practices, and professional services. But role and institutional specialization will make it extremely difficult to avoid such an outcome. In the name of objectivity, we can be looking for commitment. But that is not where the smart money will be placed.

THE RULES   In developing societies, where rapid social change is taking place, including industrialization, migration, and urbanization, instability has the potential to open up the religious market.[37] The previously dominant religions, faced with profound changes in what institutions exist and what they do, at minimum would be strained.[38] Sensing market opportunity, proponents of alternative religious offerings would be expected to appear. Assuming that political interference does not prematurely decide what expressions are appropriate, the religion marketplaces should be lively.

In time, however, "the religion rush" would be over. The market would again become fairly settled. As in more advanced countries like Canada, certain religious companies would emerge with varying shares of the religion market. To the extent that they became more and more stable with time and menu diversification, the market would become increasingly tight.

THE COMPANIES IN ACTION: A LATIN AMERICAN PREVIEW   Professor Merlin Brinkerhoff and I have examined some of these issues in the course of carrying our examination of Conservative Protestant church growth to a very different setting, Latin America.[39] We have looked at developments in three countries — Brazil, Bolivia, and Peru.

Since approximately the late sixteenth century, the Roman Catholic Church has been solidly entrenched as the number one religious company in each of these three societies. The acceleration of industrialization since around 1950, however, has partially loosened traditional bonds. Migration accompanying industrialization has broken down the support system of large extended families and close-knit communities. Millions of Latin Americans find themselves socially and spiritually uprooted.[40]

The Latin American religion market is therefore potentially more open in the face of social change. The key to any variations in the historic Roman Catholic monopoly depends first upon the Catholic Church's ability to adapt to changing conditions, and second on the ability of competitors to provide alternative and residual market offerings.

In the midst of the turbulence, aspiring rivals have arrived on the scene, joining others who had tried earlier to penetrate the market. For example, Lutherans and some other Protestant groups descended on these three countries around 1900, Pentecostals came to Brazil in 1910, and Bahais to Bolivia in 1956.[41]

The general impression is that the newcomers have been making sizeable market gains. McGill political scientist Thomas Bruneau notes that Pentecostals appear to be flourishing in areas of high urbanization and industrialization, meeting a market need for social ties and a personal style of religion.[42] Other observers say that Pentecostals have not been as successful in a country like Bolivia because of that country's low degree of urbanization. To put it another way, the market for religion Pentecostal-style has not yet developed there.

Brinkerhoff and his research aides spent a number of months going over the written and oral records of eighty-four Conservative Protestant congregations in Brazil, Peru, and Bolivia. Their sample included more than thirteen different denominations, including Christian and Missionary Alliance, Baptist, Friends, Pentecostal, and Salvation Army. Tedious though it was, they catalogued all the new additions for the period 1978-82.

What they found was that, first, church growth has been fairly limited. The eighty-four congregations averaged an attendance increase of only eighteen people per church per year. As for actual membership, the churches had an annual average increase of six new members. One in five had come from other evangelical churches, and another one in five had Conservative Protestant parents. The remaining three were recruited primarily from Roman Catholicism.

However, we analysed these findings further alongside information on Roman Catholic affiliation and involvement in the charismatic movement. What we found was that in the face of social upheaval and the aggressive proselytizing activities of other groups, the Roman Catholic Church had displayed remarkable stability. Seen in national perspectives, the gains of the opposing companies have been very modest. Since 1900, Protestants, for example, have grown from 1% to 9% in Brazil, 0% to 4% in Bolivia, and 0% to 3% in Peru. Over the same period, the Roman Catholic hold on Bolivia has changed little, has declined only slightly in Brazil, and has actually increased in Peru (see TABLE 10.3).

Clearly, the Catholic Church's religious monopoly has not been broken. Competitors, in order to experience significant numerical gains, face the difficult task of having to recruit Roman Catholics.

TABLE 10.3.　**Religious Affiliation in Three Latin American Countries: 1900, 1970, 1980**　*(In %s)*

	1900	1970	1980
BRAZIL			
Roman Catholic	96	92	89
Protestant	1	8	9
Other	4	7	10
None	0	1	1
BOLIVIA			
Roman Catholic	94	94	93
Protestant	0	4	4
Other	6	2	2
None	0	1	1
PERU			
Roman Catholic	95	99	99
Protestant	0	2	3
Other	5	1	1
None	0	0	0

Derived from Barrett, 1982. Totals exceed 100 because of multiple adoptions.

Because of their small sizes, they cannot go the easier route of simply adding offspring and geographically mobile members, a luxury enjoyed by Catholics in Canada, Conservative Protestants in the U.S., Anglicans in England, and, of course, Catholics in Latin America.

Menu diversification, however, appears to be making the recruitment of Catholics increasingly difficult. Earlier in this century, groups like Pentecostals offered a religious product that struck a responsive chord, a religion with emotion and social bonds, a religion that stood in sharp contrast to the formality and passive attendance of Catholicism. The Pentecostals subsequently grew. Moreover, some of the successful Pentecostal ingredients were quickly borrowed by their competitors, giving rise to strange congregational hybrids in the marketplace, such as "Baptist Pentecostals."

But the dominant company has added a new page to its menu. The Roman Catholic Church in Latin America is well known for its involvement and leadership in bringing about political and social change. Led by Father Gustavo Gutierrez of Peru, it has given birth to liberation theology, a theology that, as Harvey Cox puts it, "was not invented in the libraries of the seminaries" but which has emerged as "theologians spend hours with people who are engaged in difficult and dangerous political tasks."[43] It has actively worked for just government, human rights, and liberation from poverty. Further, as Canadian sociologist W. E. Hewitt notes, the Brazilian Catholic Church "moved symbolically closer to the most disadvantaged classes" in the 1960s by encouraging small grassroots communities, known as comunidades eclesiais de base (CEBs). There are now as many as eighty thousand CEBs throughout Brazil, reports Hewitt, with a total membership of some four million people, mostly drawn from the lower classes in rural areas or the peripheral urban zones of the larger cities.

Having developed a social program far superior to most of its competitors, the Church began to offer even more. In the decade of the 1960s, the charismatic movement arrived, providing an evangelical and spirit-filled expression of the faith, complete with an emphasis on the family of believers.

The consumer response has been overwhelming. In Brazil the number of charismatic Catholics increased from five thousand in 1970 to more than five hundred thousand by the early 1980s. Bolivia experienced an increase from a thousand to nine thousand during the same period. In Peru the jump was from a thousand to more than forty thousand.[44]

Pentecostals and others are now faced with the dilemma of offering something to the market that is not being offered within the more familiar confines of the Catholic Church. As one Canadian Baptist minister I talked to put it in discussing these findings, "Why should people leave the Roman Catholic Church and come over to us? We're no longer doing something that they aren't doing."

The South American "sleeping giant" appears to have awakened. It is diversifying its religious offerings with devastating consequences for the competition. As long as the Roman Catholic Church continues to meet the wide range of emerging consumer demands, there is little reason to believe that its dominance will be seriously challenged. With time, competing religious groups will not disappear but be officially relegated to minority status. Further, as Latin American societies become more settled, the Canadian and English patterns of co-existence could be expected to replace the current mood of competition and intergroup recruitment.

Developing societies resemble ours in having a continuing interest in the supernatural and giving a specialized place to religion. They differ in that their religious markets are, for a time at least, more open. As these societies become more stable, their markets will become more crystallized and closed.

The fragmentation of Canada's gods is characteristic of highly developed countries in general. In time, the gods will be dismantled in developing countries as well. The world that has become our "global village" includes, in its "global cultural package," gods in fragment form.

And as things stand, the twenty-first century offers the prospect of more of the same. But, then again, there is a possibility that, out of the fragment rubble, the gods will rise again.

CONCLUSION

The findings are in and the message is clear. Religion, Canadian-style, is mirroring culture. A specialized society is met with specialized religion. Consumer-minded individuals are provided with a smorgasbord of fragment choices. Culture leads; religion follows. While the situation is not unique to Canada, it *is* nonetheless the Canadian religious reality.

In this country, religion gives every indication of being something we create rather than something with a non-human dimension. To return to the question we raised at the beginning of the book, the Canadian situation strongly suggests not that the gods created us, but that we are creating the gods. The specifications are handed down by culture.

This, I stress, is not a subjective or theological observation. On the contrary, it is an objectively observable conclusion based on a simple examination of the nature of culture on the one hand and the nature of religion on the other. The correlation between the two is unmistakably strong. Few would argue that the relationship is due to religion's impact on culture. Indeed, to the extent that religion is regarded as a life-embracing system of meaning, the reality of its fragmentation leaves little doubt as to which is the artist and which the canvas.

The situation may well continue basically unchanged as we move into the next century. If so, a number of features can be expected.

RELIGION IN THE TWENTY-FIRST CENTURY

If religion continues to be so highly dependent upon culture, it will be moulded by national and global developments. Social forecasters seem to agree that, in the future, two central features will be prominent—the acceleration of both available information and technological innovation.[1] For example, the chairman of the board of the Microsoft Corporation, Bill Gates, says, "In twenty years, the Information Age will be here, absolutely. The dream of having the world database at [our] fingertips will have become a reality."[2] By the early twenty-first century, the experts say, a personal computer will be owned and operated by every child, as common as a pair of Nikes; television will give way to "sensa-vision," allowing us not only to see and hear but also to feel and smell; many of today's diseases, including cancer and arthritis, will disappear.[3]

As Gates points out, history is far from being in the process of merely repeating itself. Technology is leading us into unprecedented territory at an unprecedented pace. He argues that we cannot begin to extrapolate from the past in establishing the rate of change in even the next twenty years: "The leap will be unique. I can't think of any equivalent phenomenon in history."[4]

The increase in information and innovation will only intensify specialization both by institutions and by individuals. Religion will feel the consequences.

FRAGMENT CONSUMPTION   Specialized offerings from a wide variety of sources will be available to Canadians performing a variety of roles. The consequent consumer attitude to goods and services will continue to be applied also to religion and religious organizations. The tendency to adopt fragments will be pervasive.

This is no groundless speculation. As we have seen, analyses of religious styles by age cohort have shown that the consumption of belief, practice, and service fragments — versus identifiable commitment — is considerably more prevalent among younger Canadians than others. As the population ages, the consumption segment of the population can accordingly be expected to increase.

Religious influence will consequently be minor at the individual level.

Socially, the Churches can be expected to follow their twentieth-century pattern of officially speaking out on many matters, yet having limited impact. The editor of *The Presbyterian Record*, James Dickey, in discussing the need for closer ties among religious groups, recently observed: "Perhaps we have accomplished little because we operate from the top of the institutional structures, not the base."[5] The Canadian Conference of Catholic Bishops has similarly noted that the background preparation of statements is often limited to "dialogue with specialized elites." They stress that "unless [the background work] is constantly nurtured by the actions and reflections of popular movements and grass-roots communities, it will prove inadequate."[6] In view of the declining participation of Canadians in the churches, the statements of religious groups will increasingly lack the endorsement of a sizeable committed constituency and will therefore have less political clout and social impact.

The Roman Catholic sociologist, author, and priest, Andrew Greeley, predicts that the power of the Pope will shrink.

Today we are experiencing the last gasp of a dying order, and in twenty years most of it will be gone. There will be a new leadership more interested in listening to what the people and what the local bishops say. The present condition in the church is transitional.[7]

Religion will without question be with us as we move into the twenty-first century. Despite his skepticism about the future influence of the papacy, Greeley predicts that in twenty years "no one is going to claim . . . that we don't need religion, even though some people obviously will not have strong 'religious sensibilities.'" If anything, according to Greeley, there will be an increased emphasis upon the non-rational aspects of religion — the emotional, mystical, and poetic.[8]

Freud was wrong in expecting that "the illusion," as he called it, would be left "to the angels and the sparrows" as civilization increasingly opted for science and reason.[9] But in fairness to

Freud, it is obvious that the religions of the present age, characterized by "fragmented gods," are extremely abridged versions of the life-embracing systems envisaged by their founders.

OLD AND NEW COMPANIES   The twenty-first century should see the continued presence of organized religion, primarily in its present dominant forms. But there will be no lack of an ongoing stream of new companies. Proponents of "consumer cults" can be expected to work hard to legitimize their "products." Because of the profit potential in dollars and human lives, aggressive promotion through the varied available means of mass marketing can be expected. Harvey Cox of Harvard University suggests that, in order to be popular in the United States, at least, the new entries will "have to offer a mixture of religion, scientific theories, psychological techniques, and ecological lore." Cox cites Scientology as an example of such a viable market candidate.[10]

But the Canadian religion market, beyond the possibility of supernatural fragment contributions, is extremely tight, and there are few signs that it will open up. Further, because of the specialized nature of our society, rivals of the established religious groups will probably fare no better than Christianity in attempting to have an impact on the whole of people's lives. Some of the new competitors— the New Age Movement, for example — may be resisted and strongly opposed as too different. Most, however, will probably be either ignored or allowed a retail outlet to supplement the prevailing beliefs and practices.

DECREASING INVOLVEMENT   If religious groups continue to operate essentially as they are at present, what can be projected with a high degree of confidence is a continued drop-off in regular attendance at services. The most notable determinant of adult affiliation and attendance is parental and church socialization in childhood. Sean O'Sullivan's observation receives solid support from research: "Faith, after all, is not something that comes suddenly or grows in isolation; it is passed on in large measure by the simple, devout faith of parents and others."[11] Bruce Hunsberger, a psychologist at Wilfrid Laurier University in Waterloo, Ontario, is among those who, for some time, have been finding that "the reported emphasis placed on religion in one's childhood home is one of the best predictors of later religiosity."[12] But the surveys have revealed that the regular attendance levels of both adults and school-age children have decreased from two-thirds to one-third over the second half of this century.

Some will argue that many Canadians will return to church — that the "baby-boomers" will eventually find their way back. However, the PROJECT CANADA surveys have found very little support for such an argument. They have included a core of more than a thousand people who participated in 1975 and 1980 and almost six hundred people who have participated in all three surveys. What we have found is that there is a slight increase in attendance for some who marry and have children. But such an increase does not characterize the majority.[13]

These national findings are consistent with some interesting detailed findings for Anglicans in the Toronto Diocese. Asked to trace their involvement patterns over time, both actives and inactives indicated their participation tended to decline during their teens. Those who proceeded to become active as adults were inclined to become more involved during their late twenties and thirties. On the other hand, adult inactives — who outnumber the actives five to one — never did re-establish their childhood levels of participation (see TABLE C1).

TABLE C1.   **Church Involvement Over Time: Toronto Diocese Anglicans**
% indicating "highly motivated"

	Pre-Teens	13–17	18–24	25–29	30–39	40–49	50–59	60+
Actives	57	49	28	33	47	56	56	54
Inactives	59	48	21	17	20	18	13	6

SOURCE: Bibby, *ANGLITRENDS*, 1986:91.

The Anglican case may well be fairly typical of the general Canadian pattern: decreases in church involvement are not random but, rather, are powerfully related to age. Large numbers of people drop out in their teens and early twenties. Some return; many do not.

The truth of the matter is that large numbers of Canadians are not going to return to the churches because they have little to which to return — many were never really there. The religious socialization that so many of us experienced when young is simply not as common among our children.

What might future attendance levels look like? If the rate of attrition of the 1950s, 1960s, and 1970s continues, it will mean that the drop from two-thirds to one-third between 1945 and 1985 will be followed by a drop from one-third to one-sixth in another forty years (by around the year 2025). That's a very big "if," since much of Canada's attendance drop-off resulted from the modernization of Quebec. Still, it's interesting and perhaps significant that, at present, the proportion of Canadians between the ages of 18 and 29 who attend services weekly stands at about 16% — one-sixth of that cohort.

Although attendance projections are bleak, religious organizations are assured of continued contact with Canadians. The desire of people to have churches perform rites of passage surrounding birth, puberty, marriage, and death guarantees the religious groups at least a service role well into the twenty-first century—that is, if they want it.

FINANCIAL PROBLEMS   Although the vast majority of Canadians will continue to identify with religious groups and turn to them for the provision of fragments, the bills will not be paid. Faced with dwindling attendance and a decline in revenues, religious organizations will be forced to re-evaluate the role of their physical assets. For some, neighbourhood churches will probably give way to regional buildings, close to major transportation arteries and capable of servicing a large number of geographically dispersed people. Architecture and personnel would be expected to concentrate increasingly on the performance of rites of passage.

Diminishing revenues will undoubtedly cause religious groups to make more use of existing facilities, rather than building and maintaining their own. Among these will be major shopping centres. And here what started out as an analogy will become a reality: the religious organization will take its place alongside other retail outlets in providing a specialized product.

Another problem should be noted, though it will be somewhat less common. Thanks largely to the affluence of a small supporting core or perhaps the legacies of deceased members, some small congregations will find themselves occupying huge buildings. In the words of a Presbyterian inner-city minister, Gordon Fish, they will be "downtown hulks that once housed large, prosperous and active congregations in our major cities [but now] are all but 'bone dry.' "[14] Laity and executive will have to decide how to salvage such questionable operations.

MENUS, MERGERS, AND MAYHEM   The twenty-first century should see the country's dominant religious groups continue to diversify their offerings in conscious — or often unconscious — efforts to meet the varied product demands of their consumer-minded affiliates.

This general pattern of diversification can be expected to contribute to the polar tendencies of ecumenicism externally and conflict internally. The denominational menu diversification means that over a period of time many of the religious outlets across Canada will look very much the same. The result is that they will have opportunities for somewhat closer ties. It may even be that they will feel so comfortable with one another that there will be a measure of merging. In some instances, financial difficulties will expedite such tendencies, and theological virtues will be made of economic necessities.[15]

At the same time, *within* denominations, the extremities of this range of items can be expected to create increasing tension between advocates of different emphases. The United Church Renewal Fellowship, discussed earlier, is an example of a movement that a group might find hard to accommodate, and vice-versa. Schism is certainly not out of the question.

Thus, the ability to diversify and thereby subsume variant interests
— an integrative feature in the twentieth century—may become an
important source of both unity and division in the twenty-first.

GLOBAL RELIGION   The "global village" created by transportation and communication and the "global economy" created by
economic interdependence should be increasingly accompanied
by "global religion." What I have in mind here is closer international ties both within the world's dominant religions and between
them. While the Catholics and, to a lesser extent, the Anglicans
are already international organizations, denominations such as the
Baptists and Lutherans have established global associations — the
Baptist World Alliance and the Lutheran World Federation, respectively. Conservative Protestants, moreover, have been having international gatherings on themes such as "the Believers' Church."
These and further international gatherings and associations will
undoubtedly only increase.

Closer ties should also characterize the major world religions.
As with the "global village" and "global economy," this does
not mean there will be a loss of national expressions of religion.
The Canadian findings, for example, show that those expressions
are intrinsically tied to personal and cultural identity; they will
persist. But the major world religions can be expected to practise
increasing dialogue, co-operation, and mutual respect. Such
co-operative efforts, as Harvey Cox points out, may strengthen
the voice of world religions in facing global issues like nuclear
weapons and ecological problems.[16]

Indicative of such an emerging emphasis was the establishment
in 1964 by the Roman Catholic Church of a Secretariat for Non-
Christians — completely separate from its Sacred Congregation
for the Evangelization of Peoples. Its mandate has been to search
for ways of opening dialogue with non-Christians, with the goal
of enabling Christians and non-Christians to understand and appre-
ciate each other.[17] Other major groups, notably the United and
Anglican Churches, have shown a similar interest in dialogue.

MICRO-MINISTRY   In the fall of 1986, a computer donated to
an Eastern Orthodox monastery in Finland was blessed, with

modified traditional Orthodox rituals of prayer and the sprinkling of water. The monks prayed that the computer would be used in the pursuit of truth, peace, justice, and the sacredness of life.[18]

The computer is potentially of great use to religious groups. Astronomer and geophysicist Walter Roberts argues that the computer is not a new intruder to be feared but a resource to be tapped:

> *The computer won't be in charge. Like the TV set, the book [and] the screwdriver, the computer will remain but a tool for [us] to use as [we] will. But the computer of the future will be a tool of unprecedented power. . . . It will be a liberating force, if [we] choose to make it so.*[19]

The co-option of modern technology may dramatically alter both the nature and the effectiveness of ministry. The United Church's Division of Communication, for example, has for some time been exploring the role of computers at the national, regional, and local levels. The Division's Task Force on Information Flow looked at technological needs in conference offices and helped to pick out suitable computers. The conferences are currently linked to the national office and to each other.[20] As for possible uses at the local church level, Mike Milne writes in *The United Church Observer*:

> *The distributors of one church software package estimate that a computer system, designed for a 200-family congregation, would cost about $8,000. For this, the computer could handle a host of functions, ranging from typing sermons, reports or mailing lists, to keeping track of available volunteers and minding the finances.*[21]

A central finding of the PROJECT CANADA research has been that most affiliates are not lost to the religious groups. They are still out there, giving organizations the opportunity to continue to minister to them. Consequently, a basic task of religious groups is to locate these people, primarily through survey techniques, and to establish a good record-keeping system. Beyond the local level, there needs to be good inter-congregational communication in order to keep track of the geographically mobile. Here the arrival of the computer, with its awesome information-storage capabilities, seems like "a gift from the gods."

Once constituents are identified, when religious groups want to "access" them, they have the possibility of drawing upon new and exciting forms of communication. The range is vast and ever-growing; one always needs the most recent program to follow the players in this game.

For starters, groups can draw on video and sound equipment for education, worship, and entertainment purposes. Some are beginning to do so. The Canadian Baptist Federation, for example, produces and distributes VHS videos for Bible-study purposes. Reflecting an outlook similar to that of the Finnish monks, Philip Karpetz of the Ontario and Quebec Communication and Stewardship Department quips, "In this age of automation, why not baptize the machinery for God's use?"[22]

Religious groups will undoubtedly make increased use of video cassettes and other computer-generated visual and written materials made available by technology. Naisbitt, for example, sees the day when newspapers "will offer self-selected stocks printed out by individual order each afternoon on individual home computers," with such a service being as common as today's telephone.[23] Home computers likewise can be expected to be a vital link between the churches and their active members, as well as a yet-to-be-determined number of their non-involved affiliates.

To be effective, of course, information systems will have to be put to imaginative and creative use, or they will fail even to reach the eyes and ears of affiliates, let alone clear the next hurdle of being significant sources of information. David Byrne, the articulate lead singer of the rock group "Talking Heads," makes the important point that computers, for example, are not a substitute for thought and creativity:

> When it comes to the arts, they're just big or small adding machines. And if they can't "think," that's all they'll ever be. They may help creative people with their bookkeeping, but they won't help in the creative process.[24]

IMPLICATIONS FOR THE NATION

Throughout history some have seen the erosion of religion as leading to the downfall of societies. The eighth-century prophets Hosea and Isaiah warned the Israelites that if they did not return to the ways of God they would be destroyed. Hosea claims to pass on this message from God:

> It was I who knew you in the desert,
> In the land where there was no water.
> But when they fed they stuffed themselves;
> They were fed to the full, their hearts grew proud
> And they forgot me.
> [So] I will destroy you, Israel;
> Who can help you?[25]

In like manner, Isaiah proclaims:

> Now the Lord says:
> Because this people draws near to me only in words
> And honours me with no more than lip-service,
> While their hearts are far from me,
> And their reverence for me is a rule
>   they have learned by heart,
> See, I will deal with them in a way
>   that will astonish them
> And leave them filled with amazement and wonder![26]

The decline of the mighty Roman Empire has been attributed to moral decay by many observers. And in the 1880s, the man whom many regarded as Toronto's leading intellectual, Goldwin Smith, maintained that religion and the fear of eternal punishment were all that saved society from disintegration. He insisted again and again that the questioning of traditional beliefs could undermine civilization.[27]

Such a view continues to be expressed by many today among laity as well as clergy. A 66-year-old Baptist from Regina comments, "If there were no God, no one would strive to do what is right." A firefighter in Saint John says, "I believe the whole problem with society today is the lack of God in homes and businesses." Sister Mary Jo Leddy, founder and former editor of *Catholic New Times*, told a March 1987 Edmonton audience that the preoccupation of North Americans with goods and services was "a lifestyle that preceded the downfall of the Roman Empire." It "could indeed lead to the downfall of our society," she continued, "unless a new belief, a new faith, and a new strength to change our ways becomes a reality."[28]

Recently, from All Souls College, Oxford, has come a thoughtful assessment of some of the negative personal and social characteristics of advanced, secular societies. The observations warrant serious examination. They come from Bryan Wilson, the aforementioned highly respected sociologist who has spent a lifetime studying secularization. The data base for his observations is extensive: he has examined British society, American society, the major world religions, and new religious movements worldwide.[29]

Over the years, Wilson's position has never changed: modern societies have been experiencing secularization—"the process by which religious institutions, actions, and consciousness lose their social significance."[30] But all is far from well with the operation of contemporary societies. An increasing proportion of individuals, he argues, are disturbed by "the facelessness of modern bureaucracies," the impersonality of relationships, and—despite elaborate leisure and recreational opportunities—boredom. Wilson maintains that, in addition, social problems are growing "at an alarming rate," citing as examples crime, vandalism, neurosis, mental breakdown, the disruption of marriage, addiction, gambling, loneliness, and suicide.[31]

Modern societies, continues Wilson, not only "fail to cope with these problems" but, indeed, seem to be "partly responsible for their emergence."[32] A number of important stabilizing functions in western society that in the past were supplied and supported by religion may now be left unperformed. He goes so far as to say that

the consequences . . . for the standards of civic order, social responsibility, and individual integrity may be such that the future of western society itself may be thrown in jeopardy.[33]

Wilson's observations have to be taken seriously. However, they also have to be assessed not by means of speculation, but by examining available data. In the light of our findings for Canada, it is extremely difficult to agree with such "gloom and doom" assertions.

First, we have found little difference in the values and social concerns of people who are religiously committed and those who are not. They have very similar values and social concerns and view and relate to other Canadians in very much the same way.

Second, the values, concerns, and interpersonal attitudes that most people regard as important are highly pervasive, indicating that these characteristics have a number of social sources, of which religion is just one.

Third, social-problems theory and research would seriously question the claims of Wilson and others that social problems have been getting worse.[34] Global communication and, yes, the widespread prevalence of humanitarian values, have resulted in our "seeing" more problems than ever before. Most of the conditions have always been there. Apartheid did not start in the 1980s. Child abuse did not come into being in the 1970s. Gender discrimination did not arise *ex nihilo* in the 1960s. Poverty did not appear for the first time in the 1950s. Let's be clear about what has been taking place: it is precisely because people are more concerned about each other that more discrepancies between the ideal and the real are being "discovered." The conditions are not new; what is new is the extent of our exposure to global problems and our pro-human response to them.

The findings, supplemented by readily observable social concern across the country, indicate that the movement towards the adoption of religious fragments is *not* having a negative impact on Canadian society.In terms of valued characteristics such as equality, interpersonal relations, and general standard of living, even the most superficial reading of Canadian history will make it readily apparent that the present easily excels the past.

Perhaps, in Wilson's phrase, it is because we, along with other western cultures, are living "off the borrowed capital of [our] religious past."[35] If so, we seem to have spent the inheritance well. We are now pretty much living off our own money.

IMPLICATIONS FOR INDIVIDUALS

A t the personal level, we have seen that the committed and the uncommitted report similar levels of wellbeing. Of considerable importance is the fact that Canadians, whether highly religious or not, are inclined to claim high levels of happiness and satisfaction.

The much-publicized ills of boredom and loneliness, anxiety and despair, are concerns for some, but not personal experience for most. The key reason: the centrality of relationships, of family, friends, and love. Our contemporary society may feature rationality and impersonal interaction ("hot tech and cold touch"), but computers are no match for caring and community; the world of sight and sound doesn't replace relationships. Rather it is co-opted by them. As Don Posterski and I noted in *The Emerging Generation*, teenagers, for example, might have the most sophisticated stereo equipment wired to their heads. But it speaks volumes about what is of primary value when two such young people walk along a beach together, connected by a patch-cord.[36]

Relationships remain number one in Canadian life and, I am sure, in other modern societies. Civic groups, educational institutions, politicians, the media, and the so-called "helping professions" are all officially attempting to enrich the lives of Canadians, socially as well as individually.

Whatever religion's role in the promotion and enhancement of interpersonal bonds, it is clear that relationships are enjoyed just as readily by the non-religious as by the devout; that the movement from religious commitment to religious consumption is not having negative effects on the wellbeing of individual Canadians.

DEATH: AN IMPORTANT FOOTNOTE While the surveys and supplementary data indicate that religion makes little difference in how Canadians live, it does make a difference in how they die. By this I mean that the committed and uncommitted have different responses to death; they also have different beliefs about life after death.

Canadians as a whole are divided almost evenly among five *dominant responses* to death: mystery, no particular feeling, sorrow, fear, and hope (see TABLE C2). People with no religious affiliation tend to say that they have no particular feeling (39%); only 4% of the religious Nones indicate hope.

Differences between the committed and uncommitted are striking. The most prevalent response of the devout is hope (30%); the uncommitted tend to cite no particular feeling (29%) or mystery (27%). Sorrow and fear are just about as common to both categories.

TABLE C2. **Responses to Death by Religious Group** *(In %s)*

"What would you say is your primary response to the idea of death?"

N	Nat (1308)	RCOQ (217)	RCQ (247)	UC (241)	Ang (154)	Cons (88)	Luth (32)	Pres (59)	Oth (141)	None (129)
ALL AFFILIATES										
Mystery	24	21	23	30	30	14	29	23	16	23
No particular feeling	21	12	27	16	15	24	10	19	25	39
Sorrow	20	21	19	22	19	17	15	23	20	15
Fear	18	26	18	16	18	10	18	13	11	10
Hope	17	20	13	17	18	35	28	22	12	4
COMMITTED										
Hope	30	28	19	26	30	58	44	42	36	na
Sorrow	22	30	21	24	15	11	10	21	19	na
Mystery	19	14	21	29	21	18	11	7	15	na
Fear	18	24	20	10	29	5	29	11	9	na
No particular feeling	11	4	19	11	5	7	6	19	14	na
UNCOMMITTED										
No particular feeling	29	25	35	18	21	45	15	21	12	na
Mystery	27	29	26	32	38	8	55	29	18	na
Sorrow	19	10	19	20	22	25	23	27	11	na
Fear	18	26	17	18	9	17	3	16	24	na
Hope	7	11	4	12	10	5	4	8	8	na

SOURCE: PROJECT CAN80. NOTE : na = Not applicable.

Differences between religious groups are also pronounced. Committed Roman Catholics outside Quebec tend to cite sorrow, hope, and fear while, among Catholics in Quebec, all five responses are equally common. Among the committed who are United Church, mystery, hope, and sorrow are the dominant reactions. For the committed in the remaining groups, and especially among the Conservative Protestants, the primary response is hope. Fear characterizes approximately three in ten committed Anglicans and Lutherans and about two in ten committed and uncommitted Catholics. But fear is not common among Canadians who have severed ties with organized religion. As noted, it characterizes only about one in ten people with no religious affiliation.

The uncommitted also vary considerably by religious group in how they respond to death. Roman Catholics are characterized by no particular feeling, mystery, and fear; the United Church, Anglican, and Lutheran non-devout primarily by mystery. The uncommitted among the Conservative Protestants tend to indicate no particular feeling, uncommitted Presbyterians are diffuse, and the religious Others lean towards fear and mystery.

These general patterns become much more comprehensible when we examine the *beliefs* that committed and uncommitted Canadians have about life after death. The committed clearly are more likely than the uncommitted to hold some firm, positive idea about what happens to people after they die, believing in heaven, hell, reincarnation, and so on (see TABLE C3). This clarity of belief in turn is associated with a greater feeling of hope. The uncommitted, on the other hand, are almost equally divided between believing there is life after death but "having no idea what it is like" and not believing in life after death at all. Therefore, they are understandably much more likely to indicate that their dominant response to death is either no particular feeling or mystery—they simply do not know what to expect.

These findings once more suggest the influence of culture on belief. A society that emphasizes the importance of the here and now is one that is not likely to encourage individuals to ponder questions such as what happens after we die. The result is that, even though Christianity has historically had much to say about

TABLE C3. **Belief in Life After Death by Commitment and Religious Group** *(In %s)*

	Nat	RCOQ	RCQ	UC	Ang	Cons	Luth	Pres	Oth
N	(1308)	(217)	(247)	(241)	(154)	(88)	(32)	(59)	(141)
COMMITTED									
Positive*	47	47	44	25	40	88	68	33	54
Unclear	38	42	37	52	53	9	19	42	23
Negative	15	11	19	23	7	3	13	25	23
UN-COMMITTED									
Unclear	42	64	49	48	49	37	55	40	24
Negative	40	31	32	37	35	31	22	26	56
Positive	18	5	19	15	16	32	23	34	20

SOURCE: PROJECT CAN80.

*Positive: "Life after death, no punishment"; "Life after death, rewards for some, punishment for others"; "Reincarnation"; any others as specified (open-ended option provided).

Negative: "I don't believe that there is life after death."

Unclear: "I believe that there must be something beyond death, but I have no idea what it may be like."

the issue of dying and life after death, it is not culturally fashionable to give much attention—perhaps even any attention—to such "pie in the sky by and by" matters. So far as culture dictates religion's emphases, it is only to be expected that concern with the after-life would not be given a high priority by some and perhaps most of the country's groups.

The surveys show that this is the case. Fewer than five in ten of the committed actually express positive beliefs in life after death. Vagueness is particularly characteristic of people associated with the United Church: only 25% of committed United affiliates claim some kind of clear, positive belief in the after-life. This finding suggests that the United Church is giving relatively little attention to the question; even people who are committed to its version of Christianity are coming away with unclear beliefs about what will happen after they die. To a lesser extent, the same charge can be levelled at the other groups. The one exception appears to be the Conservative Protestants — decisive belief in life after death is claimed by almost nine in ten of the committed.

Keeping in mind these variations, my point is that religious commitment tends to be associated with a definite belief about what happens after death. It also creates a feeling of hope both as one experiences bereavement and as one approaches death oneself. These findings suggest that as commitment declines and is further coloured by culture, there will be a loss: Canadians will no longer be as likely to have a clear view of the life beyond or to feel hope in the face of death.

Culture has little to say about death. That's the main reason why it is taboo as a subject of discussion, ignored or covered over with those well-known, vague euphemisms — "if something happens to you"; "he passed away"; "she is no longer with us."

If there is no life after death and no basis for hope, then the loss of a message that there is "something beyond" is unfortunate but unavoidable and overdue. In that case, the time has come for resignation — grim or otherwise. Comfort in the face of the loss of loved ones will have to be solely social. Our immortality will have to be seen in terms of living on through our children and theirs, or in the impact we might have on future generations.[37]

But many would like to hope for much more. As Woody Allen put it in *Hannah and Her Sisters*, "I don't want to gain immortality through my work. I want to gain immortality by not dying." If religion *does* have something to say about dying, death, and hope, then the time has come for groups to quit echoing culture's non-message. If they have something to say on the topic, they need to speak.

Christianity, for example, has historically had much to say about the topic. Some, like priest Sean O'Sullivan — whose leukemia makes his life a precarious day-to-day experience — believes it has much to say in our age. The former Member of Parliament and aide to John Diefenbaker writes,

> *Soon, I may be summoned home. But sing no sad songs for me; for I am a Christian. . . . To other cancer victims and their families, to Catholics and all people of goodwill, I say: Remain steadfast, keep stout hearts and hold unwavering hope. Fear not, our God is still at work. However dark the*

coming days, He will triumph and be with us always, even until the end of time.[38]

Speaking sociologically and not theologically, I would suggest that the reluctance of Canada's religious groups to speak on the subject is a poignant commentary on the extent to which they have become spokespeople for culture rather than for the gods.

IMPLICATIONS FOR RELIGIOUS GROUPS

In assessing the future of organized religion in Canada almost two decades ago, John Webster Grant turned to Montreal's Expo 67, "Man and His World."[39] He suggested that the two religion exhibits at Expo graphically symbolized the religious alternatives being offered to Canadians. The first was "The Christian Pavilion," the showpiece of the Roman Catholic, United, Anglican, and Orthodox Churches. The sell was soft—no explicit preaching, just a series of audio-visual experiences depicting human suffering and human indifference. It ended with a meditation room where quiet music, pastoral murals, and Scriptural texts gently hinted at the possibility of redemption.

The second exhibit was sponsored by Conservative Protestants. Entitled, "Sermons in Science," its religious message was clear and direct: a creating God offering the world his redeeming love through Jesus Christ. Two exhibits, two choices—the first experimental, the second traditional. In Grant's opinion, the former would be only a temporary posture, "for men and institutions can bear to live out of suitcases for a relatively short time."[40] Yet he also felt that "the golden age of belief" recalled by "Sermons in Science" would be unlikely to return, although "it would continue to be a source of reassurance and a standard for judgment." [41]

The "experimental" and "traditional" capsules, I think, aptly describe the two dominant responses of religion to the modern age. On the one hand, there is an inclination to respond to the new with the new; on the other hand, there are many who want to respond to the new with the old. From a sociological point of view, both responses are inadequate. Let me explain why.

MEETING THE NEW WITH THE NEW   The experimental approach is probably the more prevalent of the two and is particularly characteristic of Canada's United and Anglican Churches, and possibly the Roman Catholic Church in parts of Quebec. The shrinking role of religion is treated as almost inevitable. Times are changing, and it is only to be expected that religion's nature and role will also change.

Rather than bemoaning the movement from commitment to consumption, some advocates of this approach view the increasingly specialized roles of both the Church and religion as "a good thing." Now that society has taken more responsibility for tasks like education, medicine, leisure, and social services, the Churches can get on with the more appropriate, specific task of dealing with religion.[42] It's not the Church's place to dominate society. Rather, it is called to be the "leaven" or "the salt," to exert a positive, godly influence on society. Rouleau, for example, writes that the Catholic Church in Quebec will not recover the power it had before the 1960s. But he goes on to say that the Church is not looking for a return to societal dominance: "It is on the level of what is properly its own — the religious level — that the Church will continue to try to serve the people of Quebec."[43]

Further, the fact that individuals are adopting fragments is also a good sign. People are working out their personal expressions of faith, selecting those aspects that are most important to them. They are creating their own personal expression of religion, instead of mindlessly accepting pre-packaged sets of beliefs and private practices. Individual struggle, search, and journey are replacing the assembly-line production of Canada's committed. Here, as in the social spheres, it is not the role of the Church to indoctrinate and suffocate. It should rather provide fragments, including rites of passage, and leave much of the development of faith up to individuals.

This position of an ever-changing, dynamic faith is not without potential problems. In attempting to meet the new with the new, religious organizations come precariously close to letting culture dictate the content and the forms of faith. The demands of the market can become the key criteria for determining the nature and the shape of religion.

For example, an approach that stresses cultural relevance can easily find itself asking, not "What *should* people believe?" but rather, "What *can* people believe?" Symbols and theology may then be rewritten largely in accordance with what the public views as credible and palatable. If some have difficulty with supernatural elements, then those elements may be "demythologized." If people cannot believe in "a God in the sky," then he may be grounded — with "he" becoming gender-inclusive if people object to a masculine term. If people cannot believe in the divinity of Jesus, then he may have to be humanized. If life after death sounds too far-fetched for some people to handle, it, too, may have to be reinterpreted in more digestible terms. Such rewriting of concepts and theology is "legitimized" on the basis of everything from revelation through the need to translate to the sheer need to update.

I must stress, at this point, that my critique has little to do with whether such content modifications are right or wrong, appropriate or inappropriate. Sociologically, what is significant about these attempts to get in step with modernity is that culture calls most of the shots, and there is a fine line between translating the message and transforming it altogether.

Those who would meet the new with the new also tend to take their directives from culture when it comes to the *forms* of religion. Liturgy and educational curricula are modified to match the language, the understanding, and the moods of the day. Church programs contract to eliminate culturally passé emphases such as temperance and expand to include current culturally sanctioned emphases, ranging from physical fitness to concern about Latin America.

And while religious leaders may claim that the updating of programs and structures has been based on insights from the gods, the cultural sources are usually anything but subtle. Take, for example, some recent developments in the United and Anglican

Churches that many leaders have heralded as progressive advances. The willingness to consider the ordination of women and homosexuals, along with the movement towards more inclusive theological language, hardly had their beginnings in revelation or Scriptural authority. When western societies had declared the equality of women and men, it seemed culturally inappropriate for Anglicans to find themselves still refusing to ordain women, or for the United Church to have gone sixty years without electing a lay woman as its moderator. It is also no longer appropriate to see God in purely masculine terms. And homosexuals, if they really are only exercising a sexual preference, should also have the right to be ordained.

When religion becomes so wedded to culture, it finds that its authority is further eroded. If culture is going to be allowed to inform and instruct, then culture also insists on being admitted to the priesthood.

The result is that some strange self-ordained cultural high priests and prophets rise up to pronounce judgement on religions' failure to embrace culture properly. Foremost are the media. Newspaper editorial writers, for example, recently took it upon themselves to applaud the Church of England's albeit belated willingness to ordain women as priests. An editorial in *The Edmonton Journal* informed us:

> *Such a move is long overdue. Yet it's puzzling why male domination in the church has persisted for so long and why it continues among a minority of members. Sexual discrimination would not be tolerated in the workplace or in politics. . . . Yet a minority of the Church of England persists in the belief that one sex is better able than the other to deliver God's message.*[44]

If religion is nothing more than culture in sanctimonious clothing, then, indeed, let journalists and others tell religion when it is right and when it is wrong. But if there are elements of religion that transcend culture, ideas that claim to have more than only a cultural source, then religion on occasion at least should find itself — recalling Robert Smith's words — "contradicting the times" and at odds with the media and perhaps a good many others. Pierre Berton, in *The Comfortable Pew*, put it this way:

> *The Christian Church is not a commercial television network. Though it has for centuries seemed to be largely an agency for the comfort of its congregations, it cannot long survive unless, like its founder, it stirs up the people by making large numbers of them acutely uncomfortable.*[45]

What is sociologically interesting is that some groups, notably the Roman Catholic Church, along with Conservative Protestants and Mormons, do sometimes say what culture doesn't want to hear (on sexuality, for example). On occasion, they make people angry! The Catholic Church further remains firm on limiting the priesthood to males and in opposing divorce — very unpopular stands. In examining the relationship between religion and culture, the issue is not whether one agrees or disagrees with the positions of these religious groups. The point is that they make an effort to stand up against culture, to say something to culture that culture is not already saying to itself. As mentioned earlier, the Catholics and Conservatives may frequently be doing little more than trying to impose old culture on new culture. But at least there's an effort to challenge current culture.

Obviously, this process whereby religion becomes a cultural product starts off with good intentions; surely religion needs to be "in touch with the times." But the practical result of the effort to meet the new with the new is that religion can be almost totally determined by culture. Peter Berger pointed out a number of years ago that when religion tries to learn from culture it seldom bargains as an equal — it takes in far more than it gives out:

> *The theologian who trades ideas with the modern world . . . is likely to come out with a poor bargain, that is, he will probably have to give far more than he will get. To vary the image, he who sups with the devil had better have a long spoon.*[46]

In interacting with science, for example, religion is not an equal partner. As Durkheim once put it, religion is unable to deny anything that science affirms, or affirm anything that science denies. [47] Religion's conversations with science as a consequence have always led to retreat and reformulation. The damage to religion's content and forms can be considerably more severe.

A religion that merely reflects culture is without a unique message — it is only a mirror. To simply meet the new with the new is to run the risk of acknowledging that there is nothing of substance to one's faith that transcends both space and time. As leading Roman Catholic Cardinal Joseph Ratzinger put it in an April 1986 lecture in Toronto, theology will "dissolve into arbitrary theory" unless it exists in and from the Church, with personal conversion at the heart of the theologian's teaching. If this doesn't happen, says Ratzinger, "if the theologian does not live and breathe Christ through the Church . . . then I suggest we are not dealing with a theologian at all, but a mere sociologist, or historian, or philosopher."[48]

Religious organizations, of course, are perfectly free to serve up fragments, to offer Canadians religion à la carte. But if they really are interested in truth, they should at least recognize what they are doing.

Religious groups that make fragments available are largely responding to contemporary culture, imitating rather than initiating. In meeting a specialized age with a specialized religion, religious organizations are offering little more than a commodity, manufactured according to cultural guidelines.

MEETING THE NEW WITH THE OLD The second dominant response of Canadian religious groups is to try to recover the religion of old. Many people who feel disenchanted with the present and want positive, identifiable beliefs and values nostalgically seek solace in the past. As Bryan Wilson points out, nostalgia is an important measure of disenchantment.[49]

This emphasis on the past, including the features of faith that are seen as unchanging, is associated with many Conservative Protestant denominations, the United Church Renewal Fellowship, and sizeable segments of the charismatic movement. Seen by its detractors as trying to bring back "that old-time religion," the response emphasizes experiential religion, traditional beliefs, the importance of Scripture, private prayer, personal morality, and the centrality of the Christian community. In addition, many who would meet the new with the old want to retain not only "the old content" but also "the old forms." Church attendance, for example, is supremely valued as indicative of devotion. This emphasis on implementing the old is also associated with some aspects of the Roman Catholic Church, particularly in its perceived inflexibility in matters such as sexuality and the ordination of women, along with its caution concerning lay involvement.

With its strong emphasis on personal faith, the traditional response stands in stark contrast with the experimental in its tendency to go to the other extreme and *ignore* culture. The major developments characterizing our era are frequently of limited interest. For some of the traditionalist groups, culture is seen almost as an adversary that must be battled and is accorded the half-personifying term, "the world." Opposition to cultural change becomes an end in itself, a sign of steadfastness in the face of pressures being exerted by "the world." Biblical verses such as "Come ye out of the world and be ye separate" are commonly invoked.

The tendency of Protestants to resist culture in designing religious forms can be seen in a familiar illustration. The "two-service Sunday," complete with 11 A.M. and 7 P.M. starting times, was a staple feature of rural Protestant life. Many of today's Conservative Protestant groups continue to stress the importance of attending two services (frequently at these same starting times), even though contemporary urban life with its time demands may have rendered the concept obsolete. Commitment to what might be regarded as an outdated form is nonetheless commonly viewed as a measure of one's commitment to the faith. Falling evening attendance, for example, is not infrequently decried as a sign of the secular times.

This tendency to resist and ignore culture has also meant that the traditionalists have been fairly ineffective in changing culture. Many evangelical Protestants, while emphasizing that religion should influence the entirety of life, have tended to focus upon individuals and personal morality to the exclusion of culture and social structure. The result is that, until very recently, many traditionalists have made few attempts to address social issues at the key levels of potential influence. Prayer has been viewed as more important than public participation, example more effective than exhortation of government.

The tendency to turn inward has not only characterized Conservative Protestants. Such an inclination among Catholic charismatics has been a very real concern of the Roman Catholic Church. A 1975 message on charismatic renewal from the Canadian Conference of Catholic Bishops included this note of caution:

> We should question the indifference — even reluctance — of some groups to take an active interest in the needs of those around them. Their predominant tendency is to self-centeredness. The joy they experience from togetherness gives rise to a sentiment of personal satisfaction that transforms their groups into ghettos. Such groups become closed circles, providing a few hours of escape from reality, rather than being as they should be — spring-boards for plunging into the world.[50]

The inclination to respond to the new with the old has also meant that many of the traditionalists often have been slow to make use of culture. The Roman Catholics, for example, have seldom turned to television in either Canada or the United States. Dean Hoge notes that "there are no nationally-known Catholic preachers today, and no TV preachers."[51] It should be added, however, that to the extent that Catholics want sheer exposure, the Pope is without question a media event in and of himself.

Conservative Protestants have never had a Vatican II and often have failed to recognize that the old *content* may need to be translated if it is to be understood, and that the old *forms* may need to be torn down in order for the old and valued product to be transmitted with success.

A message that is judged by the traditionalists to be timeless nonetheless will take on a dated appearance if the traditionalists fail to show an awareness of contemporary culture — its nature and its needs, its strengths and its weaknesses. They also forgo invaluable resources if, in the course of ignoring cultural strengths, they fail to draw on the rich resource of available technology in their efforts to communicate effectively what they call their "unchanging message."

There is almost always one major problem with trying to impose the past on the present. Whatever may have seemed to be good also carries with it the bad — which, through the wonders of selective memory, we have conveniently forgotten. The "good old days," the "good old group," and "the good old gospel" have one basic feature in common — things in reality were never "all good."

In the case of old-time religion, the tendency of many of its proponents to turn inward and become oblivious to broader social issues would be seen as "good" by few today. Similarly, the inclination of its advocates to view "self" as something to be minimized and even denied altogether would fail to gain substantial applause. We readily recognize that one of the keys to sound emotional health and human compassion is to have sound self-images, taking seriously the Biblical admonition to love God and our neighbour as we love ourselves.

Canada of the present and future needs more than merely to recapture the religion of its past. Religious groups that simply try to meet the new with the old will be presenting a religion that is not very marketable. Much more seriously, they will betray the cultural flexibility religion is capable of exhibiting and negate the cultural resources religion is capable of using.

BEYOND FRAGMENTS: THE GREAT POSSIBILITY

The experimental position contributes little to culture because of its excessive dependence on culture. The traditional position also offers little to culture because it largely ignores culture. The first tends to be a listener; the second refuses to listen. Neither approach can be expected to have a significant impact on this country's personal and social life.

A religion that will have a significant place in the Canada of the present and future is a religion that is doing something special, doing something that is different. If experimentalist religious organizations are primarily social-issue interest groups, counselling agencies, or leisure-activity centres, for example, they are going to be obliterated by superior secular competitors. These services have extremely limited markets. As Berger has asked, "Why should one buy psychotherapy or racial liberalism in a 'Christian' package, when the same commodities are available under purely secular . . . labels?"[52] Journalist Ted Byfield recently made the same point: "If the practice of the Christian faith is reduced to mere political tub-tumping most people will say, 'Why bother? We have the NDP, what do we need the church for?' "[53]

The current cores of older, committed individuals in these groups were never drawn to them primarily because of such emphases; they have simply stayed on as these thrusts have become more central. When this supporting, aging minority dies off in two or three decades, religious groups characterized by such emphases are going to face severe numerical and financial problems.

Likewise, traditionalists who look back to the past are going to have a head-on collision with the future. Their sons and daughters who are exposed to national and global culture through mass media and formal education will crash through the subcultural walls of these religious groups. They will become readily aware of the positive features of evolving science and technology and the necessity of caring going well beyond the boundaries of one's own group. These offspring will either fuse faith and culture or, more probably, reject "a faith that looks backwards" as incompatible with life as they know it.

If religion is to interact effectively with culture, then it has to be able to transcend culture, so that it has something to bring, and be responsive to culture, so that it knows how to bring it. If religious groups think they have nothing unique to bring to culture, then the future of religion in Canada and the modern world looks bleak. Religious organizations accordingly should see the writing on the wall and begin to wind down their operations and cut what may be mammoth financial losses in the early part of the twenty-first century.

But they don't have to. In the light of the historical nature of religion and the contemporary nature of culture, religious groups do have an extremely marketable product—if they are capable of rediscovering and disseminating it.

A number of years ago, the writings of the renowned social psychologist George Herbert Mead were gathered together by his students and others under the title, *Mind, Self, and Society.*[54] It seems to me that religion can have an important place in Canada and the rest of the modern world if, in a slight modification of that book title, it can reconnect *God, self and society.* Sociologically speaking, these are areas where consumer demand is very high —there is a market for them. Religiously speaking, they embrace the heart of religion. There is widespread interest in precisely what religion has historically claimed to be and do.

GOD   Bryan Wilson, while pessimistic about religion's possibility of having a significant influence in the present and future, nonetheless concedes, "The contingencies of human life occasionally force people to ask fundamental questions about meaning and purpose. . . . Here, then, might be a place for religion."[55] John Webster Grant has said that "one of the clearest messages being received" is that "the dimension of meaning once provided by the churches is still very much in demand."[56] An Italian futurist, Aurelio Peccei, reflecting on the world as a whole, has written that

> *humanity, although the prisoner of materialistic motivations, has a profound need for spirituality. . . . We humans feel that we are living in a dangerous void, that we must restore communion with spheres that transcend those motivations.*[57]

In assessing the impact of "the Information Age," Bill Gates cautions that there is a danger that people will feel worthless and overwhelmed by the amount of available data. "We'll find out what the human brain can do," he says, "but we'll have serious problems with the purpose of it all."[58]

Consistent with such assertions, the PROJECT CANADA findings for both adults and teenagers reveal no decline in the inclination to raise the so-called "ultimate questions" concerning life and death.

As long as such questions are asked, and as long as the limits of scientific answers are felt, a market for religious and other supernaturally based explanations of reality will continue to exist.

An Orwellian world in which "God is Power" and in which there is "no more curiosity" has yet to be realized.[59] Religion's role extends beyond merely "consoling" and "compensating," "offering hope" and "promoting charity," and therefore cannot, as in *Brave New World*, be readily replaced by a "soma"-like drug.[60] Charles Templeton, the former evangelist and now a successful novelist, recalls that in the midst of his doubts before he left the ministry, "I wanted very much to believe; there was in me then as there remains now an intense . . . longing for a relationship with God."[61] Templeton is far from alone.

When it comes to providing ultimate meaning, even the most sophisticated computer or micro-electronic instrument comes up short. Historically, the provision of meaning has been perhaps the central component of religion. Indeed, social scientists have found themselves defining religion as "a system of meaning used to interpret one's world."[62] Religions assert that our existence has meaning preceding that which we as humans decide to give to it. Such meaning is not cultural in origin; it literally comes from the gods.

In contrast, non-religious, humanist perspectives work from the assumption that existence has no meaning beyond that which we ourselves provide. While religion is concerned with life's meaning, humanist viewpoints attempt to make life meaningful. Bertrand Russell stated the difference well: "I do not think that life in general has a purpose. It just happened. But individual human beings have purposes."[63]

Religions have the potential to address the meaning issue, providing that do they not allow themselves to be recast strictly as human products. Robertson Davies points out that one of two possible roots of the word "religious" is *relegere*, "meaning a careful observation and heedfulness toward the numinous—whatever inspires awe or reverence."[64] The desire for the numinous, he maintains, is widespread, evident in interest in everything from astrology, through eastern religions, to science fiction.

In the quest for cultural relevance, many of those who try to meet the new with the new have somehow lost a sense of the numinous, of the supernatural dimension of religion. They under-emphasize God in the course of trying to speak to life. Much is said about human relations and social issues. But God is either missing altogether or is so implicit as to be unidentifiable.

Religion, historically understood, is equipped to make a significant, unique contribution to the human quest for meaning. As Stark and Bainbridge have argued, the questions about the meaning of life and what lies beyond death are questions that only the gods can satisfy.[65] The reason is simple: they lie beyond the pale of human experience.

If the supernatural or numinous source of information can be rediscovered, religion has the potential to speak with an authoritative voice about the meaning of life and the meaning of death. During his 1984 visit to Ottawa, Pope John Paul II said:

If the world no longer dares to speak about God, it expects from the Church . . . a word which witnesses to God with strength and conviction . . . without ever reducing the greatness of the message to the expectation of the listeners.[66]

Not everyone will listen. But my research and that of others indicate that many will.

SELF   Religion has frequently been associated with the denunciation of self. Christianity, for example, in both its Roman Catholic and Protestant expressions, has not lacked for emphasis upon human sinfulness, the need to deny self, the importance of being poor in spirit, the acknowledgment of one's being capable of nothing apart from the grace of God.

In the process, self has often been impoverished. The laity have, in some instances, been virtually immobilized. I recall a clergyman offering the simple observation to his congregation that they often ask God to do things that they themselves are perfectly capable of doing. It seemed to come as something of a revelation to more than a few.

A religion like Christianity has, in fact, a Biblical emphasis upon the importance, worth, and potential of self. In admonishing people to be concerned about those around them, the assumption of Jesus, for example, was that people already felt good about themselves — why else tell people to love others as much as they loved themselves?

This is a day when large numbers of people are being attracted to programs and groups that stress the realization of human potential. Historian and social critic Christopher Lasch has written that mass culture, consumption, and a lack of faith in the future have turned people in on themselves. Personal wellbeing, health, and psychic security are "in":

> *Having no hope of improving their lives in any of the ways that matter, people have convinced themselves that what matters is psychic self-improvement: getting in touch with their feelings, eating health food, taking lessons in ballet or belly-dancing, immersing themselves in the wisdom of the East, jogging, learning how to "relate," overcoming the "fear of pleasure."*[67]

John Naisbitt writes that the new self-help or personal growth movement, which eventually became the human potential movement, has been directly related to the emergence of high tech and its impersonal nature. "In reality, each feeds the other," he says, "high tech/high touch."[68] A sampling of well-known titles tells much of the personal growth movement story — *Winning, Don't Say Yes When You Want to Say No, Looking Out for #1, Pulling Your Own Strings, Necessary Losses*. Individuals like Leo Buscaglia, the author of *Loving Each Other* and other books, have become renowned for their emphasis upon the importance of love and tenderness, joy and touch. The centrality of self can be seen in the following, taken from *Loving Each Other*:

> *We are totally responsible for ourselves. We cannot look for reasons outside of us. . . . We only grow when we assume responsibility for our own joy and happiness. These cannot be generated from outside of us. Lasting happiness and peace come from within.*[69]

More than three hundred thousand people participated in Werner Erhard's widely known *est* (Erhard Seminars Training) program, one of the first and most successful self-motivational packages ever to appear.[70] The information society has given birth to specialists who compete to provide information on just about any phase of personal activity. Myriad courses, seminars, and workshops are available for members of every segment of the population that wants to pursue excellence.

A central thrust of many of these offerings is the idea that you and I are scarcely tapping our capabilities — that we can excel and be even more successful by taking more personal responsibility for our life performances. There is scarcely a limit to human potential.

Religion has much to say about the unrealized capabilities of individuals. In its historical form, Christianity asserts that people made in the image of God have incredible potential. In right relationship with God, that potential can be realized to its fullest. Consequently, the much-publicized call for repentance and change is also a call to experience optimum living, whereby one's potential can be fully realized. But that's not all. When people reach their own personal limits, says the religious tradition, additional resources are also available.

As a sociologist, it seems to me that such a human potential-plus product has the potential itself to be a formidable market entry. A religion that can legitimately — and therefore with conviction — speak of the good news of the potential of individuals will find an audience. An emphasis upon the numinous coupled with a healthful view of self is two-thirds of religion's "Great Possibility."

SOCIETY   One hardly needs to be reminded that relationships remain supremely important in the modern age. The American trend experts Naisbitt[71] and Toffler[72] observe that in the United States people are showing a renewed interest in identification characteristics, such as region, ethnicity, and religion. A number of commentators have noted the trend towards organizational decentralization.

Consistent with such observations is the strong tendency of people in Canada to retain the religious affiliations of their parents and to place a high value on being Canadian. Both patterns are strong, for adults and young people. As we have seen, there is no indication that the pattern will change in the foreseeable future.

But the surveys say more. Nothing is of greater importance to Canadians than relationships. Some 90% of the country's adults and young people report that they place paramount value on relationships and being loved. Intimacy, caring, community — these are traits of supreme significance as Canadians move into the twenty-first century.

Religion could not be much better equipped to respond to such a reality. Beyond God and the individual, religion is a social phenomenon. People share faith. They gather together. The Christian faith specifically, says Gregory Baum, "has always understood itself as a community" characterized by "fellowship, interdependence, mutuality, exchange, communication."[73] Gordon Turner writes that Christians "need the warmth of each others' faith, the compassion of each others' tears, and the vibrancy of each others' joy."[74]

Christianity is among the religions that further call people not only to love God and self but also to love their neighbours. In Turner's words, "A Christian faith which does not address injustice and inhumanity in its global village is not worthy of the name."[75] Don Posterski recently suggested to me that "while religion without conviction is innocuous, religion without compassion is terrifying." Christians are expected not only to find in their Creator their reason for being, but also to be right with self and others. As the Presbyterian college teacher Clarence McMullen puts it, the transcendent element "does not mean a withdrawal from the human world or from our individual humanity. It only puts them in perspective."[76] The God-self-others triangle is to be inseparable.

While community begins with people who share faith, it bursts through the boundaries of those who would keep religion for themselves and speaks to all of life. Social issues become personal issues, because they involve people. A religion like this is not the slightest bit intimidated by culture. Rather, it studies and assesses culture and extends applause or criticism as warranted. At its best, in Berger's words, religion "permits a confrontation with the age in which one lives in a perspective that transcends the age and thus puts it in proportion."[77]

THE NECESSITY OF RECONNECTION

In Canada and elsewhere, there is a market for God, self, and society. Let me be clear: I am not suggesting that religion simply respond to these three consumer demands but that these three central emphases of religion are very much in demand in contemporary life.

Much of the problem to date is that religious groups have had considerable difficulty in putting the three emphases together. And when any one of the three dimensions is missing, the product loses much of its market value.

Many who subscribe to the idea of meeting the new with the new are strong at the self and society levels, primarily with respect to general social concern, but weak on the numinous dimension. For example, McMullen says of Presbyterians:

> *I am inclined to believe that in Sunday worship, the traditional rituals and the sermon dominate. . . . We attach a halo, a kind of charisma, to the Order of Service and attempt to confine the mystery of God and faith to intellect alone. The expressions of our spirituality are neat and tidy, structured and rational-logical. But they are only expressions.*[78]

His critique has obvious applicability beyond his own denomination. The alleged lack of experiential religion is among the sources of renewal and charismatic movements within the Roman Catholic, United, and Anglican Churches.

Another Presbyterian, Robert Bernhardt, warns about a danger churches face when speaking out on social justice matters:

> *Within the Christian community we must always be concerned that declarations on contemporary issues reflect the distinctiveness of our position. Our biblical perspective needs always to be clearly identified, lest we become mere parrots of unexamined popular sentiments.*[79]

In contrast to those who are strong on the self and social dimensions but weak on the numinous, people who would meet the new with the old tend to be strong on God but, beyond their own group levels, weak on the social dimension. As mentioned, they frequently have been reluctant to grapple with major social issues. Further, their emphasis upon human sin and human limitations has meant that they have not scored high in endorsing human potential. Clearly the themes of the numinous, self, and society have to be reconnected in Canada and elsewhere if religion is to have a significant impact upon the modern world. Mine is not an isolated viewpoint. *United Church Observer* writer Bob Bettson recently cited these thoughts of an Australian Methodist evangelist, Sir Alan Walker:

> *There are few greater needs in the church today than to find a synthesis between personal evangelism and social witness. Across the world and especially in America, there is a tragic division . . . [which] has inhibited the power of Christian witness.* [80]

A variety of Canadian religious leaders concur. Former moderator Clarke MacDonald maintains that the "polarization in the United Church is due to the failure on the part of those of us who have a high commitment to social action to be seen as evangelical, and the failure of evangelicals to realize the fullness of the Gospel." Faith and action, he says, are like two wings of a bird; the bird can't fly without both wings flapping. [81] Roman Catholic Bishop Remi De Roo points out that Jesus' incarnation shows "that God loves the whole of creation and is in the process of transforming the whole of creation. That's why religious values and Bible insights have to be brought into every dimension of life. We cannot split reality into these two dimensions." [82] Anglican delegates were reminded at their 1986 General Synod in Winnipeg, "If we tell of salvation and do not seek after justice, we will be dismissed as hollow." [83]

Brian Stiller is similarly calling Conservative Protestants to link social concern with concern for evangelism; retired Anglican Bishop Desmond Hunt writes of Stiller, "He's not just saying that we're interested in the social issues. He *is* interested in coming to grips with them.''[84] Salvation Army members worldwide have recently been reminded by their international leader, General Eva Burrows, in her *Manifesto for Global Mission*, that "social action and compassionate service must be seen to be based in Christian motivation and witness.''[85] Presumably all of these pleas, along with those of other leaders, include the clear recognition of the worth of the individual.

Despite the hopes and ideals of leaders, this is not to say that reconnection will be easy. The United Church's Rodney Booth points out that churches "committed to the prophetic tradition find themselves at times in the impossible position of trying to be both glue and yeast at the same time!'' One half of society demands the preservation of old mores, he says, while the other half calls on the church to take the lead in changing them.[86] Sean O'Sullivan maintains that there are two Roman Catholic Churches emerging, led by priests, theologians, and activists. One side, he says, will become a remnant of the traditional Church.

Its adherents will place extra emphasis on fidelity to the Pope and pronouncements from Rome. Those on the other side will view themselves as reform-minded Catholics although, in fact, they are little more than neo-Protestants.[87]

Nonetheless, the reconnection of God, self, and society needs to be made. If my analysis is accurate, then religious groups currently stressing these three dimensions will tend to be the denominations and individual congregations experiencing the best responses. Time-conscious, consumption-minded Canadians will be finding that they are encountering more than merely culture, that self does not have to be suppressed, that the desire for community and concern for others is being realized.

A religion like that will not get a positive response from everyone. But, if I read our culture accurately, it cannot help but gain a positive response from many.

The Church of St. John the Divine in Victoria seems to be among the churches that are trying to cover all three bases. Its rector, the Reverend Robert MacRae, explained in a recent interview that his church attempts to preach a Biblically sound gospel and is aware of the need to address questions of meaning and purpose. While encouraging people to look back at the roots of faith, MacRae says an effort is also made to cultivate a respect for new scholarship. The congregation has become known for its stand on social issues such as race relations and the nuclear question. Perhaps less well known is the fact that groups of such activist-minded people meet each week "to study the Scriptures on peace and justice, trying to establish Scriptural bases for action." MacRae stresses that "one part of the Christian pilgrimage is to live in community and, living in community, you cannot stay away from the issues that impact on people."[88]

There are others who are similarly aspiring to bring about the God-self-society connection. Much has been made of the Catholic Bishops' 1983 New Year's Day statement on the economy, *Ethical Reflections on the Economic Crisis*. What is less known is that, in the same report, the Bishops called for Christians to reread the Scriptures in order to hear God's call to justice. As Gregory Baum points out, "This step reveals that the commitment to social justice is a spiritual event . . . the Christian struggle for social justice is not 'activism'; it includes faith and the transformation of consciousness."[89] Elsewhere he sums up the balance succinctly: "The two orders, the natural and the supernatural, are seen to cohere in a single history."[90]

When religion claims to be more than culture, it has the possibility of having authority over culture, and becomes worth listening to. As Bertrand Russell once said in explaining why he, as a non-believer, would on occasion go to hear a particular preacher: "I don't believe in God, but he does." When religion doesn't stop with God but reaffirms the potential of individuals, and further is concerned about interpersonal ties both proximate and global, it has the possibility of having a measure of influence over how lives are lived.

Fragments are chosen over religion in part because religion has frequently been seen as primarily a human phenomenon, awkwardly intruding on life, and making it more difficult to live in the process. When religion fails to integrate adequately the critical meaning, self, and community dimensions of one's life experience, it should hardly be surprising that many people find it "irrelevant," that it just doesn't "seem to work." The inclination to adopt fragments may well be the product of a specialized world; but even individuals with the best intentions cannot apply a religion to life that leaves out God *or* self *or* others. They have no choice but to opt for fragments.

A religion that features the numinous, the value of self, and the importance of relationships, and which thereby enriches life, is far less likely to be preferred in small parts and small doses.

Robertson Davies suggests another possible root from which the word "religion" is derived—*religare*, meaning to reconnect.[91] If religion in Canada and elsewhere is to move beyond its current state of impoverishment, the numinous, self, and society must be linked in the manner historically insisted upon by religion.

The gods are currently fragmented. They lie dismantled, in pieces. But the recognition of religion's poverty can lead to the rediscovery of its potential. Reconnection is not beyond the realm of possibility.

APPENDIX

THE PROJECT CANADA NATIONAL ADULT SURVEYS

To date, three *PROJECT CANADA* adult surveys have been carried out, in 1975, 1980, and 1985.

DATA COLLECTION METHOD All three surveys — self-administered questionnaires — have been conducted by mail. Each of them has used eleven-page, three-hundred-plus variable questionnaires, constructed to yield extensive information pertaining to social issues, intergroup relations, and religion. The 1975 procedures of mailing the questionnaire with a front-page cover letter, sending a follow-up postcard, and mailing a second questionnaire have been followed, with minor variations, in all three surveys.

SAMPLING A randomly selected sample of about eleven hundred cases is sufficient to claim a confidence level of 95% and a confidence interval of four percentage points when attempting to generalize to the Canadian adult population. Gallup, for example, customarily draws a sample of just under eleven hundred people in making those confidence claims.

Size and *representativeness* are the two key criteria in being able to generalize with accuracy from a sample to a population; considerable care, therefore, has been taken to ensure that both standards have been met. First, concerning size, an interest in provincial comparisons resulted in 1,917 cases' being gathered in 1975; in 1980, the sample numbered 1,482; in 1985, 1,630.

Second, with respect to representativeness, the nation has been stratified by province (ten) and community size (>100,000, 99-10,000, <10,000), with the sample drawn proportionate to the national population. As resources have improved, the number of communities involved has increased from thirty in 1975 to forty-three in 1980 to one hundred and four in 1985. Participants have been randomly selected using telephone directories (as of 1985, 98.2% of Canadian households owned telephones). Discrepancies between the sample and population characteristics have been corrected by weighting (1975: province, community size, gender; 1980: those three variables as well as age; 1985: province, gender, age). Each of the three samples has been weighted down to about twelve hundred cases in order to minimize the use of large weight factors (i.e., three or more).

As can be seen in TABLE A1, the 1975, 1980, and 1985 *PROJECT CANADA* samples are highly representative of the Canadian population. Samples of this size and composition, as noted, should be accurate within about four percentage points on most questionnaire items, nineteen times in twenty similar surveys. Comparisons with similar Gallup poll items, for example, have consistently found this to be the case. (See, by way of illustration, findings concerning attitudes towards the courts, capital punishment, beliefs, and practices in the same survey years.)

THE PANEL COMPONENT   A major interest of the ongoing national surveys has been monitoring social change and stablility. Consequently, while the first, 1975 survey was a typical cross-sectional survey with 1,917 participants, the *PROJECT CAN80* sample of 1,482 people included 1,056 who had also been involved in 1975. Similarly, the 1,630 *PROJECT CAN85* cases included 566 people who had participated in *both* 1975 and 1980, along with 170 respondents who had filled out the 1980 questionnaire only; 894 were first-time cases.

RETURN RATES   I hold the somewhat unconventional view that return rate is not necessarily a critical issue if one can establish that a representative sample of sufficient size has been attained.

TABLE A1. **Population and Sample Characteristics: 1975, 1980, 1985**

		1975 Pop	1975 Samp	1980 Pop	1980 Samp	1985 Pop	1985 Samp
Community Size	100,000 +	55	55	51	52	52	54
	99,000 – 10,000	13	13	15	15	15	16
	<10,000	32	32	34	33	33	30
Gender	Male	49	50	49	51	49	50
	Female	51	50	51	49	51	50
Age	18-34	39	37	43	40	41	42
	35-54	35	36	31	31	32	33
	55 & over	26	27	26	29	27	25
Marital Status	Married	70	69	67	67	66	65
	Never Married	22	18	23	20	24	23
	Widowed	7	10	7	10	6	7
	Divorced	1	3	3	3	4	5
Income	under $5,000	13	16	5	6	—	—
	under $10,000	—	—	—	—	7	10
	$5,000-14,999	49	49	23	26	—	—
	$10,000-14,999	—	---	—	—	10	10
	$15,000-24,999	29	25	32	32	19	25
	$25,000 & over	9	10	40	36	—	—
	$25,000-39,999	—	—	—	—	30	30
	$40,000 & over	—	—	—	—	34	26
Education	Secondary-	65	61	59	52	54	50
	Less Post-Secondary +	35	39	41	48	46	50
Religion	Protestant	46	46	46	50	41	45
	Anglican	12	12	12	12	10	12
	Baptist	3	3	3	3	3	3
	Lutheran	3	3	3	3	3	3
	Pentecostal	1	1	1	1	1	1
	Presbyterian	4	4	4	5	3	3
	United Church	18	18	18	18	16	16
	Other/ Unknown	5	5	5	8	5	7
	Roman Catholic	44	42	44	36	47	42
	Jew	2	2	2	2	1	1
	None	5	8	5	10	7	11
	Other	3	2	3	2	4	1
Ethnicity	British	45	49	*	*	40	46
	French	28	20	*	*	27	29
	Other	27	31	*	*	33	25

POPULATION SOURCE: Statistics Canada. * = Not available.

With ample resources, including time and endurance, a return rate can readily be increased. However, it may be that one merely nails down the procrastinators in the population rather than gaining the participation of people who are different in some salient way from the early respondents demographically, socially, or psychologically.

Nevertheless, for a national survey, the PROJECT CANADA return rates have been relatively high—52% in 1975, 65% in 1980, and 60% in 1985. In the case of the panels, it appears that, in preparation for PROJECT CAN80, about 75% of the 1975 participants were located; in turn, 1,056 (73%) submitted questionnaires. In 1985, again about 75% of 1975-80 respondents were found, with 566 (71%) filling out questionnaires. Approximately 75% of the new sample additions in 1980 could be located for PROJECT CAN85; 170 (63%) responded. Return rates for people involved in the surveys for the first time have been very consistent—52% in 1975, 51% in 1980, and 54% in 1985.

Between 1975 and 1980, 45% of the original 1,917 participants were lost, with a further 25% disappearing from the panel between 1980 and 1985. In addition to geographical movement and non-response, death is a major attrition factor (as of 1975, proportionate to the Canadian population, one-quarter of the sample was 55 or older). Because of the high attrition and diminishing size of the panels, no claim is being made that they are sufficiently representative or large enough to permit accurate generalizations to the Canadian population. The panels are strictly used as unique and valuable resources, assisting in the exploration of changes within the population.

FUNDING The 1975 survey was carried out for a cost of about $14,000 and had four major sources: the United Church of Canada ($2,000), the Canadian Broadcasting Corporation ($3,000), the Solicitor General of Canada ($5,000), and the University of Lethbridge ($4,000). In 1980, the panel portion of the survey was made possible by grants from the Social Science and Humanities Research Council of Canada ($10,000) and the United Church of

TABLE A2. **Year of Origin and Return Rates:**
1975, 1980, and 1985 Surveys

| Survey Year | YEAR OF ORIGIN | | | Totals |
	1975	1980	1985	
1975	1917/3686 52%	—	—	1917/3686 52%
1980	1056/1438 73%	426/842 51%	—	1482/2280 65%
1985	566/793 71%	170/270 63%	894/1666 54%	1630/2729 60%
Retained	566/1917 30%	170/426 40%	—	736/2343 31%

Canada ($2,000). The second phase of *PROJECT CAN80*, which involved filling the core out into a full national sample, cost approximately $8,000 and was funded primarily by the University of Lethbridge. *PROJECT CAN85* was funded completely by the Social Sciences and Humanities Research Council of Canada ($45,000).

RELIGIOUS GROUP SAMPLE NUMBERS The number of cases for Canada's religious groups reported in Chapters 5, 8, and 9 are proportional to their share of the nation's population. As such, however, they clearly are not large enough to allow generalization to the groups with a high level of accuracy—especially in instances in which they fall below one hundred (e.g., the Conservative Protestants, Lutherans, Presbyterians). Where possible, 1985 and 1980 Lutheran and Presbyterian cases have been combined (the cases are different). Despite the relatively small size of these religious group samples, the findings at minimum suggest patterns and tendencies that need to be interpreted in the light of other available information. The survey findings offer something of "a start"; additional data should be pursued through individual group surveys. To my mind, an objective and fair response to what I report is not denunciations based on inadequate Ns, but rather a more elaborate examination that either corroborates or negates my findings.

THE THREE OTHER STUDIES

PROJECT TEEN CANADA   This national survey of teenagers aged 15 to 19 was carried out in collaboration with Toronto youth expert Don Posterski in the late spring and early fall of 1984. Some thirty-six hundred students in one hundred and seventy-five high schools (public, separate, and private) across Canada composed the sample which, even prior to minor weighting, was highly representative of the country's 15- to 19-year-olds still in school. The questionnaire was designed to provide a comprehensive profile of teenagers. For purposes of intergenerational comparison, it included considerable material from the *PROJECT CANADA* adult surveys. Self-administered, the questionnaires were filled out in classroom settings under the supervision of school guidance counsellors or similar designates. Complete methodological details can be found in Bibby and Posterski, 1985, *The Emerging Generation: An Inside Look at Canada's Teenagers* (Toronto: Irwin Publishing).

ANGLITRENDS   In order to produce an in-depth profile of Anglicans in the Toronto Diocese — Canada's largest — I conducted an extensive survey between July and October of 1985. The nineteen-page questionnaire comprised seventy sections and more than four hundred items and was distributed by mail. Because only one in four census Anglicans appear on Toronto Diocese parish lists, two samples were drawn, one comprising active Anglicans and the other inactives. The active sample, numbering 1,158, was drawn from parish lists; the inactive sample of 562 people comprised people on parish lists who viewed themselves as inactive (440), along with people whose names were submitted by parish priests (122). The sample of actives appears to be highly representative of active Anglicans. The inactive sample closely resembles inactive Anglicans in the diocese socially and demographically. While undoubtedly more sympathetic to the denomination by virtue of having completed the questionnaire, the sample inactives provide an interesting preliminary "peek" at the cultural Anglican. The summation report, *ANGLITRENDS*, provides full methodological information. (It is available from the Anglican Book Store, Toronto.)

THE CIRCULATION OF THE SAINTS   This project, carried out in collaboration with Merlin Brinkerhoff, has involved the ongoing examination of the kinds of people being added to the membership rolls over time at twenty randomly selected evangelical churches in Calgary. The first period probed was 1966-70 in 1971; in the fall of 1982, additions to the same churches for 1976-80 were examined. New members have been classified with the help of church personnel as evangelicals, offspring of members, and outsiders at the point of joining. The main purpose has been to explore the extent of evangelical church outreach. Further methodological specifics can be found in Bibby and Brinkerhoff, 1973 and 1983.

NOTES

INTRODUCTION

1 Berton, 1965.
2 Allport, 1950.
3 See, for example, Weber, 1963; Niebuhr, 1929.
4 Freud, 1962.
5 Durkheim, 1965.
6 Marx, 1970.
7 Thielicke, 1960.
8 Berton, 1965:13.
9 Beaucage and LaRoque, 1983:31. For expositions of some of the major features of Indian and Inuit religion in Canada before the days of European settlement, see, respectively, Jenness, 1976 and Balikci, 1976.
10 Davies, 1987:188.
11 Malcolm, 1985.
12 Garnsworthy, 1984.
13 Kristofferson, "Sunday Morning Coming Down," CBS, Inc.
14 See, for example, Crysdale, 1965; Johnson and Cornell, 1982; Driedger, Currie, and Linden, 1983.
15 See Bibby and Posterski, 1985.

CHAPTER 1

1 CCCB, *Lay People's Survey,* 1986:20.
2 Turner, 1982:69.

3 Grant, 1972:161.
4 Wolfe, *Canada Lutheran*, 1986:16-17; quote slightly abridged.
5 Grant, 1972.
6 Turner, 1982:67.
7 *United Church Observer*, January, 1987:9-12.
8 *Canadian Churchman*, April, 1987:10.
9 Byfield, *Edmonton Sun*, March 1, 1987.
10 CCCB, *The Meaning of Sunday*, 1986:3.
11 CCCB, *Twenty Years Later*, 1986:5,46,54.
12 CCCB, *Twenty Years Later*, 1986:5.
13 CCCB, *Lay People's Survey*, 1986:10-13.
14 Bibby, 1979:111.
15 Anne Roche Muggeridge, 1986.
16 Davies, 1987:188.
17 Newson in Baum and Greeley, 1978:57.
18 Rouleau, 1977:9.
19 Hoge, 1986:292.
20 Hryniuk and Yereniuk, 1983:150,152.
21 Schoenfeld, 1978:220-21.
22 Lazerwitz and Harrison, 1979.

CHAPTER 2

1 Quoted in *Canada Lutheran*, October 1986:13. For an exposition of how a religion-oriented program like *Man Alive* is unique among such offerings in Canada, see Bonisteel, 1980:17-23.
2 Canadian Press release, December 12, 1986.
3 *Canadian Baptist*, January, 1987:9.
4 Gallup, 1985.
5 Kelley, 1972.
6 Bibby, 1979.
7 Bibby and Brinkerhoff, 1973, 1974, 1983.

NOTES 283

8 Barker and Currie, 1985.
9 Ontario and Quebec Baptist Yearbook, 1903.
10 Bibby and Brinkerhoff, 1983.
11 Templeton, 1983:92-93.
12 Harpur, *Toronto Star*, February 8, 1987:A7.
13 cccb, *Lay People's Survey*, 1986:6.
14 Pettersson, 1986:392.
15 DeGroot, *Edmonton Journal*, December 20, 1986:D5.
16 *Maclean's*, January 5, 1987:60.
17 Templeton, 1983:93-94.
18 *Toronto Star*, April 6, 1987:A1,A4.
19 *Maclean's*, December 4, 1978:26.
20 *Maclean's*, December 4, 1978:26.
21 Hexham et al., 1985. For an excellent overview of new religious movements, see Hexham and Poewe, 1986.
22 Bird and Reimer, 1982.
23 Brinkerhoff and Mackie, 1986:161.
24 Stark and Bainbridge, 1985.
26 See Bibby and Weaver, 1985.
26 Personal visit in Vancouver, July 1983.
27 Ferguson, 1980.
28 MacLaine, 1983 and 1985.
29 Burrows, 1986.
30 Luckmann, 1967.
31 Sinclair-Faulkner, 1977:401.
32 For detailed expositions of these and other studies, see Bibby, 1983c.
33 Cottrell, 1980.
34 Cottrell, 1980:18.
35 For details, see Bibby, 1983c.
36 Stark and Bainbridge, 1985:3.
37 See, for example, Berger, 1963.
38 Comte, 1966.
39 Freud, 1962.
40 Bibby and Weaver, 1985.

Chapter 3

1 See, for example, Lutherans in *Canada Lutheran*, November, 1986:27.
2 Bibby, 1979.
3 Westhues, 1976b:206.
4 Bibby and Posterski, 1985:124.
5 A remark of Archbishop Garnsworthy to priests gathered in Toronto for the release of the study *Anglitrends*, April 1986.
6 Westhues, 1978:246.
7 Bibby, 1979:111.
8 Orr, 1936:114.
9 Schoenfeld, 1986:8.
10 Schoenfeld, 1986:9-10.
11 Sklare, 1971.
12 Berton, 1982:47.
13 See Bibby, 1983b.
14 Tarr, 1986.
15 Cited in Walsh, 1956:23.
16 Cited in Beaucage and LaRoque, 1983:32.
17 *United Church Observer*, October 1986.
18 *Anglican Churchman*, April 1987:4.
19 Vatican, *Attitudes Toward Other Religions*, 1984:13.
20 Cited in *Canadian Baptist*, September 1986:42.
21 Canadian Institute of Public Opinion, November 12, 1984.
22 Canadian Press release, October 1984.
23 Camp, fund-raising letter in support of the Canadian Civil Liberties Association, 1985:1.
24 Camp, 1985:1.
25 Stiller, 1985:5.
26 Canadian Institute of Public Opinion, February 21, 1979.
27 Hiller, 1978:185.
28 Garnsworthy, 1986.
29 Fallding, 1978:148.
30 Boillat, *Canadian Baptist*, October 1986:57.
31 Cited in Orr, 1936:39.

CHAPTER 4

1 See, for example, Robinson, 1963; Altizer, 1966; Cox, 1965.
2 Canadian Institute of Public Opinion, 1949, 1975, 1985.
3 *Weekend Magazine*, December 1977.
4 Davies, 1987:190.
5 *United Church Observer*, August 1986:2; see also the *Observer* issues of October 1986:5 and March 1987:2.
6 Canadian Institute of Public Opinion, 1960, 1969, 1976.
7 Jenness, 1976:78.
8 Canadian Institute of Public Opinion, November 4, 1981.
9 Canadian Institute of Public Opinion, January, 1960.
10 See, for example, Glock and Stark, 1965:151-68; Hay and Morisy, 1978 and 1985.
11 Bibby and Posterski, 1985:116.
12 Currie, King, and McCombs, 1982:22.
13 Glock and Stark, 1965.
14 Gordon, *Toronto Star*, February 8, 1987:B7.
15 Wilson, 1982:172.
16 Bibby, 1986b.
17 Rennie in *Faith Today*, July-August, 1986:37.
18 Grant, 1972.
19 Naisbitt, 1984:260.
20 Huxley, 1932:52.
21 Currie, 1976.

CHAPTER 5

1 See, for example, *United Church Observer*, July 1982, versus the issue of June 1986.
2 Hiller, 1976:381.
3 Bibby and Posterski, 1985:169.
4 Orr, 1936:20, 40, 109, 114.
5 For an example of the rationale for using age as an indicator of era, see Stark, 1973.

6 Fulford, 1987:12.
7 Freud, 1962.
8 Davies, 1987:188.

CHAPTER 6

1 Walker, 1986:202.
2 CCCB, *Twenty Years Later*, 1986:42.
3 See Westhues, 1976.
4 Westhues, 1978:255.
5 Westhues, 1978:253.
6 *United Church Observer*, June 1985:28.
7 *United Church Observer*, March 1985:24.
8 Cited in *United Church Observer*, March 1985:28.
9 Peake, 1983:55; regarding the background of Anglican leaders, see Porter, 1965: 515, and Nock, 1979.
10 Hiller, 1978:191.
11 Stiller, 1985.
12 Schoenfeld, 1978.
13 See, for example, Glock, 1974; Hadden, 1969.
14 O'Sullivan, 1986:190.
15 Fallding, 1978:153.
16 Cited in *United Church Observer*, September 1986:10.
17 CCCB, *Lay People's Survey*, 1986.
18 See, for example, Glock and Stark, 1965:123-50; Blizzard, 1957 and 1985.
19 *Canada Lutheran*, November, 1986:24.
20 Interview on *Cross Country Checkup*, Easter 1985.
21 For an analysis of these patterns among Calgary Conservative Protestants, see Bibby and Brinkerhoff, 1983.
22 Milner and Milner, 1976:163, 171.
23 Hughes, 1976:189.
24 Milner and Milner, 1976:166.
25 Cited in Betcherman, 1975:92.

26 Berton, 1976:150.
27 Penton, 1976:95-97.
28 Mol, 1985:91.
29 Grant, 1972:20.
30 Grant, 1972:20.
31 Penton, 1976:85.
32 Penton, 1976:5-6.
33 Shupe and Bromley, 1979.
34 Hexham, personal conversation, April 1987.
35 Naisbitt, 1984.
36 Fallding, 1978:154.
37 Schoenfeld, 1978:217.
38 Donald G. Bastian, personal observation, February 1987.
39 Arnold, 1983:106.
40 McCullum, *United Church Observer*, October 1986:9-10.
41 Robert Smith, *United Church Observer*, September 1986:34.
42 Coffin, *Canadian Baptist*, 1987:10.
43 Stiller, 1986.
44 See, for example, *Equality for All*, 1986; *Uncharted Waters*, 1986; *Child Care*, 1986.
45 *ChristianWeek*, April 7, 1987:1.
46 *Canadian Churchman*, February 1987:3.
47 *Anglican Renewal Ministries*, 1987.
48 CCCB, "Charismatic Renewal," 1975.
49 *United Church Observer*, January 1987.
50 *United Church Observer*, March 1987:5.
51 *Alberta Report*, April 7, 1986:46.
52 *United Church Observer*, September 1986:33.
53 *United Church Observer*, January 1987.
54 *United Church Observer*, February 1987:3.
55 See, for example, Grant, 1972:192ff, and Hiller, 1976:373ff.
56 Stark and Bainbridge, 1985.
57 *Canadian Baptist*, February 1986:9.
58 *Canadian Baptist*, March 1986:10.
59 *Presbyterian Record*, July-August 1986:21-22.
60 Turner, 1982:69-70.

CHAPTER 7

1 A personal experience related to the author by Dr. Samuel Southard.
2 Incidents related to the author.
3 Durkheim, 1964.
4 Fallding, 1978:151.
5 Fallding, 1978:151.
6 Berger, 1963:106.
7 See Bibby, 1983c.
8 Durkheim, 1964.
9 Marx, 1970:83.
10 Cited in Giroux, 1978:19.
11 Giroux, 1978:220-221.
12 Falardeau, 1976:111.
13 Chrétien, 1985:3-4.
14 Rouleau, 1977:10.
15 Bibby, 1986c.
16 Durkheim, 1965: 431.
17 Luckmann, 1967:103.
18 Hexham et al., 1985.
19 Wilson, 1976:80.
20 Mann, 1962:138ff.

CHAPTER 8

1 CCCB, *Twenty Years Later*, 1986:51.
2 Associated Press release, March 10, 1987.
3 EFC brief, *Equality for All*, 1986:8-9.
4 *Cross Country Checkup*, Easter 1985.
5 Bibby, 1986b.
6 Associated Press release, March 10, 1987.
7 Vatican, *Educational Guidance in Human Love*, 1983:30.
8 Vatican, *Educational Guidance in Human Love*, 1983:32.
9 *United Church Observer*, January 1986:18.

10 See the *Toronto Star*, July 26, 1986, and *Presbyterian Record*, September 1986:4ff.

11 *United Church Observer*, January 1986:26.

12 Bibby, 1986b:86.

13 Canadian Press release, March 4, 1987.

14 DeGroot, *Edmonton Journal*, March 22, 1987:A3. *United Church Observer*, March, 1987:6.

15 Bibby, 1986b:31.

16 EFC brief, *Uncharted Waters*, 1986:6.

17 Cited in *Faith Today*, December-January 1986:27.

18 CCCB, *Ethical Reflections*, 1983:2.

19 *United Church Observer*, February 6, 1985:20.

20 Wilson, 1982:47.

21 Canadian Press release, March 12, 1987.

22 Harpur, 1986:30.

23 Naisbitt, 1984.

24 Hordern, 1966:46.

25 Robert Smith, *United Church Observer*, September 1986:34.

26 Wilson, 1982.

27 Rokeach, 1973.

28 Canadian Institute of Public Opinion, December 1, 1982.

29 Bibby and Posterski, 1985:21.

30 Berger, 1961.

31 Berger, 1986:44. For a statement of secular humanism in perhaps its extreme form, see "Humanist Manifesto II" in *The Humanist*, September-October 1973:4-9.

32 Rouleau, 1977:11.

33 Chrétien, 1985:37.

34 Bibby and Posterski, 1985:51ff.

CHAPTER 9

1 Some of the material in this chapter is based on Bibby, 1986a.

2 Kirkpatrick, 1949.

3 Stark and Glock, 1968.

4 Rokeach, 1969.

5 Rushby and Thrush, 1973.
6 Nelson and Dynes, 1976.
7 Gorsuch and Aleshire, 1974.
8 Malcolm, 1985:56.
9 Cited in Malcolm, 1985:58.
10 Bibby, 1987.
11 Bibby, 1987:158.
12 Baum, 1979:203-204.
13 *Mennonite Reporter*, February 16, 1987:1.
14 *Calvinist Contact*, April 3, 1987:1.
15 Galatians 3.28, Revised Standard Version.
16 See Canadian Institute of Public Opinion release of June 2, 1983.
17 Hiller, 1976:368.
18 *Prairie Messenger*, April 6, 1987:6.
19 Douglas, 1987:136.
20 Crysdale, 1976.
21 CCCB, *Twenty Years Later*, 1986:61.
22 *Canadian Churchman*, March 1987:9.
23 Sjoberg, *Canada Lutheran*, January 1986:15.
24 Baum, 1984.
25 Bibby and Posterski, 1985:120.
26 For a thorough review of studies, see Bibby and McCormick, 1984.
27 Bibby and McCormick, 1984.
28 Redekop, *ChristianWeek*, April 7, 1987:5.
29 *United Church Observer*, January 1985:11.
30 *Toronto Star*, April 12, 1987:A11.
31 *Canadian Churchman*, April 1987:1.
32 *United Church Observer*, January 1985; *Western Catholic Reporter*, March 16, 1987; *Canadian Churchman*, April 1987.
33 *Faith Today*, July-August 1986:32,35.
34 *Faith Today*, March-April 1987. A readership poll of the magazine involving 300 Conservative Protestants and conducted in late 1986-early 1987 found 76% in favour of reinstatement. Those favouring ranged from 92% for Alliance members through 88% for Pentecostals, to 78% for Baptists.

35 Bibby and Posterski, 1985:150.
36 CCCB, *Challenge of Moral Living*, 1986:19.
37 Some of the material here is based on Bibby, 1986a.
38 Rokeach, 1965.
39 See, for example, Lee and Clyde, 1974.
40 See, for example, Boisen, 1939; Holt, 1940; Frazier, 1964; White, 1966 re: Canadian rural-urban migrants; and Hill, 1971.
41 Connecticut: Lindenthal et al., 1970; California, Stark, 1971.
42 St. George and McNamara, 1984:361.
43 W.I. Thomas, 1928.
44 Canadian Institute of Public Opinion, January 29, 1972.
45 Canadian Institute of Public Opinion, November 1963.
46 Canadian Institute of Public Opinion, January 29, 1972.
47 *Maclean's*, January 6, 1986:15.
48 St. George and McNamara, 1984:361-62.
49 DeGroot, *Calvinist Contact*, April 3, 1987:1.
50 Cited in *United Church Observer*, September 1986:33.
51 Bibby and Posterski, 1985:32.
52 Baum, 1984:93.

CHAPTER 10

1 See Westhues, 1978; Fallding, 1978; Hiller, 1978; Schoenfeld, 1978. For an excellent examination of national variations in secularization in the western world, especially its political aspects, see Martin, 1978.
2 The American data here are drawn from Gallup, 1985.
3 Cited in McGuire, 1987:92,94.
4 Gallup, 1985:12.
5 Gallup, 1985:10.
6 Gallup, 1985:12.
7 Gallup, 1985.
8 Bellah et al., 1985:225.
9 Westhues, 1978:258.
10 Berton, 1982:36.

11 Berton, 1982:58.
12 Cited in Fallding, 1978:145.
13 See, for example, Wilson, 1970; Hiller, 1978; Stark and Bainbridge, 1985.
14 Fallding, 1978:146.
15 Wills, 1978.
16 Sigelman, 1977:290.
17 Martin, 1967:55.
18 Hay and Morisy, 1978 and 1985.
19 See, for example, Towler, 1985.
20 Hay and Morisy, 1978 and 1985.
21 Martin, 1967:55.
22 Martin, 1967:76.
23 See Gallup, 1986:2 and Sigelman, 1977:290.
24 Cited in Martin, 1967:53.
25 Martin, 1967:76.
26 Barrett, 1982:700; Martin, 1967:19.
27 Martin, 1967:44.
28 Barrett, 1982:700; Martin, 1967:40.
29 Reeves, 1986:194.
30 Moss, 1986:22.
31 Walker, 1986:202.
32 Walker, 1959:418.
33 Barrett, 1982:702-5.
34 See, for example, Martin, 1967:51.
35 Reeves, 1986:191.
36 Bailey, 1986.
37 Some of these ideas have appeared in Brinkerhoff and Bibby, 1985.
38 See, for example, Durkheim, 1964; Weber, 1958; Redfield, 1941.
39 Brinkerhoff and Bibby, 1985.
40 Simons, 1982.
41 Barrett, 1982.
42 Bruneau, 1974:62-63.
43 Cox, 1984:136.
44 Barrett, 1982.

CONCLUSION

1 For excellent review of literary and social science futurists, see McHale, 1969:241-64, and Toffler, 1983: 196-98. For a recent set of prognoses, see Long, 1987: 36-40, 94-100.
2 Gates in Long, 1987:38.
3 See Long, 1987.
4 Gates in Long, 1987:38.
5 Dickey, *Presbyterian Record*, January 1986:4.
6 CCCB, *Twenty Years Later*, 1985:28.
7 In Long, 1987:98.
8 In Long, 1987:98.
9 Freud, 1962.
10 In Long, 1987:98.
11 O'Sullivan, 1986:40.
12 Hunsberger and Brown, 1984:239.
13 Bibby, 1983a.
14 Fish in *Presbyterian Record*, January 1987:8.
15 Demerath and Hammond, 1969.
16 Cox in Long, 1987:98.
17 Vatican, *Attitudes Toward Other Religions*, 1984:8.
18 Cited in *Presbyterian Record*, January 1987:41.
19 Roberts, 1969:80.
20 *United Church Observer*, December 1985.
21 Milner, *United Church Observer*, December 1985:11.
22 Karpetz, *Canadian Baptist*, May 1986:4.
23 Naisbitt, 1984:19.
24 Byrne in Long, 1987:94.
25 Hosea 13:5-6,9, Phillips translation.
26 Isaiah 29:13-14, Phillips translation.
27 Fulford, 1987:10.
28 Leddy, *Western Catholic Reporter*, 1987:23.
29 See, for example, Wilson, 1966, 1976, 1982.
30 Wilson, 1982:149.
31 Wilson, 1982:46.
32 Wilson, 1982:46.
33 Wilson, 1982:88.

34 See, for example, Mauss, 1975.
35 Wilson, 1982:88.
36 Bibby and Posterski, 1985:29.
37 See, for example, Viorst, 1986:342-64.
38 O'Sullivan, 1986:235.
39 Grant, 1972:224-25.
40 Grant, 1972:225.
41 Grant, 1972:225.
42 For expositions of this argument, see, for example, Parsons, 1964; Greeley, 1972; Grant, 1976:218ff.
43 Rouleau, 1977:20-21.
44 *Edmonton Journal*, March 2, 1987:A3.
45 Berton, 1965:54.
46 Berger, 1969:27.
47 Durkheim, 1965:430.
48 Ratzinger, *Catholic New Times*, May 4, 1986:1.
49 Wilson, 1982:167.
50 CCCB, *Charismatic Renewal*, 1975:11.
51 Hoge, 1986:290.
52 Berger, 1969:26.
53 Byfield, *Edmonton Sun*, March 1, 1987.
54 Mead, 1934.
55 Wilson, 1982:49.
56 In Slater, 1977:19.
57 Peccei, 1981:25.
58 Gates in Long, 1987:38.
59 Orwell, 1948:273.
60 Huxley, 1932:69.
61 Templeton, 1983:67.
62 See, for example, Glock and Stark, 1965; Yinger, 1970; McGuire, 1987.
63 Cited in Bibby, 1986a:386.
64 Davies, 1987:187.
65 Stark and Bainbridge, 1985.
66 CCCB, *Challenge of Moral Living*, 1986:7.
67 Lasch, 1979:31; see also Lasch, 1984.

68 Naisbitt, 1984:36.
69 Buscaglia, 1984:181.
70 Burrows, 1986:19.
71 Naisbitt, 1984:259.
72 Toffler, 1983:161.
73 Baum, 1978:vii.
74 Turner, 1982:67.
75 Turner, 1982:67.
76 McMullen, *Presbyterian Record*, February 1987:23.
77 Berger, 1969:21.
78 McMullen, *Presbyterian Record*, February 1987:23.
79 Bernhardt, *Calvinist Contact*, March 20, 1987:7.
80 Walker, *United Church Observer*, September 1986:32.
81 MacDonald, *United Church Observer*, September 1986:33.
82 Interview with Joanne Helmer, *Lethbridge Herald*, November 18, 1985:A6.
83 *Canadian Churchman*, August-September 1986:1.
84 Hunt, *ChristianWeek*, April 7, 1987:11.
85 Burrows, *The War Cry*, March 14, 1987.
86 Booth in *Canada Lutheran*, July-August 1986:22-23.
87 O'Sullivan, 1986:210-211.
88 Interview on CBC's *Cross Country Checkup*, Easter 1985.
89 Baum, 1984:30-31.
90 Baum, 1984:60-61.
91 Robertson Davies, 1987:187.

BIBLIOGRAPHY

Abella, Irving, and Harold Troper. 1983. *None Is Too Many*. Toronto: Lester and Orpen Dennys.

Allport, Gordon. 1950. *The Individual and His Religion*. New York: Macmillan.

Altizer, Thomas. 1966. *The Gospel of Christian Atheism*. Philadelphia: Westminster Press.

Anglican Renewal Ministries. 1987. "Renewal Leaders Conferences, June, 1987" (Brochure). Nepean, Ontario: ARM.

Arnold, Abraham. 1983. "New Jerusalem on the Prairies: Welcoming the Jews." In Benjamin G. Smillie (ed.), *Visions of the New Jerusalem*. Edmonton: NeWest Press, 91-107.

Bailey, Edward. 1986. "The Religion of the People." In Tony Moss (ed.), *In Search of Christianity*. London: Firethorn Press, 178-88.

Balikci, Asen. 1976. "The Netsilik Eskimo." In Stewart Crysdale and Les Wheatcroft (eds.), *Religion in Canadian Society*. Toronto: Macmillan, 86-99.

Baptist Convention of Ontario and Quebec. 1903. "Report of the Committee on the State of Religion." *1903 Baptist Yearbook for Ontario, Quebec, Manitoba, and The North-West Territories and B.C.* Orillia, Ontario: The Baptist Convention of Ontario and Quebec.

Barker, Irwin R., and Raymond F. Currie. 1985. "Do Converts Always Make the Most Committed Christians?" *Journal for the Scientific Study of Religion* 24:305-13.

Barrett, David B. (ed.). 1982. *World Christian Encyclopedia*. Nairobi: Oxford University Press.

Baum, Gregory. 1979. *The Social Imperative*. New York: Paulist Press.

Baum, Gregory, and Duncan Cameron. 1984. *Ethics and Economics: Canada's Catholic Bishops on the Economic Crisis*. Toronto: James Lorimer.

Baum, Gregory, and Andrew Greeley (eds.). 1978. *Communication in the Church*. New York: Seabury Press.

Beaucage, Marjorie, and Emma LaRoque. 1983. "Two Faces of the New Jerusalem: Indian-Metis Reaction to the Missionary." In Benjamin G. Smillie (ed.), *Visions of the New Jerusalem.* Edmonton: NeWest Press, 27-38.

Bell, Daniel. 1977. "The Return of the Sacred: The Argument on the Future of Religion." *British Journal of Sociology* 28:419-49.

Bellah, Robert. 1967. "Civil Religion in America." *Daedalus* 96:1-21.

Bellah, Robert, Richard Madsen, William M. Sullivan, Ann Swidler, and Steven M. Tipton. 1985. *Habits of the Heart.* New York: Harper and Row.

Berger, Peter L. 1961. *The Noise of Solemn Assemblies.* New York: Doubleday.

1963a.   Invitation to Sociology. New York: Doubleday

1963b.   "A Market Model for the Analysis of Ecumenicity." *Social Research* 30:77-93.

1967.   *The Sacred Canopy: Elements of a Sociological Theory of Religion.* New York: Doubleday.

1969.   *A Rumour of Angels: Modern Society and the Rediscovery of the Supernatural.* New York: Doubleday.

1979.   *The Heretical Imperative: Contemporary Possibilities of Religious Affirmation.* New York: Doubleday.

1986.   "Religion in Post-Protestant America," *Commentary* 81: 41-46.

Berger, Peter L., and Richard John Neuhaus (eds.). 1976.   *Against the World for the World: The Hartford Appeal and the Future of American Religion.* New York: Seabury Press.

Berton, Pierre. 1965.   *The Comfortable Pew.* Toronto: McClelland and Stewart.

1976.   *My Country.* Toronto: McClelland and Stewart.

1982.   *Why We Act Like Canadians.* Toronto: McClelland and Stewart.

Betcherman, Lita-Rose. 1975.   *The Swastika and the Maple Leaf: Fascist Movements in Canada in the Thirties.* Toronto: Fitzhenry and Whiteside.

Beynon, Erdmann, D. 1938.   "The Voodoo Cult among Negro Migrants to Detroit." *American Journal of Sociology* 43:894-907.

Bibby, Reginald W. 1978.   "Why Conservative Churches Really Are Growing: Kelley Revisited." *Journal for the Scientific Study of Religion* 17:129-37.

1979.   "The State of Collective Religiosity in Canada: An Empirical Analysis." *The Canadian Review of Sociology and Anthropology* 16:105-16.

1983a.   "Religionless Christianity: A Profile of Religion in the Canadian 80s." *Social Indicators Research* 13:1-16.

1983b.   "The Moral Mosaic: Sexuality in the Canadian 80s." *Social Indicators Research* 13:171-84.

1983c. "Searching for Invisible Thread: Meaning Systems in an Industrialized Canada." *Journal for the Scientific Study of Religion* 22:101-19.

1985. "Religious Encasement in Canada: An Argument for Protestant and Catholic Entrenchment." *Social Compass* 32:287-304.

1986a. "Religion." In Robert Hagedorn (ed.), *Sociology* (3rd edition). Toronto: Holt, Rinehart and Winston, 381-415.

1986b. *Anglitrends: A Profile and Prognosis.* Toronto: Anglican Diocese of Toronto.

1986c. "Social and Lifestyle Trends in Canada." Presented at The International Conference on Dynamics of Social Change. Edmonton, July.

1987. "Bilingualism and Multiculturalism: A National Reading. In Leo Driedger (ed.), *Ethnic Canada: Identities and Inequalities.* Toronto: Copp Clark Pitman, 158-69.

Bibby, Reginald W., and Merlin B. Brinkerhoff. 1973. "The Circulation of the Saints: A Study of People Who Join Conservative Churches." *Journal for the Scientific Study of Religion* 12:273-83.

1974. "When Proselytizing Fails: An Organizational Analysis." *Sociological Analysis* 35:189-200.

1983. "Circulation of the Saints Revisited: A Longitudinal Look at Conservative Church Growth." *Journal for the Scientific Study of Religion* 22:253-62.

Bibby, Reginald W., and Armand L. Mauss. 1974. "Skidders and Their Servants: Functions of a Skid Road Rescue Mission." *Journal for the Scientific Study of Religion* 13:421-36.

Bibby, Reginald W., and Peter McCormick. 1984. "Religion and Party Preference in Canada: Toward an Overdue Demystification." Presented at the annual meeting of The American Sociological Association, San Antonio, August.

Bibby, Reginald W., and Donald C. Posterski. 1985. *The Emerging Generation: An Inside Look at Canada's Teenagers.* Toronto: Irwin.

Bibby, Reginald W., and Harold R. Weaver. 1983. "The Pendulum That Never Swung: A Rational Look at Irrationality." Presented at the annual meeting of The Pacific Sociological Association, San Jose, April.

1985. "Cult Consumption in Canada: A Further Critique of Stark and Bainbridge." *Sociological Analysis* 46:445-60.

Bird, Frederick, and William Reimer. 1982. "Participation Rates in New Religious Movements." *Journal for the Scientific Study of Religion* 21:1-14.

Blizzard, Samuel W. 1985. *Protestant Parish Minister: A Behavioral Science Interpretation.* Storrs, Connecticut: Society for the Scientific Study of Religion.

Boisen, Anton. 1939. "Economic Distress and Religious Experience." *Psychiatry,* May.

Bonisteel, Roy. 1980. *In Search of Man Alive.* Toronto: Totem Books.

Booth, Rodney. 1984. *The Winds of God.* Winfield, B.C.: Wood Lake Press.

Brinkerhoff, Merlin B., and Reginald W. Bibby. 1985. "Circulation of the Saints in South America." *Journal for the Scientific Study of Religion* 24:253-262.

Brinkerhoff, Merlin B., and Marlene M. Mackie. 1986. "The Applicability of Social Distance for Religious Research: An Exploration." *Review of Religious Research* 28:151-67.

Bruneau, Thomas C. 1974. *The Political Transformation of the Brazilian Catholic Church.* London: Cambridge University Press.

Burrows, Robert J.L. 1986. "Americans Get Religion in the New Age." *Christianity Today,* May 16, 1986:17-23.

Buscaglia, Leo F. 1984. *Loving Each Other: The Challenge of Human Relationships.* New York: Fawcett Columbine.

Canadian Conference of Catholic Bishops. 1983. *Charismatic Renewal.* Ottawa: CCCB.

———. 1983. *Ethical Reflections on Respect for Life.* Ottawa: CCCB.

———. 1985a. *An Appeal to Youth's Dynamism and Faith.* Ottawa: CCCB.

———. 1985b. *Twenty Years Later.* Ottawa: CCCB.

———. 1986a. *The Challenge of Moral Living.* Ottawa: CCCB.

———. 1986b. *The Meaning of Sunday in a Pluralistic Society.* Ottawa: CCCB.

———. 1986c. *First Compilation of Synod 87 Lay People's Survey.* Ottawa: CCCB.

Chalfant, Paul H., Robert E. Beckley, and C.E. Palmer. 1981. *Religion in Contemporary Society.* Palo Alto, Calif: Mayfield Publishing Company.

Chrétien, Jean. 1985. *Straight from the Heart.* Toronto: Key Porter Books.

Clark, S.D. 1948. *Church and Sect in Canada.* Toronto: University of Toronto Press.

Cogley, John. 1968. *Religion in a Secular Age.* New York: The New American Library.

Comte, Auguste. 1966. *System of Positive Polity.* New York: Burt Franklin Research and Source Works Series.

Cottrell, Melanie. 1980. "Invisible Religion and the Middle Class." Presented at the Third Consultation on Implicit Religion, Ilkley, England.

Cox, Harvey. 1965. *The Secular City.* New York: Macmillan.

———. 1984. *Religion in the Secular City.* New York: Simon and Schuster.

Crysdale, Stewart. 1961. *The Industrial Struggle and Protestant Ethics in Canada.* Toronto: Ryerson Press.

1965. *The Changing Church in Canada: Beliefs and Social Attitudes of United Church People.* Toronto: United Church of Canada.

Crysdale, Stewart, and Les Wheatcroft (eds.). 1976. *Religion in Canadian Society.* Toronto: Macmillan.

Currie, Raymond. 1976. "Belonging, Commitment, and Early Socialization in a Western City." In Stewart Crysdale and Les Wheatcroft (eds.), *Religion in Canadian Society.* Toronto: Macmillan.

Currie, Raymond, Leo. F. Klug, and Charles R. McCombs. 1982. "Intimacy and Saliency: Dimensions for Ordering Religious Experiences." *Review of Religious Research* 24:19-32.

Davies, Robertson. 1987. "Keeping Faith." *Saturday Night,* January: 187-92.

Davis, Kingsley. 1949. *Human Society.* New York: Macmillan.

Demerath, N.J. 1969. "Irreligion, A-Religion, and the Rise of the Religion-Less Church." *Sociological Analysis* 30:191-203.

Demerath, N.J., and Phillip E. Hammond. 1969. *Religion in Social Context.* New York: Random House.

Douglas, Tommy. 1987. "The Radical Gospel." *Saturday Night,* January: 136-38.

Driedger, Leo. 1974. "Doctrinal Belief: A Major Factor in the Differential Perception of Social Issues." *The Sociological Quarterly,* Winter: 66-80.

Driedger, Leo, Raymond Currie, and Rick Linden. 1983. "Dualistic and Wholistic Views of God and the World: Consequences for Social Action." *Review of Religious Research* 24:225-44.

Durkheim, Emile. 1964. *The Division of Labor in Society.* Glencoe: Free Press.

1965. *The Elementary Forms of the Religious Life.* New York: Free Press.

Dyer, Wayne W. 1978. *Pulling Your Own Strings.* New York: Avon Books.

Evangelical Fellowship of Canada. 1986a. Submission to the Minister of Justice Concerning *Equality for All.* Willowdale, Ontario: EFC.

1986b. *Child Care.* An EFC Reponse to The Special (Parliamentary) Committee on Child Care. Willowdale, Ontario. EFC.

1986c. *Uncharted Waters.* An Examination of The Federal Government's Plan to Include "Sexual Orientation" in The Human Rights Act of Canada. Willowdale, Ontario: EFC.

Falardeau, Jean-Charles. 1976. "The Seventeenth-Century Parish in French Canada." In Stewart Crysdale and Les Wheatcroft (eds.), *Religion in Canadian Society.* Toronto: Macmillan, 101-12.

Fallding, Harold. 1978. ''Mainline Protestantism in Canada and the United States of America: An Overview.'' *Canadian Journal of Sociology* 3:141-60.

Fensterheim, Herbert, and Jean Baer. 1975. *Don't Say Yes When You Want to Say No.* New York: Dell.

Ferguson, Marilyn. 1980. *The Aquarian Conspiracy.* Los Angeles: J.P. Tarcher.

Frazier, E. Franklin. 1964. *The Negro Church in America.* New York: Schocken Books.

Freud, Sigmund. 1962. *The Future of an Illusion.* New York: Doubleday.

Fulford, Robert. 1987. ''1887.'' *Saturday Night.* January:7-12.

Gallup, George, Jr.. 1985. *Religion in America, 50 years: 1935-1985.* May, Report No. 236. Princeton: The Gallup Report.

1986. *Emerging Trends.* October, Vol. 8, No. 8. Princeton: Princeton Research Center.

Garnsworthy, Lewis S. 1984. *The Archbishop's Charge to the 132nd Synod.* Toronto: Anglican Diocese.

1986. *The Archbishop's Charge to the 134th Synod.* Toronto: Anglican Diocese.

Geertz, Clifford. 1968. ''Religion as a Cultural System.'' In Donald Cutler (ed.), *The Religious Situation.* Boston: Beacon.

Glock, Charles Y. (ed.). 1974. *Religion in Sociological Perspective.* Belmont, Calif: Wadsworth.

Glock, Charles Y., and Rodney Stark. 1965. *Religion and Society in Tension.* Chicago: Rand McNally.

Gorsuch, Richard, and Daniel Aleshire. 1974. ''Christian Faith and Ethnic Prejudice: A Review and Interpretation of Research.'' *Journal for the Scientific Study of Religion* 13:281-307.

Grant, John Webster. 1972. *The Church in the Canadian Era.* Toronto: McGraw-Hill Ryerson.

1977. ''Religion and the Quest for National Identity.'' In Peter Slater (ed.), *Religion and Culture in Canada.* Toronto: Canadian Corporation for Studies in Religion: 7-21.

Greeley, Andrew. 1972. *The Denominational Society.* Glenview, Ill.: Scott Foresman.

Harpur, Tom. 1986. *For Christ's Sake.* Toronto: Oxford University Press.

Hay, David, and Ann Morisy. 1978. ''Reports of Ecstatic, Paranormal, or Religious Experiences in Great Britain and the United States: A Comparison of Trends. *Journal for the Scientific Study of Religion* 17:255-68.

1985. ''Secular Society, Religious Meanings: A Contemporary Paradox.'' *Review of Religious Research* 26:213-27.

Herberg, Will. 1960. *Protestant, Catholic, Jew.* (Revised edition). New York: Doubleday.

Hewitt, W.E. 1986. "Strategies for Social Change Employed by CEBs in the Archdiocese of Sao Paulo." *Journal for the Scientific Study of Religion* 25:16-30.

Hexham, Irving, and Karla Poewe. 1986. *Understanding Cults and New Religions.* Grand Rapids, Michigan: William Eerdmans.

Hexham, Irving, Raymond Currie, and Joan Townsend. 1985. "New Religious Movements." In *The Canadian Encyclopedia.* Edmonton: Hurtig.

Hiller, Harry H. 1976a. "The Sociology of Religion in the Canadian Context." In G.N. Ramu and Stuart D. Johnson (eds.), *Introduction to Canadian Society.* Toronto: Macmillan, 349-400.

——— 1976b. "Alberta and the Bible Belt Stereotype." In Stewart Crysdale and Les Wheatcroft (eds.), *Religion in Canadian Society.* Toronto: Macmillan, 372-83.

——— 1978. "Continentalism and the Third Force in Religion." *Canadian Journal of Sociology* 3:183-207.

Hobart, Charles. 1974. "Church Involvement and the Comfort Thesis in Alberta." *Journal for the Scientific Study of Religion* 13:463-70.

Hoge, Dean R. 1986. "Interpreting Change in American Catholicism: The River and the Floodgate." *Review of Religious Research* 27: 289-99.

Holt, John B. 1940. "Holiness Religion, Cultural Shock and Social Reorganization." *American Sociological Review* 5:740-47.

Hordern, William. 1966. *New Directions in Theology Today,* Volume 1, Introduction. Philadelphia: The Westminster Press.

Hryniuk, Stella, and Roman Yereniuk. 1983. "Building the New Jerusalem on the Prairies: The Ukrainian Experience." In Benjamin G. Smillie (ed.), *Visions of the New Jerusalem.* Edmonton: NeWest Press: 137-52.

Huel, Raymond. 1983. "Gestae Dei Per Francos: The French Catholic Experience in Western Canada." In Benjamin G. Smillie (ed.), *Visions of the New Jerusalem.* Edmonton: NeWest Press, 39-53.

Hughes, Everett. 1976. "Action Catholique and Nationalism: A Memorandum on the Church and Society in French Canada, 1942." In Stewart Crysdale and Les Wheatcroft (eds.), *Religion in Canadian Society.* Toronto: Macmillan, 173-90.

Hunsberger, Bruce. 1980. "A Reexamination of the Antecedents of Apostasy." *Review of Religious Research* 21:158-70.

——— 1983. "Apostasy: A Social Learning Perspective." *Review of Religious Research* 25:21-38.

——— 1984. "Religious Socialization, Apostasy, and the Impact of Family Background." *Journal for the Scientific Study of Religion* 23:239-51.

1985. "Parent-University Student Agreement on Religious and Non-religious Issues." *Journal for the Scientific Study of Religion* 24: 314-20.

Huxley, Aldous. 1932. *Brave New World.* New York: Harper and Row.

Jenness, Diamond. 1976. "Canadian Indian Religion." In Stewart Crysdale and Les Wheatcroft (eds.), *Religion in Canadian Society.* Toronto: Macmillan, 71-78.

Johnson, Douglas W., and George W. Cornell. 1972. *Punctured Preconceptions: What North American Christians Think about the Church.* New York: Friendship Press.

Kelley, Dean. 1972. *Why Conservative Churches Are Growing.* New York: Harper and Row.

Kilbourn, William (ed.). 1966. *The Restless Church: A Response to the Comfortable Pew.* Toronto: McClelland and Stewart.

Kirkpatrick, Clifford. 1949. "Religion and Humanitarianism: A Study of Institutional Implications." *Psychological Monographs* 63(9).

Lasch, Christopher. 1979. *The Culture of Narcissism.* New York: Warner Books.

1984. *The Minimal Self: Psychic Survival in Troubled Times.* New York: W.W. Norton.

Lazerwitz, Bernard, and Michael Harrison. 1979. "American Jewish Denominations: A Sociological and Religious Profile." *American Sociological Review* 44.

Lee, Gary, and Robert Clyde. 1974. "Religion, Socioeconomic Status, and Anomie." *Journal for the Scientific Study of Religion* 13:35-47.

Lenski, Gerhard. 1961. *The Religious Factor.* New York: Doubleday.

Lindenthal, Jacob, Jerome Myers, Max Pepper, and Maxine Stern. 1970. "Mental Status and Religious Behavior." *Journal for the Scientific Study of Religion* 9:143-49.

Long, Marion. 1987. "The Seers' Catalog." *Omni*, January:36ff.

Luckmann, Thomas. 1967. *The Invisible Religion.* New York: Macmillan.

MacLaine, Shirley. 1983. *Out on a Limb.* New York: Bantam Books.
1985. *Dancing in the Light.* New York: Bantam Books.

Malcolm, Andrew H. 1985. *The Canadians.* New York: Times Books.

Mann, W.E. 1962. *Sect, Cult, and Church in Alberta.* Toronto: University of Toronto Press.

Martin, David. 1967. *A Sociology of English Religion.* London: SCM Press.
1978. *A General Theory of Secularization.* London: Harper Row.

Marx, Karl. 1970. *Critique of Hegel's Philosophy of Right* (Annette Jolin and Joseph O'Malley (trans.)). Cambridge, Mass.: Harvard University Press.

Mauss, Armand L. 1969. "Dimensions of Religious Defection." *Review of Religious Research* 10:128-35.

1975. *Social Problems as Social Movements.* Philadelphia: Lippincott.

McGuire, Meredith B. 1987. *Religion: The Social Context.* Belmont, Calif: Wadsworth.

McHale, John. 1969. *The Future of the Future.* New York: George Braziller.

McLeod, Henry. 1982. "A Comparison of Trends in Protestant Church Membership in Canada:. 1946-1979." *Yearbook of American and Canadian Churches.* New York: Abingdon.

Mead, George Herbert. 1934. *Mind, Self, and Society.* Chicago: University of Chicago Press.

Milner, Sheilagh H., and Henry Milner. 1976. "Authoritarianism and Sellout in Quebec in the 1930s." In Stewart Crysdale and Les Wheatcroft (eds.), *Religion in Canadian Society.* Toronto: Macmillan, 161-72.

Milton, Ralph. 1981. *This United Church of Ours.* Winfield, B.C.: Wood Lake Press.

Mitchell, Robert. 1976. "Polity, Church Attractiveness, and Ministers' Careers." *Journal for the Scientific Study of Religion* 5:241-58.

Mol, Hans. 1976. "Major Correlates of Churchgoing in Canada." In Stewart Crysdale and Les Wheatcroft (eds.), *Religion in Canadian Society.* Toronto: Macmillan.

1985. *Faith and Fragility: Religion and Identity in Canada.* Burlington, Ontario: Trinity Press.

Moss, Tony. 1986. "Christianity in Crisis." In Tony Moss (ed.), *In Search of Christianity.* London: Firethorn Press, 13-22.

Muggeridge, Anne Roche. 1986 *The Desolate City: The Catholic Church in Ruins.* Toronto: McClelland and Stewart.

Naisbitt, John. 1984. *Megatrends.* New York: Warner Books.

Nelson, L.D., and Russell Dynes. 1976. "The Impact of Devotionalism and Attendance on Ordinary and Emergency Helping Behavior." *Journal for the Scientific Study of Religion* 15:47-59.

Niebuhr, H. Richard. 1929. *The Social Sources of Denominationalism.* New York: Holt and Company.

Nock, David. 1979. "Anglican Bishops and Indigenity: John Porter Revisited." *Studies in Religion* 8:47-55.

O'Sullivan, Sean. 1986. *Both My Houses: From Politics to Priesthood.* Toronto: Key Porter Books.

Orr, J. Edwin. 1936. *Times of Refreshing: 10,000 Miles of Miracle through Canada.* Toronto: Evangelical Publishers.

Orwell, George. 1948. *Nineteen Eighty-Four.* London: Secker and Warburg.

Parsons, Talcott, 1964. "Christianity and Modern Industrial Society," In Louis Schneider (ed.), *Religion, Culture, and Society.* New York: John Wiley.

Peake, Frank. 1983. "Anglicanism on the Prairies." In Benjamin G. Smillie (ed.), *Visions of the New Jerusalem.* Edmonton: NeWest Press, 55-68.

Peccei, Aurelio. 1981. *One Hundred Pages for the Future: Reflections of the President of The Club of Rome.* New York: Pergamon Press.

Penton, M. James. 1976. *Jehovah's Witnesses in Canada.* Toronto: Macmillan.

Pettersson, Thorleif. 1986. "The Audiences' Uses and Gratifications of TV Worship Services." *Journal for the Scientific Study of Religion* 25:391-409.

Porter, John. 1965. *The Vertical Mosaic: An Analysis of Social Class and Power in Canada.* Toronto: University of Toronto Press.

Posterski, Donald C. 1985. *Friendship: A Window on Ministry to Youth.* Scarborough: Project Teen Canada.

Quebedeaux, Richard. 1978. *The Worldly Evangelicals.* San Francisco: Harper and Row.

Redfield, Robert. 1941. *The Folk Culture of Yucatan.* Chicago: The University of Chicago Press.

Reeves, Donald. 1986. "Radical Christianity." In Tony Moss (ed.), *In Search of Christianity.* London: Firethorn Press,. 192-200.

Ringer, Robert J. 1977. *Looking Out for #1.* New York: Ballantine Books.

Rioux, Marcel. 1978. *Quebec in Question.* James Boake (trans.). Toronto: James Lorimer.

Roberts, Walter Orr. 1969. *A View of Century 21.* Claremont, Calif: Claremont University Center.

Robinson, John T. 1963. *Honest to God.* Philadelphia: Westminster.

Rokeach, Milton. 1965. "Paradoxes of Belief." *Information Service,* National Council of Churches, February 13:1-2.

1969. "Religious Values and Social Compassion." *Review of Religious Research* 11:3-23.

1973. *The Nature of Human Values.* New York: The Free Press.

Roof, Wade Clark, and Dean R. Hoge. 1980. "Church Involvement in America: Social Factors Affecting Membership and Participation." *Review of Religious Research* 21:405-26.

Rouleau, Jean-Paul. 1977. "Religion in Quebec: Present and Future." *Pro Mundi Vita: Dossiers* Nov-Dec, No. 3.

Rushby, William, and John Thrush. 1973. "Mennonites and Social Compassion." *Review of Religious Research* 15:16-28.

Schner, George P. (ed.). 1986. *The Church Renewed: The Documents of Vatican II Reconsidered.* Lanham, Md.: University Press of America.

Schoenfeld, Stuart. 1978. "The Jewish Religion in North America:

Canadian and American Comparisons." *Canadian Journal of Sociology* 3:209-31.

1986. "Integration into the Group and Sacred Uniqueness: An Analysis of Adult Bar Mitzvah." Presented at the annual meeting of *The Association for the Sociology of Religion*, August, New York.

Shupe, Anson D., Jr., and David G. Bromley. 1979. "The Moonies and the Anti-Cultists: Movement and Countermovement in Conflict." *Sociological Analysis* 40: 325-34.

Sigelman, Lee. 1977. "Multi-nation Surveys of Religious Beliefs." *Journal for the Scientific Study of Religion* 16:289-94.

Simons, Marlise. 1982. "Latin American New Gospel." *New York Times Magazine*, November 7, 45ff.

Simpson, John H. 1985. "Status Inconsistency and Moral Values." *Journal for the Scientific Study of Religion* 24:155-62.

Sinclair-Faulkner, Tom. 1977. "A Puckish Look at Hockey in Canada." In Peter Slater (ed.), *Religion and Culture in Canada*. Toronto: Canadian Corporation for Studies in Religion, 383-405.

Sklare, Marshall. 1971. *America's Jews*. New York: Random House.

St. George, Arthur, and Patrick McNamara. 1984. "Religion, Race and Psychological Well-Being." *Journal for the Scientific Study of Religion* 23:351-63.

Stark, Rodney. 1971. "Psychopathology and Religious Commitment." *Review of Religious Research* 12:165-76.

Stark, Rodney, and Charles Y. Glock. 1968. *American Piety*. Berkeley: University of California Press.

Stark, Rodney, and William Sims Bainbridge. 1985. *The Future of Religion*. Berkeley: University of California Press.

Stiller, Brian. 1985. Brochure outlining the nature and goals of The Evangelical Fellowship of Canada.

1985. Letter to Dalton Camp, October 1, on behalf of The Evangelical Fellowship of Canada.

Tarr, Leslie. 1986. "Does Canada Need a Moral Majority?" *Faith Today*, March-April: 18-24.

Templeton, Charles. 1983. *Charles Templeton: An Anecdotal Memoir*. Toronto: McClelland and Stewart.

Thielicke, Helmut. 1960. *Our Heavenly Father*. John Doberstein (trans.). New York: Harper and Row.

Thomas, W.I. 1928. *The Child in America*. New York: Knopf.

Toffler, Alvin. 1972. *The Futurists*. (Edited Works.) New York: Random House.

1983. *Previews and Promises*. New York: Bantam Books.

Towler, Robert. 1985. *The Need for Certainty: A Sociological Study of Conventional Religion*. Boston: Routledge and Kegan Paul.

Turner, Gordon Bruce. 1982. *Being: The Christian Story*. Toronto: United Church of Canada.

Vatican, The. 1983. *Educational Guidance in Human Love: Outlines for Sex Education.* Rome.

1984. *The Attitude of the Church towards the Followers of Other Religions.* Rome.

Viorst, Judith. 1986. *Necessary Losses.* New York: Ballantine Books.

Viscott, David. 1972. *Winning.* New York: Pocket Books.

Walker, Andrew. 1986. "The Third Schism." In Tony Moss (ed.), *In Search of Christianity.* London: Firethorn Press, 202-17.

Walker, Willison. 1959. *A History of the Christian Church.* New York: Oxford University Press.

Wallis, Roy, and Steve Bruce. 1984. "The Stark-Bainbridge Theory of Religion: A Critical Analysis and Counter-Proposals." *Sociological Analysis* 45: 11-28.

Walsh, H.H. 1956. *The Christian Church in Canada.* Toronto: Ryerson Press.

Weber, Max. 1930. *The Protestant Ethic and the Spirit of Capitalism.* London: George Allen and Unwin.

1958. *The City.* Glencoe: The Free Press.

1963. *The Sociology of Religion.* Boston: Beacon Press.

Westhues, Kenneth. 1976a. "The Adaptation of the Roman Catholic Church in Canadian Society." In Stewart Crysdale and Les Wheatcroft (eds.), *Religion in Canadian Society.* Toronto: Macmillan, 290-306.

1976b. "Religious Organization in Canada and the United States." *International Journal of Comparative Sociology* 17:206-25.

1976c. "Public vs. Sectarian Legitimation: The Separate Schools of the Catholic Church." *The Canadian Review of Sociology and Anthropology* 13:137-51.

1978. "Stars and Stripes, the Maple Leaf, and the Papal Coat of Arms." *Canadian Journal of Sociology* 3:245-61.

Westley, Frances. 1978. " 'The Cult of Man': Durkheim's Predictions and New Religious Movements." *Sociological Analysis* 2:135-45.

Wills, Gary. 1978. "What Religious Revival?" *Psychology Today,* April: 74-81.

Wilson, Bryan. 1966. *Religion in Secular Society.* London: Watts.

1970. *Religious Sects.* New York: McGraw-Hill.

1976. *Contemporary Transformations of Religion.* London: Oxford University Press.

1982. *Religion in Sociological Perspective.* London: Oxford University Press.

Wuthnow, Robert. 1974. "Religious Commitment and Conservativism: In Search of an Elusive Relationship." In Charles Y. Glock (ed.), *Religion in Sociological Perspective.* Belmont, Calif.: Wadsworth.

Yinger, Milton J. 1970. *The Scientific Study of Religion.* New York: Macmillan.

INDEX

Agnosticism, 64
Aleshire, Daniel, 177-78
Allen, Woody, 250
Allport, Gordon, 2
Anglican Church in Canada, 4, 7, 8,
35, 58, 123, 132, 240, 251, 254,
268
abortion, 163
acceptance of others, 178-90 *passim*
age composition, 117
Anglican Renewal Ministries, 128-29
Anglitrends, xi, xii, 7, 51-52,
134-36, 237-38, 278-79
Barnabas Ministries, 128
beliefs, 102, 103
charismatic renewal, 23, 128, 129,
267
Church of England, 4, 56, 114,
222-28, 231, 254
commitment, 106, 107, 108, 152-53
company model, 114-15
culture and, 252*ff*
death and, 247, 248
Diocese of Toronto study. *See* Anglican Church in Canada, *Anglitrends*
education, 202
experience of religion, 104
finances, 16
gender roles, 203, 204
happiness, 207-11 *passim*
inactive members, 51-52, 55, 76-78

law, 196-98 *passim*
membership, 13-15
national policies and, 184
personal concerns, 173
politics, 193-96 *passim*
prejudice, 179, 180
proportion of population, 48-51
regional strength, 115, 116
rites, 108, 109
sex and, 155, 156, 157-58, 159
social concerns, 171, 190-93
passim, 199
values, 167, 168
war, 198-200 *passim*
Anka, Paul, 219
Arnold, Abraham, 127
Astrology, 23, 41, 74-75, 82, 95, 147,
262

Bahai, 229
Bailey, Edward, 226-27
Bainbridge, William, 39, 43, 132,
263
Bakker, Jim, 32, 35, 36
Baptists, 26, 27-28, 30, 115, 188,
190, 205, 214, 215, 229, 231, 232,
240
attendance, 13-15
Baptist Convention of Ontario and
Quebec, 30

Canadian Baptist Federation, 26, 61, 133, 242
growth, 25
Barker, Irwin, 30
Baum, Gregory, 182-83, 191-92, 213, 266, 270
Becker, Howard, 84
Bellah, Robert, 217
Berger, Peter, 6, 141, 169, 255, 260, 266-67
Bernhardt, Robert, 267
Berton, Pierre, 1, 3, 56, 123, 215, 218, 255
Betcherman, Lita-Rose, 123
Bethel Pentecostal Church (Ottawa), 26
Bettson, Bob, 268
Bird, Frederick, 38
Boesak, Allan, 165
Boillat, Maurice, 61
Bonisteel, Roy, 24
Booth, Rodney, 269
Bousquet, Madeleine, 164
Brinkerhoff, Merlin, xii, 28-31, 38, 228, 229, 279
Bromley, David, 125
Bruneau, Thomas, 229
Buddhism, 8, 22, 48, 115, 116
Zen Buddhism, 38
Burnaby Christian Fellowship, 25
Burrows, Eva, 269
Buscaglia, Leo, 264
Bush, George, 31
Byfield, Ted, 16, 260
Byrne, David, 242

Calderwood, William, 130
Camp, Dalton, 59-60
Campbell, Kenneth, 57
Canadian Charter of Rights and Freedoms, 4
Canadian Civil Liberties Association, 59-60

Canadian Conference of Catholic Bishops, 12, 16-17, 18, 33, 35,112, 113, 119, 129, 152, 188, 205, 235, 258, 270
Canadian Interfaith Network, 34-35
Capra, Fritjof, 40
Carter, Jimmy, 27
Cartier, Jacques, 58
Charismatic movements, 23, 128-29, 231-32, 256, 258, 267. See also Pentecostals
Children of God, 37, 38
Chrétien, Jean, 143-44, 172
Christian and Missionary Alliance, 26, 27, 28, 115, 229
Christian Reformed churches, 28, 185
Church affiliation, 47-67, 226, 236, 265-66
stability of, 48-61, 95, 98, 121, 131-34, 149, 241-42. See also PROJECT CANADA survey data
Church attendance, 4, 6, 226, 257
drop-off, 11-12, 23, 46, 81, 95-96, 100, 132-33, 236-38
finances and, 238-39
Protestant, 12-16, 106, 135
Roman Catholic, 16-21, 106
rural, 93
television and, 32-34
theories concerning, 24-61
See also PROJECT CANADA survey data
Church building programs, 12
finances, 15
Church of Christ, Disciples, 28, 160
Cleaver, Eldridge, 27
Coffin, Richard, 26, 128
Colson, Charles, 27
Comte, August, 43
Conservative Protestants, 24, 43, 57, 90, 116, 220, 221, 227, 229, 230, 251, 277
abortion, 161, 162
acceptance of others, 178-90 passim

age composition, 117
American, 27, 115. *See also* Religion, United States
beliefs, 102, 103, 104, 115
Bible Belt, 87, 90, 108
charismatic renewal, 129
Circulation of the Saints (Calgary study), xi, 28-31, 279
commitment, 30, 104, 106, 107, 205
company model, 114, 115-16, 117
competition, 121-22, 124-25, 126
culture and, 256-59, 260
death, 247, 248, 249
definition, 246
education, 202
evangelism, 28-31, 58, 133, 229-31
experience, 104
gender roles, 204
growth pattern, 25-31, 231
happiness, 207-11 *passim*
law, 196-98 *passim*
national policies, 184, 185
personal concerns, 173, 174
politics, 193-96 *passim*
prejudice, 178, 179, 180, 186, 187
proportion, 48-50, 116
regional strength, 115-16
rites, 108, 109
sex, 154, 155, 156, 158, 159, 160, 164
small denominations, 28
social concerns, 171-72, 190-93 *passim*, 199, 268-69
values, 166, 167, 168, 169
wars, 198-200 *passim*
Cottrell, Melanie, 42
Cox, Harvey, 231, 236, 240
Crysdale, Stewart, 191
Cult. *See* New religious movements
Culture
Canadian, 180-82
religion and, 1-3, 9
Currie, Raymond, 30, 70, 83-84

Davies, Robertson, 5, 19, 64, 102-3, 262, 271
Davis, William, 15-16
DeGroot, Paul, 35, 209
Denver, John, 40
De Roo, Remi, 191, 268
Dickey, James, 235
Diefenbaker, John, 100, 250
Divine Light Mission, 147
Douglas, Tommy, 190-91
Doukhobors, 124-25
Duplessis, Maurice, 124, 143
Durkheim, Emile, 2-3, 138, 139, 146-47, 255-56
Dylan, Bob, 27

Eastern Orthodox, 115, 116, 117
Electronic Church. *See* Television evangelists
Episcopalians, 220
Erhard, Werner, 40, 264-65
ESP, 41, 42, 147. *See also* PROJECT CANADA survey data, religious beliefs, less conventional; Psychic beliefs
Evangelical Fellowship of Canada, 59-60, 115, 128, 150, 160
Evangelical Free Church, 26, 27
Evangelical Lutheran Church in Canada, 120, 191. *See also* Lutheran Churches
Evangelical Protestants, 4, 7. *See also* Conservative Protestants

Falardeau, Jean-Charles, 143
Fallding, Harold, 119, 126, 140, 215
Falwell, Jerry, 27, 32, 57
Feltmate, Donald, 26
Ferguson, Marilyn, 39
Finney, John, xii
Fish, Gordon, 239
Free Methodists, 26, 28
Freud, Sigmund
and religion, 2, 43, 73, 205, 235-36

Frye, Northrop, 180-81
Fulford, Robert, 97-98

Gallup polls, 12, 27, 32, 64, 65,
  132-33, 168, 206-7, 216, 217
Garbe, Ralph, 130-31
Garnsworthy, Lewis, 5, 51, 60
Gates, Bill, 234
Gérin, Léon, 143
Glock, Charles, xii, 41-42, 177
Gordon, Henry, 73
Gorsuch, Richard, 177-78
Gould, David, 158
Graham, Billy, 137-38, 205
Grant, John Webster, 15, 81-82, 114,
  124, 251, 261
Greek Orthodox, 116, 251
Greeley, Andrew, 41, 235
Gutiérrez, Gustavo, 231

Hare Krishna, 37, 38-39
Harpur, Tom, 31-32, 164-65
Hatton, G. Russell, 158
Hay, David, 223
Hewitt, W.E., 231
Hexham, Irving, 125, 147
Hill, Daniel, 38
Hill, Donald, 132-33
Hiller, Harry, 60, 90, 215
Hinduism, 8, 22, 68, 115, 116
Hoge, Dean, 21, 258
Homosexuality
  and religion. See Religion, homo-
  sexuality
Hordern, William, 165
Hryniuk, Stella, 22
Hubert, Bernard, 18
Hughes, Everett, 122-23
Humbard, Rex, 32
Hunsberger, Bruce, 236-37
Hunt, Desmond, 268-69
Hutterites, 124-25
Huxley, Aldous, 83

Islam, 8, 22, 115, 116

Jehovah's Witnesses, 48, 124, 188,
  189, 192
Jenkins, David, 224
Jews. See Judaism
Johnson, Benton, 121
Jones, Jim, 36-37, 38, 60
Judaism, 8, 55-56, 115, 116, 117,
  164, 186, 187, 188, 189, 220
  anti-semitism, 123
  attendance, 22
  company model, 114, 121, 126-27
  membership, 22
  proportion, 48, 49

Karpetz, Philip, 242
Keegstra, Jim, 190
Kelley, Dean, 27
King, Coretta, 4, 176
King, Jr., Martin Luther, 176
Kirkpatrick, Clifford, 176-77
Kristofferson, Kris, 5
Ku Klux Klan, 123-24
Kuhlman, Kathryn, 32
Kurbis, Ernest, 120

Lasch, Christopher, 264
Leddy, Mary Jo, 244
Lincoln, Abraham, 100
Luckman, Thomas, 40-41, 42, 147
Lutheran Churches, 13, 49, 55, 115,
  116, 220, 229, 240, 277, 278
  abortion, 162
  acceptance of others, 178-90 passim
  age composition, 117
  attendance, 113-15
  beliefs, 102, 103
  commitment, 106, 107, 108
  company model, 114
  death, 247, 248
  education, 202

experience of religion, 104
gender roles, 203, 204
happiness, 207-11 *passim*
law and, 196-98 *passim*
national policies and, 184, 185
personal concerns, 173
politics, 193-96 *passim*
prejudice, 179, 180
rites, 108, 109
sex and, 155, 156, 158, 159, 160
social concerns, 171, 190-93
  passim, 199
values, 167, 168
war, 198-200 passim

MacDonald, Clarke, 209, 268
Mackie, Marlene, 38
MacLaine, Shirley, 39, 40
MacPherson, Aimee Semple, 219
MacRae, Robert, 269-70
Mainse, David, 32, 36
Malcolm, Andrew, 5, 180, 215
Mallone, George, 25
Maloney, J.J., 123-24
Mann, W.E., 148
Martin, David, 223
Marx, Karl,
  religion and, 3, 142-43, 205
Mauss, Armand, xii, 36
McAteer, Michael, 153
McCormick, Peter, 193
McCullum, Hugh, 127
McGavran, Donald, 215
McKibbon, K.D., 130
McLeod, Bruce, 197
McMullen, Clarence, 266, 267
McNamara, Patrick, 205, 209
Mead, George Herbert, 261
Melanchuk, Allan, 190
Mennonite Brethren Church, 194
Mennonites, 26, 28, 115, 124, 177,
  185, 191
Methodists, 220, 268

Milner, Henry, 122, 123
Milner, Mike, 241
Milner, Sheilagh, 122, 123
Moddle, Harold, 131
Moral Majority, 27, 57
Morgentaler, Henry, 163
Morisy, Ann, 223
Mormons, 48, 52, 121, 164, 188,
  189, 255
Moslem. *See* Islam
Mother Teresa, 4
Muggeridge, Anne Roche, 19
Mulroney, Brian, 176, 195
Murray, Anne, 219
Muslim. *See* Islam

Naisbitt, John, 82, 125, 165, 242,
  264, 265
Nazarenes, 26, 115, 119
New Age Movement, 236
Newson, Janice, 19
Nichol, Dave, 59
Nietzsche, Friedrich, 62
Nostbakken, David, 35

Ono, Yoko, 40
Orr, J. Edwin, 91
Osler, Sir William, 97-98
O'Sullivan, Sean, 118-19, 236,
  250-51, 269

Peccei, Aurelio, 261
Pentecostals, 13-15, 23, 26, 27, 28,
  104, 115, 128, 160-63, 188, 189,
  229, 231, 232
Penton, Jim, 124
Pettersson, Thorleif, 34
Piazza, Thomas, 41-42
Pinnock, Clark, 198
Pope John XXIII, 17
Pope John Paul II, 4, 17, 23, 59,
  114-15, 154, 258, 263
Pope Paul VI, 17

Posterski, Donald, xiii, 7, 246, 266, 279
Presbyterian Church, 4, 8, 49, 113, 115, 116, 123, 133, 220, 277, 278
  abortion, 162
  acceptance of others, 178-90 *passim*
  age composition, 117-18
  attendance, 13-15
  beliefs, 102-4
  commitment, 106, 107
  company model, 114
  death, 247, 248
  education, 202
  experience of religion, 104
  gender rules, 204
  happiness, 207-11 *passim*
  law and, 196-98 *passim*
  national policies and, 184
  personal concerns, 173
  politics, 193-96 *passim*
  prejudice, 179, 186, 187
  rites, 108, 109
  sex and, 154-55, 156, 159, 160
  social concerns, 171, 190-93 *passim*, 199
  values, 167, 168, 169
  war, 198-200 *passim*
PROJECT CANADA, xi, xii, 7, 18, 38-39, 42-43, 44-45, 52, 53, 62-85, 145, 198, 261
  methodology, 273-78
PROJECT TEEN CANADA, xi, xii, 7, 50, 53, 169, 174, 198, 261, 278
PROJECT CANADA survey data
  religious beliefs, 62, 93, 95-96, 98, 100, 101, 104
  creation, 63
  God, 63, 64, 65, 72, 79, 82, 92, 98, 104
  happiness, 63
  Jesus, 63, 64-65, 66, 72, 79, 82, 98, 104

  less conventional, 74-76, 82-83, 86, 92, 93, 95, 98, 100, 104
  life's meaning, 64
  life's purpose, 63
  suffering, 63
religious commitment and 72-73, 93, 95-96, 98, 100-101, 130
  abortion, 160-63
  acceptance of others, 178-90
  bilingualism/multiculturalism, 182-90
  death, 246-51
  education, 200-202
  gender roles, 201-4
  happiness, 207-11
  interracial/interreligious marriage, 185-87
  law, 196-98
  nationalism, 182
  personal concerns, 172-75
  politics, 193-96
  prejudice, 178-80
  sex, 155-59
  social concerns, 170-72, 190-93, 199, 200
  values, 166-70
  war, 198-200
religious commitment by
  age, 33, 34, 81, 87, 89, 95-97, 98, 99, 100, 101, 108
  denomination, 87, 104-6. *See also denominations by name*
  educational status, 87, 96-100, 101, 108
  region, 11, 87-91
    Atlantic, 90
    B.C., 90-91
    Bible Belt, 87, 90, 108
    community size, 92-94
    rural, 91-94
    urban, 91-94
    See also Roman Catholics in Quebec

sex, 87, 100-102, 108
religious commitment over time,
  237-38. See also Religion,
  commitment
religious experience, 69-70, 72, 79,
  93, 95-96, 98, 100-101, 104
religious knowledge, 70-72, 79, 93,
  95-96, 98, 100-101
religious non-involvement, 83-84. See
  also Religion, non-affiliates
religious practices, 92, 93, 95-96,
  98, 100-101, 104
  Bible reading, 68, 69, 82, 104
  prayer, 68, 72, 79, 82, 101, 104
  table grace, 68-69
  rites, 76-78, 82, 89, 93, 95-96, 98,
    101, 102, 108, 109
  self-reported nature, 79-80, 84-85,
    93, 101
Protestantism, 8, 164, 177, 182, 186,
  193, 220, 257
  church attendance, 11, 14
  history in Canada, 3-4
  percentage, 21, 47, 48, 230.
  See also Protestant Churches by
    denomination
Psychic beliefs, 23, 74-76, 88. See
  also PROJECT CANADA survey data,
  religious beliefs, less conventional

Quakers, 191, 229
Queensway Cathedral, 25, 121
Quiet Revolution (Quebec), 20-21

Rajneeshism, 147
Ratzinger, Joseph Cardinal, 256
Reagan, Ronald, 31, 100, 195
Redekop, John, 194-95, 198
Reeves, Donald, 224, 226
Reiner, William, 38
Religion
  abortion and, 160-63
  acceptance of others and, 178-90

Canadian demographics,
  company model, 112-20
  competition, 121-36
  Statistics Canada, 114-18.
  See also denominations and religions
    by name; PROJECT CANADA survey
    data
Canadian history and, 3-4, 81, 91,
  94-96, 97-98, 99-100, 217-18
commitment, 5, 30, 38, 72, 73, 86,
  98, 100, 104, 137-40, 148, 226,
  227, 234-37
age and, 260
compassion and, 176-77
death and, 246-51
education and, 200-202
finances of churches and, 238-39,
  260
future of, 236-38
gender roles and, 201-4
happiness and, 206-11
implications of decline, 243-46,
  251-56
law and, 196-98
marketing of, 261-72
national policies and, 180-90
personal concerns and, 172-75
politics and, 193-96, 260
prejudice and, 177-80
significance of, 151-63, 211-13
social concerns and, 170-72, 190-93,
  199, 200, 260
traditional, 256-59
values and, 166-70
war, 198-200
See also Church affiliation; Church
  attendance; PROJECT CANADA survey
  data; Religion, fragmentation
competition, 122-25, 147-48, 217-19,
  226, 228-32
merging, 239. See also Religion,
  fragmentation
computers and, 240-42

confidence in, 52-53
consumer-oriented, 1, 3, 80-85, 94,
110, 111*ff*, 122, 126-36, 144-49,
164, 169, 175, 203, 233, 239-40
culture and, 1-3, 9, 22, 39-40, 51-52,
147, 170, 203, 213, 233, 250, 251,
253-56, 257*ff*
form vs. content, 256-59
religious possibilities for, 259*ff*
religious socialization, 39-40, 55-56,
69, 94-96, 99-100, 215, 238,
248-49
support for fragmentation, 111-36,
239-40, 256
See also PROJECT CANADA survey
data; Religion, commitment;
Religion, fragmentation
death and, 246-51
England, 222-28
Nonconformists, 225-26. See also
Anglican Church in Canada,
Church of England
evangelism and, 58-59, 127-28,
267-72. See also Conservative
Protestants; Religion, pluralism
fragmentation, 1, 3, 5, 9, 72, 80-84,
86, 92, 94, 95, 102, 108-10, 175,
213, 215, 223, 227, 232, 233,
234-36, 256, 270-71
diversification, 126-36, 239-40
uses of, 140-42, 148-49, 245, 246,
252. See also Religion, commitment; Religion, specialization
God and, 261-63
homosexuality, 2, 154-58, 159-60,
179
identification with. See Church affiliation, stability
industrialization (and post-
industrialization), 21, 41, 85,
86, 138, 144
resulting specialization, 138-40,
214, 227, 234
role conflict, 140

role consistency, 141
society, 144-46. See also Religion,
secularization
influence of, 211-13
interdenominational co-operation, 132
intergenerational stability, 50-51
interracial/interreligious marriage
and, 185-87
"invisible religion," 40-43
Latin America, 228-32
law and, 196-98
meaning systems and, 42-43
media and, 23, 24, 35-36, 37-38,
39, 53, 115, 131, 172, 219-20,
254-55. See also Television
evangelists
mental health and, 205-9
nationalism and, 180-82
Native peoples and, 3, 58-59, 67
new religious movements, 24, 37-40,
43, 131-32, 219, 228, 236
media and, 37-38, 39
opposition, 38-39
participation in, 38-40
worship, 39-40
"no religion" option, 43-45, 132
non-affiliates, 21, 43-45, 47, 49-50,
225-26
abortion and, 161, 162
acceptance of others, 178-90 *passim*
beliefs of, 44-45, 103
commitment, 106, 107, 109
death and, 247, 248
education, 202
experience, 104
gender roles, 203, 204
happiness and, 207-11 *passim*
law and, 196-98 passim
nationalism, 182, 184
personal concerns, 173
politics, 193-96 *passim*
prejudice, 179, 180, 186
sex and, 155, 159
social concerns, 171, 172, 190-93

passim, 199
values, 167, 168
war, 198-200 *passim*
non-Christian religion in Canada, 47.
See also religions by name
pluralism and, 56-61, 125, 126, 158,
163, 164, 178, 227
effect on evangelism, 61, 121,
217-18, 219, 226
politics and, 2, 193-96
pornography and, 160
"privatized" religion. *See* Religion,
consumer-oriented; Religion,
fragmentation; Religion, "invisible
religion"
relationships and, 266-67
religious leaders,
morale, 12, 52-54
views of, 52-53, 72
rites of passage and, 1, 23, 44,
55-56, 76-78, 89, 93, 238, 252
science and, 96-97, 146-48
secularism and, 41, 69, 90, 147, 169
self and, 263-65
sex and, 153-65,
sex-related rights, 158-60
significance of, 1-2
social justice and, 23. *See also*
Religious commitment, social
concerns and
social science and, 6-9, 43, 215
specialization. *See* Religion, fragmentation; Religion, industrialization
supernatural beliefs and, 2-3, 23,
41, 62, 73, 82-83, 97, 146-48,
165, 215-16, 217, 222, 227-28,
232, 236, 263
survey research and, 6-9
technology and, 234, 259
truth claims and, 2, 61, 217-18, 219,
256
Judeo-Christian, 3. *See also*
Religion, pluralism and United

States,
affiliations, 219-22
fragmentation, 214-17
values and, 166-70
war and, 198-200
women's ordination controversies
and, 254-55
*See also religions and denominations
by name*; PROJECT CANADA survey
data
Rennie, Ian, 81
Rioux, Marcel, 143
Roberts, Oral, 32, 35, 36
Roberts, Walter, 241
Robertson, Pat, 32
Rokeach, Michael, 177, 205
Roman Catholicism, 8, 59, 123-24,
142, 177, 220, 223, 225, 227, 240,
251, 255, 257
abortion, 161, 162
acceptance of others, 178-90 *passim*
age composition, 117
anti-Catholicism, 123-24
attendance, 11, 16-21,
Quebec, 19-21, 238
beliefs, 102, 103, 104
charismatic renewal, 23, 128, 258,
267
commitment, 104, 106, 107, 133-34,
152
company model, 112-13, 114,
118-19, 121
competition, 122-23, 126
culture and, 252*ff*
death and, 247, 248
education, 202
experience of religion, 104
gender roles, 203, 204
growth, 231
happiness and, 207-11 *passim*
history in Canada, 3-4, 122-23
identity, 55
laity, 119, 257
Latin America, 228-32

law and, 196-98 *passim*
lay views of, 12, 17, 18-19, 119, 152
national policies and, 180-90 *passim*
nationalism, 182
personal concerns, 173, 174
politics, 193-96 *passim*
prejudice, 179-80, 186
proportion, 21, 47, 48-51, 52
regional strength, 115, 116
rites, 108, 109
sex and, 154, 155, 156, 158, 159, 164
social concerns, 171, 190-93 *passim*, 199
television, 33
values, 167, 168, 169
Vatican II, 17-21, 119, 132, 150
war, 198-200 *passim*
Roman Catholicism in Quebec, 81, 87, 88, 90, 113, 143-44, 155, 156-57, 158, 159, 160, 161, 162, 166, 167, 168, 169, 170, 173, 174, 179, 180, 183, 187, 192, 195, 198, 203, 204, 238, 247, 248, 252. *See also* Roman Catholicism
Rouleau, Jean-Paul, 20-21, 144, 169-70, 252
Runcie, Robert, 114-15
Russell, Bertrand, 262, 270
Rutledge, Ralph, 25, 121
Ryerson, Egerton, 100

Salvation Army, 26, 27, 28, 115, 229
Satanism, 38
Schoenfeld, Stuart, 55, 215
Schuller, Robert, 32
Scientology, 37, 38-39, 236
Scott, Ted, 23
Secularism,
  in politics, 5
  Quebec, 20-21

Shupe, Anson, 125
Sikhs, 148
Sinclair-Faulkner, Tom, 41
Sjoberg, Donald, 191
Sklare, Marshall, 56
Smith, Goldwin, 243-44
Smith, Robert, 58, 127-28, 165, 254-55
Squire, Ann, 119
St. George, Arthur, 205, 209
Stark, Rodney, xii, 7, 39, 43, 132, 177, 263
Stiller, Brian, 59-60, 128, 268-69
Stratton, Allan, 65
Swaggart, Jimmy, 32
Swaren, Milton, 25

Television evangelists, 23, 27
  appeal of, 24, 31-36
  electronic church, 43
  public attitude to, 35-36
  viewing of, 32-34
Templeton, Charles, 36, 219, 262
Thielicke, Helmut, view of God, 3
Thomas, W.I., 206
Thompson, Eugene, 132-33
Thunderchild, Chief, 58
Toffler, Alvin, 265
Towler, Robert, 223
Transcendental meditation, 38, 147
Turner, Gordon, 12, 15, 135, 266
Turner, John, 176
Tutu, Desmond, 4, 191
Tweedie, John, 129-30

U.S. National Council of Churches, 27
Ukrainian Catholics, 22
Ukrainian Orthodox, 22
Unification Church ("Moonies"), 37, 38-39, 125, 147
Unitarians, 188, 189

United Church of Canada, xii, 132, 240, 251, 254, 277
abortion, 162, 163
acceptance of others, 178-90 *passim*
age composition, 177
attendance, 13-15
beliefs, 102, 103
charismatics, 128, 129, 130, 267
commitment, 106, 107, 108
company model, 112, 113-14, 117, 118
competition, 126, 127
computers, 241
culture and, 252*ff*
death and, 247, 248, 249
disenchanted members, 16, 172
education and, 202
experience of religion, 104
finances, 15-16
growth, 12
happiness and, 207-11 *passim*
identification, 55
law and, 196-98 *passim*
lay people, 119
national policies and, 184
personal concerns, 173
politics, 193-96 *passim*
prejudice, 179, 180
proportion of population, 48-51
regional strength, 115, 116
rites, 108, 109
sex and, 155, 156, 157, 158, 159

social concerns, 171, 172, 190-93 *passim*, 199
United Church Renewal Fellowship, 114, 128, 129-31, 154, 158, 239, 256
values, 167, 168, 169
war, 198-200 *passim*
United Church of Christ, 220

Vision TV, 35

Wagner, C. Peter, 215
Waite, Terry, 191
Walker, Alan, 268
Walker, Andrew, 111-12, 224
Weber, Max
and religon, 2
Westhues, Kenneth, 215, 218
Westview Church (London), 25
Wills, Gary, 222
Wilson, Bryan, 76, 147, 164, 165-66, 244-45, 256, 261
Winter, Terry, 32, 36
Wolfe, Larry, 13
Wuthnow, Robert, 41

Yereniuk, Roman, 22
Yinger, J. Milton, 41
Yoga, 38

Zen Buddhism. *See* Buddhism, Zen